Pocahontas Descendants

A Revision, Enlargement and Extension
of the List as Set Out by
Wyndham Robertson in His Book
Pocahontas and Her Descendants (1887)

*By Stuart E. Brown, Jr.,
Lorraine F. Myers*

THIRD

*Corrections
and
Additions*

Published by Genealogical Publishing Co., Inc.
1001 N. Calvert Street, Baltimore, Maryland 21202
Library of Congress Catalogue Card Number 97-72241
International Standard Book Number 0-8063-1542-3
Made in the United States of America

THIRD
CORRECTIONS
and
ADDITIONS
to

POCAHONTAS'
DESCENDANTS

by

Stuart E. Brown, Jr.   Lorraine F. Myers

THE POCAHONTAS FOUNDATION

1997

> William Byrd II of "Westover" notes that
> Maj. John Bolling "enjoyed all the profits of
> an immense trade with his countrymen, and of
> one still greater with the Indians".

Acknowledgements

Much of the data included in this volume was obtained from or through the assistance of the following persons and organizations: Richard Jeffery Alfriend III; Ellen Carter Hurt Allen; Thomas E. Barton; Suzanne Marie King Berschback; Kathrine Howard Biggs; Elizabeth ("Beth") Frances Bolling Skelly Borgman; Dorothy Perry Brawley; Phyllis Coghill Brown; Chester LeRoy Call; Elizabeth ("Betty") Rives Allen Callaway; Catherine Carlisle Canada; Steve Candela; Diana Letitia Eldridge Coleman; Thomas Webber Culpepper; Robert J. Dandridge, Jr.; Susan Elizabeth Evans; William Leroy Evans, Jr.; Josephine Clement Harrison Evarts; Harriet Elizabeth Fenner Gaines; E. Alvin Gerhardt, Jr.; W. S. Griffith; David Hadden, Jr.; Ann Randolph Hurst Harrington; Mathilde Keyser Clark Holmes; Mr. and Mrs. William Thomas Howard, Jr.; Juliet L. Hunter; Mrs. Stanard C. Jessup; Margaret Anne Dulin Joyner; Emily Virginia Parker Kendig; Janet Keene Patton Lewis; Anthony P. Martin; Shirley ("Little Dove") Custalow McGowan; Mary ("Molly") Ledwith Paul Maull; Alice Mae Callaway Moore; Robert Rives Mullen; Nancy Joy Gribble Nelson; James Samuel Patton; Frank Ladessie Perry, Jr.; Faye H. Purol; Joe Aldridge Randolph; William M. S. Rasmussen; Elizabeth ("Beth") DeHardit Richardson; Alene Carroll Rizzo; Anne Corbin Parker Romaine; Charles B. Saunders, Jr.; Abigail Alden Smith Shriver; Katherine Roseborough Spicer; Thomas Ragland Terry; Robert S. Tilton; Virginia Historical Society and Frances Elizabeth Smith Williams.

A study drawing made in 1960 by Sidney E. King, the experienced, knowledgeable Jamestown historical artist, is a summertime likeness of Pocahontas. Courtesy: Jamestown-Yorktown Foundation.

Introduction

The Pocahontas Foundation, based upon information furnished to it, has compiled a tentative list of the descendants of Pocahontas, a list set forth in a combined volume (printed in 1994 and reissued in 1997) which includes reprints of the three books POCAHONTAS' DESCENDANTS (1985), CORRECTIONS AND ADDITIONS TO POCAHONTAS' DESCENDANTS (1992) and SECOND CORRECTIONS AND ADDITIONS TO POCAHONTAS' DESCENDANTS (1994) and continues in this separate 1997 book, THIRD CORRECTIONS AND ADDITIONS TO POCAHONTAS' DESCENDANTS.

Proposed corrections and/or additions to the list are cordially invited, and should be sent by mail (together with a stamped and addressed envelope) to The Pocahontas Foundation, P. O. Box 431, Berryville, VA 22611.

Falmouth

Maureen Barbara Snow reports that the ship "Treasurer", because of bad weather, stopped at Falmouth and that Pocahontas, her infant son and companions, landing and travelling by road to London, stayed at an inn in the Cornwall village now known as Indian Queen. See SECOND CORRECTIONS AND ADDITIONS page iv.

More recently Mrs. Snow reports hearing "Indian Queen", a dance, a part of the 1651 production "The English Dancing Master" by London's John Playford.

Bolling Bible

The late Mrs. Emily Hume Alfriend Rawlings (1423221) owned what she called the "Bolling Bible" (published in London in 1769).

All of the family entries in this Bible were made in the same handwriting and probably at the same time with the exception of two entries (see below).

This suggests that the names were copied from another Bible and that Mrs. Rawlings' Bible was a gift to a descendant of the "Cobbs" Bolling family.

The entries must have been made subsequent to August 10, 1770, the date given for the death of Edward Bolling (18), which date appears to have been written in the same handwriting.

This Bible contains a list of the eighteen children (names and dates done in the same handwriting) born of the marriage of John Bolling (1) and Eliz. Blair (1).

Just before the name of their daughter Mary Bolling (14) the word "ours" is written in the handwriting of Mrs. Rawlings (she claimed her by the word "ours").

Additional support for the marriage of Elizabeth Bland Blair Bolling (1) to Richard Bland, Jr. is found in the Virginia Gazette of April 28, 1775 which announced the death of Mrs. Elizabeth Bland spouse of Col. Richard Bland of "Jordan's" in Prince George County.

This marriage resulted in Elizabeth Bland Blair Bolling (1) becoming the step mother to her daughter's husband Richard Bland III.

The last entry in Mrs. Rawlings' Bible records Mary Bolling Poythress (1431) and her death on August 26, 1802 at twelve years of age.

The date of the marriage between Elizabeth Bland Blair Bolling (1) and Richard Bland, Jr. is unknown, but it had to be sometime between August 8, 1759, the date of the death of Martha Macon Massie Bland, who was the second wife of Richard Bland, Jr., and April 22, 1775, the date of Elizabeth Bland Blair Bolling's death.

When Richard Bland, Jr., was stricken on a street in Williamsburg on October 26, 1776 while on the way to a session of the Assembly he was taken to the home of Sarah Bolling Tazewell (15) where he died after a few hours.

Mrs. Rawlings' Bible shows "Eliz. Blair youngest Daughter" of Dr. Archibald Blair.

These names and birth and death dates of the eighteen (of John and Elizabeth Bland Blair Bolling) are the same as those given on the Volta list (page 328) except that Mrs. Rawlings' Bible (using the Volta list numbers) shows:

V2 Archibald Bolling died 1747.
V4 Elizabeth Bolling born 7/19 and died "31st July following".
V7 Robert Bolling born 1738, died (different handwriting - - - see above) 7/21/1775.
V9 Ann Bolling died 1747.
Vx Mary Bolling died (different handwriting - - - see above) 9/9/1803.

POCAHONTAS MEMORIAL ASSOCIATION
WASHINGTON, D. C.
Received of Miss Matoaca Gay
April 5, 1906. $ 1.00
membership fee Jennie B. Garrison.
Assistant Treasurer.

Additional Bibliography

AMERICAN PRESIDENTIAL FAMILIES. 1933.

AUSTRALIAN DICTIONARY OF BIOGRAPHY 1851-1890. Vol. 6.

Boggs, Marion Alexander. ed. THE ALEXANDER LETTERS 1787-1900.
   Savannah 1910.

"BOLLING BIBLE".

Brawley, Dorothy Perry, and Perry, Frank Ladessie, Jr. THE
   BOLLING-GAY-GASTON-BRAWLEY PAPER TRAIL WITH ALLIED FAMILIES
   AND FRIENDS. 1995. Book contains much biographical material
   on some of the persons covered.

Brown, Stuart E., Jr. POCAHONTAS. 1989.

BURGESSES & GUILD BRETHREN OF GLASGOW 1751-1846.

GENTLEMAN'S MAGAZINE. 1793.

Henderson, Alexander. AUSTRALIAN FAMILIES. 1941.

HOLY BIBLE (two volumes). London 1751. Owned by Nathaniel
   West Dandridge, Esq.

IGI - International Genealogical Index from the Church of Jesus
   Christ of Latter Day Saints.

Irving, Joseph. THE BOOK OF EMINENT SCOTSMEN.

JONES' DIRECTORY FOR 1798 (of Glasgow). Facsimile 1973.
   Notes at end of a 1866 edition.

Lawrence-Dow, Elizabeth. AUTOGRAPHS 1701/2 - CHARLES CITY,
   PRINCE GEORGE AND SURRY COUNTIES. 1976.

Patton, James Samuel. THE FAMILY OF WILLIAM & ELIZABETH BOLLING
   ROBERTSON. Arranged by Generations in Descent with Numerical
   Identification. 1995. Revised and Indexed of 1975 edition.

POCAHONTAS AND THE POWHATANS OF VIRGINIA. 1995. Brochure by
   Jamestown-Yorktown Foundation.

Rasmussen, William S; and Tilton, Robert S. POCAHONTAS. HER
   LIFE AND LEGEND. 1994.

Smith, John Gutherie. HISTORY OF STRATHENDRICK. 1896.

Starr, Joan, MELTON PLAINS OF PROMISE.

VICTORIAN MEN OF THE TIME. 1882.

VIC BDB - Victorian Index of Births, Deaths and Marriages.

Zorn, Walter Lewis. THE DESCENDANTS OF THE PRESIDENTS OF THE
   UNITED STATES OF AMERICA. Second Revised Edition. 1955.

NOTE: Some other books, etc., relied upon in whole or in part
      are mentionned in the text.

THIRD CORRECTIONS AND ADDITIONS TO POCAHONTAS' DESCENDANTS
and/or CORRECTIONS AND ADDITIONS and/or
SECOND CORRECTIONS AND ADDITIONS

p. 6 (of POCAHONTAS' DESCENDANTS) Mary Kennon died 1742

1 Col. John Bolling (b. 1/20/1699*1700), m. 8/24/1728 Elizabeth
    Bland Blair (b. 1/20/1705*6)

    Listed, as children of Col. John Bolling, Col. William
Bolling and Benjamin Bolling but these have not been proven to
be such children (see POCAHONTAS' DESCENDANTS 327-32).

111 Elizabeth Bolling, m. William Robertson of "Belfield",
      Dinwiddie County. He and she are buried at "Cobbs".

1112   Thomas Bolling Robertson witnessed in Paris Bonaparte's
        leaving and return to Waterloo. A Louisanna Federal
        judge.

11132611 Bessie Meade Friend, m. Francis Elmore Drake
111326111 Francis Elmore Drake, Jr.

1113261121 Rebecca Beverly Cunliffe*
1113261122 Charlotte Meade Cunliffe*
1113261123 Nathaniel Isaac Cunliffe*
    * Triplets

111326321 Clabe Webster Lynn, Jr., m. Jean
1113263211 Chloe Beckwith Lynn, m. Michael Getsey
1113263212 Susan Lunsford Lynn, m. Ed Reeves

111326323 Jean Elizabeth Lynn

11132636   Hibernia McIlwaine Friend, m. James Arthur Richardson,
            Jr. (1916-1966)

111326362 John Friend Richardson, m. Margie Roadman
1113263621 Marguerite ("Cricket") Richardson, m. Joseph Evans

1113263641 Jenny Rona Richardson

111326512 Hugh Senn Hassell, m. Dorothea
1113265121 Joanna Hassell
1113265122 James Hassell
1113265123 Virginia Hassell
111326513 Andrew Morrison Hassell II

111326521 Margaret Collier Cuthbert (1943-   ), m. David
            Tilghman Broaddus
1113265211 Suzanne Everard Broaddus
1113265212 David Tilghman Broaddus, Jr.

111326522 Charles Henry Cuthbert V (1947-   )
111326523   Hibernia McIlwaine Cuthbert (1950-   ), m. 1976,
           William John Langley, Jr., M.D.

111326524 Nathaniel West Cuthbert (1956-   )

111326531 John Woodrow Davis, Jr. (1944-   ), m. Joanne Ardino

111326532 Archibald Graham Davis (1947-   )

111326533 Roger Pryor Davis (1950-   ), m. Bonnie Jean Feltes

111326536 Katherine Burwell Davis (1957-   ), m. John Russell
           Perkins

111332111 Gay Robertson Blackwell, m. Dean Richard Lally (1929-
           1987)
1113321111 Thomas Arthur Lally (1955-   ), m. Melanie Ann Wood
11133211111 Kathleen Gay Lally (1986-   )
1113321112 Dean Richard Lally, Jr. (1957-   ), m. 1980, Janet
           Alise Olson
11133211121 Kimberley Alise Lally (1985-   )
11133211122 Dean Richard Lally III (1988-   )
11133211123 Sarah Ann Lally (1990-   )
1113321113 Bryan Robertson Lally (1962-   )

111332112 Ann Gordon Blackwell, m. (1st) David Sanford
           Tillotson. M. (2nd) James McNeil. M. (3rd)
                    Sheehan
1113321121   David Sanford Tillotson, Jr., m. 4/23/1988, Barbara
           Ann Ely
11133211211 Rudyard Leroy Tillotson (1989-   )

1113321142 Caroline Gay Poggie, m. 1994, Gerald Keeney

11133212 Charles Claiborne Blackwell, m. 1921, Julia Mae Boothe
           (1898-1995)

11133212211 Keith Douglas Breckenridge
11133212212 Craig Mitchell Douglas Brenkenridge

111332123 Richard Cabot Blackwell, m. (1st) Judith Fearing
           Turner (1930-1991). M. (2nd) Nancy Tanehill
1113321231   Sarah Turner Blackwell (1961-   ), m. Peter
           Palmer (1960-   )
11133212311 Trent Richard Palmer (1991-   )
11133212312 Holly Stuart Palmer (1993-   )

1113321232   William Claiborne Blackwell (1963-   ), m. Heather
           Reade (1965-   )
11133212321 Jessica Turner Blackwell (1993-   )
1113321233   Douglas Wilsey Blackwell (1965-   ), m. Karri McGraw
           (1967-   )

1113321234 Patricia Fearing Blackwell (1967-   ), m. Clark
            Allen Peterson (1965-   )
11133241 Henry Fairfax Lynn III (1899-1978), m. 1922, Mary Eliza
          Dorsey (1902-1993)

1113324112 Walter Scott Richards (1954-   )

111332412 Henry Fairfax Lynn IV (1925-   ), m. (1st) 1949,
           Natalie Nell Clawson (1927-   )
1113324121 Henry Fairfax Lynn V (1950-   ), m. 1973, Barbara
            Gilsdorf (1950-   )
11133241211 Julie Ann Lynn (1977-   )
11133241212 Jacob Andrew Lynn (1986-   )

11133241221 Tiffany Anne Lynn (1977-   )
11133241222 Joshua James Lynn (1974-   )
1113324123 Charles Andrew Lynn (1958-   ), m. (1st) 1983, Kathy
            Hickman Hazelwood. M. (2nd) 1992, Peggy Karpus
     Children by first wife:
11133241231 Charles Andrew Lynn, Jr. (1983-   )
11133241232 James Daniel Lynn (1986-   )
11133413 Mary Frances Lynn (1926-   ), 1948, Joseph Augustus
          Cheatham, Jr.
1113324131 Joseph Augustus Cheatham III (1950-   ), m. (1st)
            1972, Frances Mary White (1951-   ). M. (2nd)
            1994, Patricia Josephs

1113324132 Debra Lynn Cheatham, m. Raymond Cottrell Hooker III
11133241321 Pamela Elizabeth Hooker (1976-   )

111332414 Caroline Jones Lynn (1928-   ), m. (1st) 1949, Thomas
           Martin Doyle (1925-   ). M. (2nd) 1994, Robert
           Harman Davis
1113324141 Thomas Martin Doyle, Jr., m. (1st) 1973, Donna Mae
            Campbell.   Div. 1975. M. (2nd) 1986, Hazel
            Elizabeth Galahan
    Children by second wife:
11133241411 Thomas Avery Doyle (1991-   )
11133241412 Patrick Allen Doyle (1993-   )
1113324142 Mary Katherine Doyle (1953-   ), m. 1975, Christopher
            Nelson Rhodes
11133241421 Jacob Nelson Rhodes (1978-   )
11133241422 Isaac Nelson Rhodes (1980-   )
1113324143 Frances Ann Doyle (1956-   ), m. Charles Martin
            Davenport
11133241431 Ashley Lynn Davenport (1986-   )
11133241432 Virginia Leigh Davenport

1113324151 Briscoe Baldwin Brown III (1951-   ), m. Angie Ponzo
11133241511 Maury Briscoe Brown

11133243 Kent Owens (1909-1911)

1113441   Walter Holmes Robertson, m. Frances Lynn Dorsey. Frances
          Lynn Dorsey m. (2nd) Ernest J. Ristedt
11134411   Frances Lynn Robertson, m. (1st) John Morpott Piercy,
           Jr. M. (2nd) 1983, Conway Loomis Seeley (1905-1995)
111344111   John Morpott Piercy III, m. Gloria Ann Hutcherson
            (1938-   )
1113441111   Melanie Ann Piercy, m. James Bowling Cook
11134411111   Alexandra Genevieve Cook (1987-   )
11134411112   Julia Ann Cook (1989-   )
11134411113   James Bowling Cook III
11134411114   John Hayden Piercy Cook
1113441112   John Morpott Piercy IV, m. Robin Whittington

111344112   Gay Lynn Piercy, m. Louis Fernand Gagnon
1113441121   Louis Fernand Gagnon, Jr., m.
1113441122   Jennifer Lynn Gagnon, m. Hunter Whitney Wood
11134411221   Mason Wood
11134411222   Whitney Wood
1113441123   Walter Holmes Robertson Gagnon
111344121   Robin Ann Billington (1944-   ), m. (1st) 1960,
            William Edward Toth (1938-   ). M. (2nd) Austin
            Edward Starbird
     Children by first husband:
1113441211   Anthony Powell Toth (1961-   ), m. 1994, Donna Rae
             Gardiner
1113441212   Edward Billington Toth (1963-   ), m. 1990, Lisa
             Marie Para
11134412121   Heather Toth
1113441213   Anne Dorsey Toth (1965-   ), m.   Rasier
11134412131   Christopher Raiser (1988-   )

111344122   Robert James Billington, Jr. (1944-   ), m. (1st)
            1972, Cathy Danna. M. (2nd) 1985, Shya-Fen Tsai
     Children by first wife:
1113441221   Peyton Christina Billington (1975-   )
1113441222   Joseph Danna Billington (1977-   )
111344123   Randall Holmes Billington, m. (1st) 1969, Lynn Fairfax
            Carr (111344331). M. (2nd) 1979, Luanne McPherson
     Child by first wife:
1113441231   Melissa Billington (1973-   )
     Children by second wife:
1113441232   Sarah Louise Billington (1980-   )
1113441233   Samuel Holmes Billington (1981-   )
111344124   James Thomas Billington (1952-   ), m. Kathy Cooper
     Child with Ginger Cummings:
1113441241   Melissa Sue Billington (1978-   )
     Child by wife:
1113441242   Thomas Lee Billington (1979-   )
111344125   John Edward Billington (1955-   ), m. 1986, Patricia
            Lynn Duncan Hennessy
1113441251   Austin Blaise Billington (1994-   )
111344126   Jeffrey Robertson Billington (1957-   ), m. 1976,
            Elizabeth Slocum
1113441261   Amy Marie Billington (1977-   )

11134413 Rita Holmes Robertson, m. (2nd) Robert Kyle Woltz
1113441311 Patrick Robert Haley
1113441312 Andrew Clarke Haley (2/11/1987-   )
1113441313 Kellen Emily Haley

1113441321 Megan Haley
1113441322 Timothy Sean Haley

1113441331 Frances Ruth Bernard (1988-   )
1113441332 Meredith Dorsey Bernard (1991-   )

111344135 Sarah Kyle Woltz (1964-   ), m. John Stuart Burns

1113442 Bolling Lynn Robertson, m. (2nd) Elizabeth Averett
          Penick (Meredith) (1895-1986)

111344221   Marianne Fairfax Lewis, m. (1st) Thomas Larson
    Child by first husband:
1113442211 Desiree Lee Larson (1971-   )
    Child by second husband:
1113442212 Robert Davis Isinger II (1979-   )
111344222 Linda Leslie Lewis (1952-   ), m. Joel Wineroth
1113442221 Joel Wineroth, Jr.
1113442222 Whitney Caroline Wineroth
1113443 Rolfe Robertson, m. (1st) Charlotte Cochran (1894-1995).
          M. (2nd) Willie Ann Peyton
    Child by first wife:
11134431   Charlotte Robertson, m. (1st) Walter Nelson Munster
           (1916-   )

111344313 Walter Nelson Munster, Jr. (1955-   ), m. Colleen
             Gavin
1113443131 Drayton Munster
1113443132 Cameron Carr Munster

111344322 Anne Peyton Robertson, m. Joseph John Procaccini, Jr.
111344323 Rolfe Robertson III, m. Debora Lynn Jeremiah

1113443233 John Rolfe Robertson (1987-   )
1113443234 James Hunter Robertson (1988-   )

1113443242 Christopher Robertson McNerney (1985-   )
1113443243 Molly Ives McNerney (1988-   )
1113443244 Conor James McNerney (twin) (1992-   )
1113443245 Ian John McNerney (twin) (1992-   )

1113443252 Forest Walker Kettler (1985-   )
1113443253 Caroline Canfield Kettler (1987-   )
1113443254 Robert Peyton Kettler (1995-   )

111344326 James Powhatan Wyndham Robertson, m. 1989, Antigone
             John Agnos (1963-   )

111344331 Lynn Fairfax Carr, m. (2nd) Jay Borton

1113443311 Melissa Billington (1973-   )
111344334 Elizabeth Murdock, m.   Hilliard

1113443412 Elizabeth Tudor Robertson (1984-   )

111344342 Elizabeth Averett Robertson, m. (2nd) 1986, Charles
            Daniel Rowe

11134435 John William Peyton Robertson, m. Edith Shepherd Brooke
111344351 Elizabeth Bolling Robertson, m. (2nd) Jeffery Laytin
    Child by first husband:
1113443511 Nevada Marquette Tinsman (1987-   )
    Child by second husband:
1113443512 Silvia Brooke Laytin (1994-   )

111344353 John William Peyton Robertson, m. Melissa Lanni

111344362 Bruce Dixon Robertson, m. 1989, Robin McGlaughlin
111344363 Ellen Peyton Robertson, m. 1985, Andrew Blake
1113443631 Camillus Andrew Blake (1990-   )

1113443711 Jessica Katherine Weisser
1113443712 Jacob Charles Weisser (1985-   )

1113443721 Victoria Marie Pierson (1988-   )
111344373 Charles Donald Butter, Jr., m. Susan Marie Dosser
            (1960-   )
1113443731 Benjamin Joseph Butter (1988-   )
1113443732 Joshua Michael Butter (1990-   )
1113443733 Andrew Thomas Butter (1992-   )
111344374 Gretchen Butter (1965-   ), m. John Hilgers
1113443741 Spencer Robinson Hilgers (1989-   )
1113443742 Heidi Louise Hilgers (1992-   )
1113443743 Margaret Jean Hilgers (1994-   )
111344375 Daniel Butter (1968-   ), m. Audra Bearman

111344411 Eileen Lynn Gruet, m. Barry Rexrode
11134442 Martha Knighton Brashears (1921-1989), m. 1944, Samuel
            Gibson (1922-1986)
111344421 James Randolph Gibson, m. Marney
1113444211 Jacquelyne May Gibson (1969-   )
1113444212 Jamey Brashears Gibson (1974-   )
1113444213 Garrett James Gibson (1976-   )
1113444214 Katherine May Gibson (1978-   )
1113444215 Jonathan Nord Gibson (1983-   )
1113444216 Lauren Robertson Gibson (1983-   )

1113444221 Jonathan Kohan (1987-   )
111344423 Gail Brashears Gibson, m. (2nd) Paul Rodland

111344431 Gay Frances Reif, m.   Olleo
1113444311 Kimberley Olleo (1970-   )
1113444312 Lisa Olleo (1974-   )
111344432 Karen Neeley Reif, m.   Tota

1113444321 Michael Tota (1976-   )
111344441 Fred Harwood Kuver, m. Michele
111344442 Nancy Lynn Kuver, m. Ron Bonanno
1113444421 Todd Bonanno (1978-   )
1113444422 Travis Bonanno (twin) (1980-   )
1113444423 Tracey Bonanno (twin) (1980-   )
111344443 Bethann Kuver, m.   Frederick
1113444431 Kimberley Frederick (1979-   )
1113444432 Ricky Frederick (1984-   )

1113451 Louise Fairfax Robertson, m. George Twyman Wood III
11134511 George Twyman Wood IV (1922-1986)

111345112 George Twyman Wood V (1952-   ), m. Katherine Suttles
1113451121 Alden Randolph Wood (1987-   )
1113451122 Caroline Fairfax Wood (1989-   )

11134512 Walter Wyvill Wood, m.(2nd) 1986, Linda Ellen Leonard

111345122 Walter Wyvill Wood, Jr., m. Carroll Goodman
1113451221 Brackston Ewing Wood (1992-   )
1113451222 Laura Kathleen Wood (1994-   )

1113461122 Grace William Campbell

1113462 Harriet Simpson Robertson (1891-1986)

111346212 Robin Robertson Chancellor
1113462121 Zachary Chancellor Hagerman (1975-   )
1113462122 Gabriel Hagerman (1984-   )

11134811 Samuel Alexander Moore, Jr. (11/11/1918-11/5/1985)

111348121 Richard Reynolds Moore, m. (2nd) 1992, Traci Wolf

1113482 Mary Fairfax Robertson (7/14/1894-1986), m. Richard
          Edgar Waterhouse, Jr. (1890-1959) (?)

1113482121 Kara Motophan Keichikan Waldron
1113482122 Brooke Tyrell Waldron

1113621112 Barbara Bradford Silk
111362112 Anne Robertson Buttenheim, m. 1988, Dat Duthin
1113621121 Elizabeth Duthin
111362113 Elizabeth Gay Buttenheim, m. 1985, James Edward
            Maxwell
1113621131 Wyndham Maxwell
1113621132 Charlotte Maxwell

1113621141 Andrew Vytas Kisielious
1113621142 Julia Gay Kisielious
1113621143 Curtis Kisielious
11136212 Frederick Clay Robertson, Jr. (9/30/1927-5/4/1988)

1113621211 Charles Clay Hulcher
1113621212 Carter Robertson Hulcher (d. at 3 months 1986)
111362122 Susan Rutledge Robertson, m. 1986, Edwin David Selby
1113621221 Mark Robertson Selby (1989-   )

1113622 Julian Hart Robertson (11/3/1899-1995, m. Blanche
          Williamson Spencer (1906-1994)

111362221 Benjamin Robert Williamson, Jr., m. 1988, Caroline
           Costner Crook
1113622211 Caroline Williamson
1113622212 Benjamin Robert Williamson III

111362321 Elizabeth Burns Robertson, m. 1985, Jean Melancon
111362322 William Marsh Robertson, m. Barbara
1113623221 Ashley Elizabeth Robertson (1991-   )
1113623222 William Kessenich Robertson (1995-   )

1113812 Wyndham Robertson III (1905-1989), m. (1st) Constance
         Keyworth (1905-1995). M. (2nd) Laura Wilson Adams
         (1903-1993)
11138121 Helen Patricia Robertson, m. (1st) 1945, Richard
          Anderson (1924-1979). M. (2nd) John Willard Griffin
          (1920-1988). M. (3rd) Arthur Sheridan Kuhns (1929-
)
   Children by first husband:
111381211 Cynthia Lynn (Anderson) Griffin (1946-   ), m. (1st)
           1963, Richard Roger Harris (1939-   ). M. (2nd)
           Roberto Gerardo Purnudi (1946-   )
   Child by first husband:
1113812111 Routy Darin Harris (1964-   ), m. Janice Marie
            Jabaga (1967-   )
11138121111 Kelly Robert Harris (1989-   )
   Child by second husband:
1113812112 Roberto Alexander Purnudi-Anderson (1984-   )
111381212 Bradley Kent (Anderson) Griffin (1947-1986), m. (1st)
           1964, Sandra Lynn Hofman. M. (2nd) 1978, Kathleen
           Jean Ruth
   Child by second husband:
111381213 Christopher Sean Griffin (1956-   ), m. 1981 Kathleen
           Louise Philbrick

1113812132 Mary Louise Griffin (1983-   )
1113812133 Amy Elizabeth Griffin (1989-   )
11138122 Wyndham Robertson IV (1927-   ), m. (1st) 1949, Gloria
          Jean Otwell (1926-   ). M. (2nd) 1961, Linda
          Alexander (1937-   ). M. (3rd) 1973, Linda Denise
          Bickford (1946-   )
   Children by first wife:
111381221 Jeffrey Wyndham Robertson, m. Judith Strawser
111381222 Stephen Eugene Robertson
   Children by second wife:
111381223 Wyndham Robertson V, m. 1993, Maria Ana Murallon
1113812231 Joshua Murallon Robertson (1993-   )

111381224   Richard Alexander Robertson (1967-   ) (twin), m.
            1986, Laura Joanne Widner
111381225 Wendy Robertson (1967-d. young) (twin)

1114 John Robertson, Judge of Virginia Circuit Court.   Born at
      "Belfield".   Author

111418113 Jennifer Shelton

111418122 Christina Andrews

1114182 Elizabeth Lewis Carter Harrison, m. William Beckler
         White

1114212 Mary Frances Munro Bolling. Add, at end (2415185).
11142121   Richard Bolling Randolph (1918-1988)

11142122 William Barksdale Randolph (1919-1994), m. Elizabeth
          Page Craven (1922-1990)

1114212211 Alexander Dressler Randolph (1987-   )

111421222 Richard Nichols Randolph, m. 1983, Mary Susan Rositzke
           (1961-   )
1114212221 Emily Ann Randolph (1987-   )

111421232 Emily Martha Hampton Crom, m. Michael Lyons
111421233 Lucy Barksdale Crom, m. Austin McNamara
1114212331

1114241 Alice Stith Barksdale (1891-1983)
1114242 Anne Robertson Barksdale, m. Bernard Hoskins Baylor
11142421   William Barksdale Baylor, m. (2nd) Elizabeth Cushing
           Herring

111424214 Margaret ("Margo") Hazen Baylor

11142431 Robert Barksdale Ooghe. Div. M. (2nd) 1972, June
          Adelaide Walker

   Children by second wife:
111424313 Robert Barksdale Ooghe, Jr. (1974-   )
111424314 Lydia Adelaide Ooghe (1980-   )

1114244 Winifred Elizabeth Lewis Barksdale (1899-1989)
1114245 Gay Robertson Barksdale (1901-1986)

111424513 William Barksdale Propert, m. 1977, Valerie Jean
           Hanson
1114245131 Matthew Barksdale Propert (1982-   )
1114245132 Emily Boyd Propert (1987-   )

111425 Infant son Barksdale (1856-   ) (twin)

11161321 Henry Skipwith Gordon III (1898-   )
11161322 Henry Skipwith Gordon IV (1900-1960), m. Frances
          Virginia Willis
111613221 Henry Skipwith Gordon V (1929-   ), m. (1st) Cornelia
          Holt Casleton. M. (2nd) Millicent Tilghman Pascault.
          M. (3rd) Johanna Hesthag Seggern
   Child by first wife:
1116132211 Henry Skipwith Gordon VI (name changed later to
          Skipwith Gordon Castleton)
   Children by second wife:
1116132212 Lydia Ann Gordon (1959-   )
1116132213 Walter Conrad Gordon (1961-   )
111613222 James Fitzhugh Gordon (1937-   ), m. (1st)
          M. (2nd)   . M. (3rd) Beverley
          Poe
   Children by third wife:
1116132221 Karen Lynn Gordon (1963-   )
1116132222 Michael James Gordon (1965-   )
1116132223 Brian Stewart Gordon (1973-   )
111613223 Sarah Elizabeth Wheeler Gordon (1938-   ), m. (1st)
          Richard Sears McCulloch II. M. (2nd) Thomas Edward
          Congalton
   Children by first husband:
1116132231 Kathleen Stewart McCulloch (1957-   )
1116132232 Sarah Elizabeth McCluloch (1959-   )
1116132233 Richard Sears McCulloch III (1961-   )
111613224 Margaret Ransom Gordon (1945-   ), m. Robert Paul
          Eben
1116132241 Debra Ann Eben (1966-   )
1116132242 Kelly Lynn Eben (1968-   )
1116132243 Paul Stewart Eben (1969-   )
1116132244 Frances Eben (1971-   )
111613225 William Stewart Gordon (1948-   ), m. Nancy Weiss
11161323 Stewart Eccleston Gordon (1905-1991), m. Mary Gardiner
          Blake (1906-1991)
111613231 Margaret Stewart Gordon (1927-   ), m. 1949, Philip
          Merrill Hildebrandt

1116132312 Margaret Ann Hildebrandt, m. (1st) Bruce Carroll
          Sampson. M. (2nd) Mark McClelland
1116132313 Grace Brooks Hildebrandt, m. (1st) Matthew Calvin.
          M. (2nd) Donald Dowell

111613232 Stewart Eccleston Gordon, Jr.
1116132321 Katherine Stewart Gordon
1116132322 Elizabeth Graham Gordon

1116132324 Stewart Eccleston ("Chip") Gordon III

1116222 Eliza Bolling Skipwith, m. Valery Gaienne Hyams
11162221 Mathilde Skipwith Hyams
11162222 John Skipwith Hyams (1908-1994), m. 1947, Myrtis
          Juanita Temple

111622222   Ouita Gayle Hyams (1952-   ), m. 1982, William
             Benjamin Bingham III
1116222221   Sarah Skipwith Bingham (1988-   )
1116222222   Alexander Hyams Bingham (1988-   )
1116222223
11162223 Henry Michael Hyams (1911-   )

11162224 Valery Gaienne Hyams, Jr. (1914-1956)
111622241   Valery Gaienne Hyams III

1116222461   Maya Flores

111622254   Randall Hartwell Pyfron, Jr., m. Shawna Hughes
1116222541   Lais Pyfron
1116222542   Randall Hartwell Pyfron III

11162256 Louis Lambkin Morris, m. Camille

1116227222   Jesse Elizabeth Carroll (1983-   )

11171 Gay Robertson Bernard, m. (as his second wife) Charles
         Tiernan (Charles had a daughter Helen, by his first
         wife (see 111713 below).
111711   Anna Dolores Tiernan, m. John Robinson Tait
111713   Gay Bernard Tiernan, m. (as his 2nd wife) Henry Augustus
         Fenwick (Henry's first wife was Helen Tiernan, the
         daughter of Charles Tiernan (see 11171 above) and his
         first wife . . . Helen was Gay's half-sister).
1117131   Henry Augustus Fenwick, Jr.
1117132   Charles Ghequierre Fenwick

1117133   Gay Bernard Fenwick, m. Margaret Mary Griffiss (1890-
          1974)

111713336   Stephen Fenwick Edelen

111713341   Guy Chance Fenwick (1948-   )
111713342   Elizabeth Fenwick, m. Rolfe Wyer

1117133521   Rosalie Fenwick

111714 Laura Cecelia Tiernan, m. Joshua Pierce Klingle

111762   Bernard Robertson Guest, m. Eliza Laurens Chisolm (1870-
          1931)
1117621   Mary Bernard Guest, m. Claiborne Watkins Beattie Gwyn

11179 Caroline Pocahontas Bernard, m. Martin Pickett Scott, son
         of John and Elizabeth Pickett Scott

111793 Lelia Bernard Scott, m. Richard Henry Alvery

1117931132

111793114 Douglas Simmons, m. Robin
1117932 Richard Henry Alvey, Jr., m.
1117933 Martin Scott Alvey, m. Emma Glass

1117941 John Bernard Scott, Jr. (1908-1995)

111794111 Virginia Robbins, m. Gary Bugg

11179422 Robert Iden Iglehart, m. (2nd) Alison Lewis
111794221 Mary Alison Iglehart
111794222 Robert Anderson Iglehart

1117a32 Robert Carleton Upton, m. Alberta Arrett Pritchett
          (1920-1993)

1117a42 Robert Gilchrist Robb, Jr. (1931-1991)

111x21111 Ann David Dandridge (1943-   ), m. (1st) William
            Stiffler III. M. (2nd) Christopher Hartman
    Children by first husband:
111x211111 Sarah Stiffler
111x211112 William Stiffler IV
111x21112 Sally Dandridge (1947-   ), m. Brian Lemco
111x211121 Nicholas Lemco

111x21121 Angus McDonald, Jr.

111x2121 Gavin Hadden, Jr., m. 1942, Carol Wolgemuth
111x21211 Gavin Hadden III (1946-   ), m. Patricia

111x21212 Linda Hadden (1950-   ), m. Ty Shen

111x21213 Susan Gay Hadden (1943-   ), m. Theodore Woodcock

111x21214 Peter Hadden (1964-   )

111x2123 David Hadden (1920-   ), m. Loris Jeffries
111x21231 David Hadden, Jr., m. Lyn Carter
111x212311 John David Hadden (1981-   )
111x212312 Katherine Carter Hadden (1982-   )
111x212313 Alexander Carter Hadden (1987-   )

111x21233 Ann Hadden (1952-   ), m. Sam Munoff

111x212411 Reilly Hadden (1986-   )

111x213111 Jennifer Franklin
111x213112 Elizabeth Franklin
111x213113 John Weed Franklin III

111x213121 John Best
111x213122 Elizabeth Best
111x213123 Barbara Best

111x213131 Churchill Halstead Franklin
111x213132 Katherine Franklin
111x213133 Lindsey Franklin

111x2132 Susan Stuart Gibson, m. Stephen Rintoul Davenport III
111x21321 Stephen Rintoul Davenport IV

111x214211 Sarah Gelb
111x214212 Yair Gelb
111x214213 Yigal Gelb

111x2143 Betty Gay Symington, m. Sanford Byrd Kauffman

111x214321 Lisa Norris
111x214322 Timothy Norris

111x215 Arthur Selden Lloyd, Jr.

111x261 Pelham Blackford, Jr. (1905-1992)
111x2611 Franklin Carter Blackford, m. (2nd) Robert Filer

111x262 James Baylor Blackford, m. (1st) Lillian Cary St. Clair
         (1912-   )
   Children by first wife:
111x2621 Gay St. Clair Blackford (1942-   )
111x2622 Ann Courtenay Blackford (1944-   ), m. 1971, Robert
          Garner
111x26221 Carson Blake Garner (1974-   )

111x2623 Susan Constant Blackford, m. Richard Hankins

111x2631 Frank Robertson Blackford, Jr. (1940-   ), m. 1965,
          Vivien Kunfi Stanton
111x26311 Loren Lindeman Blackford (1968-   )
111x26312 Evan Baldwin Blackford (1973-   )
111x2632 John Baldwin Blackford (1944-   ), m. 1971, Anne Drake
          Little
111x26321 David Little Blackford (1972-   ) (twin)
111x26322 Jacob Baldwin Blackford (1972-   ) (twin)

111x411 Frank Reade (1895-1957)

111x4121 Reade Johnson, m. (2nd) Robert Ayres Carter
111x41211 Robin Rebecca Berry, m.   Govan
111x412111 Ayanna Reade Govan (1994-   )

111x41411 Reade Maclin, m. Henry Alan Rowe
111x414111 Jonathan Reade Rowe (1989-   )
111x414112 Mary Louise Rowe (1992-   )
111x41412 Caroline Maclin, m. W. Timothy Key
111x414121 Daniel Robertson Key (1994-   )
111x4142 Elizabeth Whitman Copenhaver, m. Robert Burns Triplett,
          Jr.
111x41421 Robert Burns Triplett II (1957-   )

111x41422 William Whitman Triplett (1959-   )
111x41423 Clark Copenhaver Triplett (1966-   ), m.
111x414231 Samantha Robertson Triplett
111x41424 Elizabeth Whitman Triplett (1967-   ), m. Eric James
           Stoops

111x43 Katy Robertson, m. William Trigg Booker (1876-1952)

111x441 Katy Robertson Motley (1917-1978)

111x4412 Kenneth Armistead Grandstaff II

111x44314 Natasha Marie Kalergis (1988-   )

111x4432 Hugh Douglas Camp Motley (1954-   ), m. Kathleen
          Buchanon

111x4434 Frank Robertson Motley, Jr., m. Julie Clark

111x641 Kathleen Robertson White (1902-1981)

111x6421 Martha Norton White, m. (2nd)   Wiese

111x64212 James L. Hart, Jr.
111x6422 Claire Stone White, m.   Sahling
111x643 Mary Faukerson White, m. Frederick Alexander
111x6431 Frederick Alexander, Jr., m. (2nd) Janet Lee

111x6433 Markham Robertson Alexander

111x6442 Harry Porche Baya

111x64422 Paul Emery Baya

111x6451 Harriet White Gwathmey, m. John McGuire Chinn

111x646 William Young Conn White, Jr. (1914-1994), m. Kathleen
         Brown (1915-1986)
111x6461 Kathleen Sanders White (1946-   ), m. Benjamin
          Franklin Sheftall (1947-   )
111x64611 Katherine Russell Sheftall (1970-   )
111x64612 Rebeccah Brown Sheftall (1975-   )
111x6462 William Young Conn White III (1949-   ), m. Mary
          Katherine Russell (1957-   )
111x64621 William Young Conn White IV (1984-   )
111x64622 Elizabeth Lane White (1987-   )
111x6463 James Lowery White II (1952-   ), m. Linda Lee
          Marbury (1952-   )
111x64631 Jane Poythress White (1986-   )

111x6712 Charles Joseph Post III, m. (2nd) Anna Hamilton Phelan

111x812 Wyndham Bolling Robertson Lee, m. (2nd) Lelia Marshall
         Cabel

111x8121 Carol Holcombe Lee, m. Thomas Frederick Farrar

111x8122 Norvell Harrison Lee, m. Preston Mayo (-1990)

111x813 Francis Thompkins Lee, m. Lois Amelia Moore
111x8131 Francis Thompkins Lee, Jr. (1924-   ), m. Elizabeth
          Lowery
111x81311 Francis Norvell Lee
111x81312 Judith Carter Lee
111x81313 Nancy Lee
111x8132 Rose Marie Lee (1926-   ), m.   Grant
111x81321 Michael Lee Grant (1956-   )
111x81322 Lois Marie Grant (1959-   )

111x831 Margie Robertson (1906-1995)
111x832 Florence Robertson
111x8321 Walter Robertson Milbourne, m. Sue Dyer
111x83211 Gregory Broughton Milbourne
111x83212 Karen Elizabeth Milbourne
111x83213 Walter Robertson Milbourne, Jr.
111x83214 Margaret Henderson Milbourne

111x881 Wyndham Robertson Worden (1902-1919)

111x8842 Florence Worden, m. (2nd)   Barrett

111x8881 Lynn Worden, m. Franklin Wayne Wilson, Jr.
111x88811 Sarah Lewis Wilson (1974-   )
111x88812 Franklin Wayne Wilson III (1976-   )
111x8882 Mary Stuart Worden, m. 1976 Bryant Wallace Brooks
          (1955-   )

113 Col. William Bolling. War of 1812. Founded in America
     first institution for deaf

     The three following children attended Braidwood Institute,
Edinburgh, Scotland:

114 Mary ("Polly") Bolling

115 Thomas Bolling, Jr. Died 1/11/1836 at "Gaymont", Caroline
     County

116 John Bolling

121 Martha Bolling, m. Peter Field Archer (1756-1814), son of
     Edward Field and Mary Elizabeth (?) Archer of Chesterfield
     County
1211 Powhatan Bolling Archer (1795-   ), m. (1st) Martha Jones
      Walthall, m. (2nd) Elizabeth Westerstone Price
1212 Martha C. Archer (1794-   ), m. (1st) 5/9/1825 Chesterfield
      County, John Randolph Bolling, m. (2nd) (after 1825)
      Robert Berry

16

1213   Eleanor ("Ellen") W. Archer (1797-   ), m. 12/29/1825,
          Robert Berry
1214   Mary Archer (1798-   ), m. (1st) Edward Covington, m.
          (2nd) 5/2/1846 Chesterfield County, Augustus E. Cogbill
12141 Martha Covington, m. (1st) Julius   . M. (2nd)
          Henry Wells
1215   Lucy Ann Archer (ca. 1800-after 1868), m. 2/4/1837,
          Chesterfield County, Edward Archer (only brother to
          Branch Archer of Richmond)
12151 Brother killed C.S.A. 5/14/1864
12152 Anna Bolling Archer, m. 12/29/1868, James A. Page
12153 Girl
12154 Girl
12155 Girl
12156 Boy
12157 Boy

121x   Pocahontas Archer, m.
121x1 Son
121x11 Child
121x12 Child
121x13 Child
121x14 Child
121x15 Child
121x16 Child

124   William Archer Bolling (died in Campbell County), m. 11/2/
          1801, Catherine Payne
1241   Dr. Archibald Bolling, m. Anne Eliza Wigginton

1241271 Son of Galt lived only two days.

125   Mary Jefferson Bolling (b. ca. 1776), m. (2nd) 12/2/1815,
          in Chesterfield County, William Covington

129   Ann Bolling (7/20/1767-   ), m. 1784, Capt. Howell Lewis
1291   Warner Lewis (1810-1878), m. (1st) Margaret Akin (d.
          10/15/1842 New Madrid County , MS), m. (2nd) Mrs. Emeline
          Russel Jarrett. Warner was born in Lexington, KY, and
          was left an orphan at an early age. He was then taken to
          New Orleans and reared by his great aunt Martha Monroe.
          After obtaining his majority, he moved to New Madrid,
          MS, and married Miss Akin, a native of Cape Girardeau
          County and of Irish descent. Mr. Lewis moved near
          Farmington, MO, to St. Fracois County, MO, in 1858 where
          he purchased a farm.

       Children by Akin:

12911
12912

12913 Thomas Walker Lewis (b. 3/7/1841 New Madrid County, MO),
          m. Caroline Sebastian (b. 4/19/1845 St. Francois, MO,

                of French descent). A farmer (195 acres) west of
                Fredericktown.
129131   Edward L. Lewis
129132   Thomas E. Lewis
129133   Mary A. Lewis
129134   Cora E. Lewis
129135   Emma L. Lewis
129136   Maggie B. Lewis
129137   Carrie M. Lewis
129138   Alberta A. Lewis
129139   John W. Lewis
12913x   Deceased

    Children by Mrs. Jarrett (she had one child by her first
    husband):
12914
12915
12916
12917
12918
12919

13   Col. Robert Bolling, m. (1st) Mary Lavinia Burton (b. 1748),
       dau. of John Burton and granddau. of William Burton.

13115   John Monro Banister, Jr. An Episcopal minister (Hunts-
          ville, AL, from 1860 until his death). His wife's
          family the Broadnax lived at "Kinston", near Petersburg.
          John wore a Prince Albert coat and silk hat and carried
          a gold headed cane.

131152   William Broadnax Banister, m. Mary Carolina Noltenius

131153   Robert Bolling Banister, m. 2/ /1874 Corrilla Nations
            in Gonzales County, TX
1311531   Mary Louisa Banister (1875-1928). A concert pianist
            until her health failed. M. 1899 Truman H. Aldrich,
            Jr., son of a Birmingham congressman. Div.
13115311   Truman H. Aldrich III (1906-1955 or 1960), m. (1st)
              193   in Philadelphia,   Gloninger. Div.
            M. (2nd)   . D. in Brookhaven,
            GA. He was an architect.
131153111   Mary Louise Aldrich

1311552   Monro Banister Lanier. President of Ingalls Shipbuild-
            ing Company at Pascagoula, MS

1311562   John Monro Banister Slaughter. Mobile, AL. M.
              , granddaughter of Emily Banister of
          Virginia, a sister of 13115 John Monro Banister.

1312   Anne Robertson Bolling, m. Rev. John N. Campbell
1313   Martha Stith Bolling, m. Martin Slaughter, son of Stanton
          and Judith Pickett Slaughter.

1314   Robert Buckner Bolling (born "Weynoke", Charles City
          County), m. Sarah Melville Minge, dau. of John and Sarah
          Short Stewart Minge.
13141 Robert Bolling, M.D. (born in Philadelphia), m. Leontine
          Hagerdon
13142 John Minge Bolling (born in New York City), m. Madge
          Walker
13143 Townsend Stith Bolling (died in youth)
1315   George W. Bolling, m. Martha Nicholls, dau. of William
          Nicholls.
13151 Mary Tabb Bolling (born in Petersburg), m. 11/28/1867,
          Maj. Gen. William Henry Fitzhugh

132a   Charles Joseph Cabell (1789-11/23/1810).   Died in New
          Orleans of yellow fever.   Graduate of William and Mary.

133   Elizabeth Blair Bolling (b. ca. 1767)

1331121   Sallie Love Booker (1858-1934), m. George ("Trit")
          Booker (1849-1926)
13311211   Ella Neal Booker (1882-1958), m. W. B. ("Buck") Binford
13311212   William Watson Booker (1886-1961), m. Georgia B. Adams
          1910-1993)
133112121   William Watson Booker, Jr. (-1993), m. (1st)
          Mary Ann Wood, m. (2nd) Barbara
1331121211   William Watson Booker III, m. 1984, Maria Caroline
          Donnini
1331121212   Mark Douglas Booker
133112122   Grace Ellen Booker (1933-1976), m. Brad Barr
13311213   Richard Edward Booker (1889-1971), m. Helene Foster
          1895-1988)
133112131   George William Booker (1915-199), m. Jacqueline
          Crute
1331121311   James Foster Booker (1947-   )
1331121311   Dawn Booker
1331121312   Ann Elizabeth Booker (1948-   ), m. William Lantz
13311213121   Joshua Lantz
13311213122   Travis Lantz
13311214   Henry Theodoric Booker (1892-1953)
13311215   George West Booker (1895-   ), m. Elgie Gilliam (1907-
          1993)
133112151   Katherine Anne Booker (1928-   ), m. Edmund Wilson
          Womack (1927-   )
1331121511   Susan Glenn Womack (1951-   ), m. Linnie Wilson
          Barr (1949-   )
13311215111   Christopher West Barr (1971-   )
13311215112   Amy Barr
1331121512   Joseph Wilson Womack (1954-   ), m. Joyce Marie
          Linville (1953-   )
133112152   Edward G. Booker (1930-1959)
13311216   Norman Courtney Booker (1897-1956)
13311217   Mary Elizabeth Booker (1902-1988)
1331122   Richard Glover Booker (1855-   ), m. Carrie Cole
1331123   Walter T. Booker (1865-   ), m. Mrs. Fannie Foster

```
1331124   Norman Courtney Booker (1867-    )
1331125   Lou Emma Booker (1869-1945), m. Jesse T. Adams
13311251  Ella Kate Adams
13311252  Jack Adams
13311253  Edwin Glover Adams, m. Eudora Saunders
133112531 Eugenia Lou Adams, m.            Young
13311254  Jessie Love Adams, m. Gordon Anderson
133112541 Grace Gilliam Anderson
13311255  Louisa Adams (      -1993), m. R. F. Burke Steele (   -
          1969)
133112551 Louise Scott Steele, m. Robert E. Kanich
133112552 R. F. Burke Steele, Jr., m. Elizabeth Virginia Scarff
133112553 Alice Booker Steele (     -1979)
13311256  Richard Thomas Adams, m. Geraldine Scott
133112561 Richard Thomas Adams, Jr.
133112562 James E. Adams
133112563 Robert Clark Adams
1331126   George Richard Booker


13312  Thomas West Jones, m. 1846, Martha Jones

1331211922321 Pauline Elizabeth Jackson, m. Randy Gilchrist
13312119223211 Aaron Cameron Gilchrist
13312119223212 Catherine Elizabeth Gilchrist
1331211922322 Charlie Richard Jackson.  Name changed to
               Christopher Joseph Evans after divorce from
               his father.  M. Christy Deas


13313  Mary Ann Jones, m. Thomas Richard Marshall

13314  William Saunders Jones m. 1846, Virginia Judith Moorman
       (1826-     )
133141   James Saunders Jones, m. Evelyn Hunter
1331411  Edna Jones
1331412  Jamie Jones (    -1936), m. Charles Edward Wildasin
13314121 Evelyn Hunter Wildasin
13314122 Margaret Handy Wildasin, m.        Story
13314123 Charles Edward Wildasin
13314124 Jamie Jones Wildasin
133142   Thomas M. Jones, m. Betty Bonsack
1331421  William Jones
1331422  Ruth Jones
1331423  Eula Jones, m.          Smith
1331424  Carrie Moorman Jones
1331425  Herbert S. Jones
133143   Elizabeth Clark Jones, m. William D. Price
1331431  Elizabeth Virginia Price, m. Charles P. Marshall
1331432  Anna M. Price.  Unm.
1331433  Mary ("May") Price, m. Frank Womack
1331434  Samuel (William?) Jones Price.  Unm.
133144   Martha West Jones (1853-1908), m. William Chatham Abbitt
          (1848-1916)
1331441  William Jones Abbitt (1875-1936), m. Olive West Gilliam
13314411 Ralph Abbitt (12/26/1901-     )
```

```
13314412   Janie Abbitt (8/27/1906-1992), m. William T. Smith
               (2/22/1904-    )
13314413   Thomas Gilliam Abbitt (10/9/1909-1973)
13314414   Olive ("Sis") Abbitt (9/9/1911-4/  /1991)
13314415   Robert ("Bud") Abbitt (11/28/1914-    )
13314416   William Jones ("Jerry") Abbitt (2/15/1918-    )
1331442    Benjamin Bolling Abbitt (1876-1940), m. Gertrude Green
               (1879-1957)
13314421   Sarah West Abbitt (1906-1906)
13314422   Gertrude Mae Abbitt (1910-1986)
1331443    James Curry Abbitt (1879-1955), m. Mary Frances Moss
               (1871-1961)
1331444    Harry West Abbitt (1881-1957), m. Margaret Linda Dixon
               (1890-1989)
13314441   Margaret Dixon Abbitt (1914-    ), m. Cleon Walton
               Goodwin (1907-197 )
133144411  Cleon Walton Goodwin, Jr. (1943-    ), m. Susan Rye
1331444111   Claire Goodwin (1975-    )
1331444112   Brian Addison Goodwin (1981-    )
133144412  Harry Abbitt Goodwin (1945-    ), m. Ann Jenning
1331444121   Harry Abbitt Goodwin, Jr. (1974-    )
13314442   Harry West Abbitt, Jr. (1919-    ), m. Catherine
               Margaret Thomas
13314443   Jean Dixon Abbitt (1917-1994), m. John Riddick Harriss
               (1917-    )
133144431  Jean Abbitt Harriss (1942-    ), m. Wylie Paul Waller,
               Jr.
1331444311   Wylie Paul Waller III (1969-    )
1331444312   Allen Dixon Waller (1972-    )
133144432  Sarah Riddick Harriss (1944-    ), m. Armand R. Emrick
               III
1331444321   John Armand Emrick (1970-    )
1331444322   Samuel Riddick Emrick (1974-    )
133144433  Diana Binford Harriss (1946-    ), m. (1st) G. W.
               Marsh, m. (2nd) Carl Edison Wallace
1331444331   John Harriss ("Marsh") Wallace (1973-    )
1331444332   Brian Elkins Wallace (1977-    )
1331444333   William Wallace (1979-    )
133144434  Margaret Dixon Harriss (1952-1991), m. James Lynn
               Daniell
1331444341   Margaret West Daniell (1977-    )
13314444   Russell Dixon Abbitt (1921-1991), m. Saralee Griffeth
13314445   Julia West Abbitt (192 -1973), m. (1st) Herbert Liles
               Rives, Jr., m. (2nd) C. M. Davis
1331445    Lola Virginia Abbitt (1884-1971), m. Jesse Jennings
               Harvey (1877-1960)
13314451   Lola Virginia Harvey (1905-    ), m. Houston M. Crowder
               (    -1975)
133144511  Houston Crowder
133144512  Nancy Crowder, m. Larry Owen Peters
13314452   Chatham Harvey (1907-1913)
13314453   Jesse Jennings Harvey, Jr. (1909-1973), m. Lucy Downs
13314454   William Clifton Harvey (1909-1910)
```

13314455 Benjamin Curry Harvey (1920-1969), m. Frances Plunkett
          1918-   )
133144551 Jane Abbitt Harvey (1949-   )
133144552 Mary Frances Harvey (1952-   ), m. Danny Ray Bryant
          (1953-   )
1331445521 Andi Elizabeth Bryant (1980-   )
133144553 Martha A. Harvey (1955-   ), m. R. Kent Ramsey
          (1955-   )
1331445531 Jamie Katherine Ramsey (1980-   )
1331446 Mary Ann Abbitt (1885-1967), m. Henry Theodoric Terry
          (1872-1952)
13314461 Mary West Terry (4/26/1912-9/ /1992), m. Patrick
          Alexander Robinson (1899-1964)
133144611 Patrick Alexander Robinson, Jr. (1940-   ), m. (1st)
          Susan Bagley Mann, m. (2nd) Mary E. Shubert (7/1/
          1950-   )
1331446111 Patrick Alexander Robinson III (1964-   ), m. 1986,
          Danielle Boram (1966-   )
13314461111 Alexandra Danielle Robinson
13314461112 Patrick Alexander Robinson IV
1331446112 Melissa Ruth Robinson (1968-   )
1331446113 James Nelson Robinson (1970-   )
1331446114 Natalie Rose Robinson (1981-   )
1331446115 Mary Elizabeth Robinson (1985-   )
133144612 Lucian Dabney Robinson III (1946-   ), m. Susan
          Beller (1946-   )
1331446121 Bronwyn Robinson (1974-   )
1331446122 Bambi Robinson (1975-   )
1331446123 Christopher Scott Robinson (1985-   )
13314462 Nathaniel Chatham Terry (10/4/1913-   ), m. Nannie
          Ruth Cooper (1913-2/ /1986)
133144621 Mary Sue Terry (1947-   )
133144622 Ruth Cooper Terry (10/ /1949-   ), m. George
          Dickerson, Jr.
1331446221 George Dickerson III (1969-   ), m. Victoria Hilton
13314462211 Katherine Ann Dickerson (1992-   )
1331446222 Benjamin Chatham Dickerson (1975-   )
133144623 Sally Ann Terry (1/ /1951-   ), m. Warren Lee Rodgers
1331446231 Warren Lee Rodgers, Jr. (1978-   )
1331446232 Margaret Abbitt Rodgers (1981-   )
1331446233 William Nathaniel Rodgers (1985-   )
13314463 Joseph Benjamin Terry (10/7/1915-4/19/1991), m. 4/30/
          1941, Mary Elizabeth Featherston (8/13/1912-1/20/
          1977)
133144631 Joseph Benjamin Terry, Jr. (8/26/1946-   ), m.
          5/ /1975, Delores Ann Vawter
133144632 Thomas Ragland Terry (10/5/1951-   )
13314464 Henry Theodoric Terry, Jr. (1918-1981), m. Ellen Ruth
          Blattspieler (1923-1982)
13314465 George Abbitt Terry (11/13/1920-   ), m. Lulie
          Greenhow Jones (10/26/1921-   )
13314466 Sallie Love Terry (2/2/1923- 1/ /1983), m. (1st) Bill
          A. Chandler (1921-1956), m. (2nd) Robert Langdon
          Baillio (-1983)

```
133144661  Terry Hays Chandler (1947-1970)
133144662  Linda Sue (Chandler) Baillio (1955-    )
13314467  Elizabeth Virginia Terry (11/1/1926-    ), m. Herman
          Cleveland Wingfield (1/14/1919-    )
13314468  Ann Bolling Terry (11/ /1929-1993), m. Irving Werner
          Lindenblad (1929-    )
133144681  Irving Werner Lindenblad, Jr. (11/1/1960-    )
133144682  Nils Bolling Lindenblad (1963-    ), m. Susan Lieber
1331446821  Beth Ann Lindenblad (1994-    )
1331447  Stella Watkins ("Billie") Abbitt (1886-1952), m. James
         Blair Wilson (1880-1957)
13314471  James Blair Wilson, Jr.
13314472  Ellen MacCorkle Wilson (1912-1964), m. E. Douglas
          McClure (1904-1981)
1331448  George Dallas Abbitt (1890-1957), m. Bertha Hanson
133145  William Ansalem Jones, m. Lacey Lee Hunter
1331451  Lena Virginia Jones, m.         Winston
1331452  Elsie Lee Jones, m. M. C. Goggin
1331453  James Saunders Jones
1331454  Minnie Hunter Jones, m.         Gaskill
1331455  Erna William Jones, m. Will Blanks
1331456  William Benjamin Jones
1331457  Lillian Estelle Jones, m.         Gulledge
1331458  Iva Childs Jones, m.         Harvey
1331459  Micajah Clark Jones
133146  Samuel Dewes Jones, m. Elizabeth Harrison
1331461  Harrison Jones (1887-    ), m. Kathryn Gordon
13314611  Harrison Jones, Jr.
13314612  Gordon Jones, m. Ann Creekmore
133146121  Harrison Jones III
1331462  Saunders Jones
1331463  Lula Dean Jones, m. Beverly Means DuBose
13314631  Beverly Means DuBose, Jr., m. Frances Woodruff
133146311  Beverly Means DuBose III
13314632  Betty DuBose
1331464  Bolling Jones, m. Dorothy Hodgson
13314641  Bolling Jones, Jr.
13314642  Saunders Jones
133147  Micajah Clark Jones, m. Annie Brazeal
133148  Bolling Henry Jones, m. Lula Harrison
133149  Ella Virginia Jones (1965-1951)
13314x  Emma Lillian Jones (1867-1927), m. Howlett Hunter
        (1852-1927)
13314x1  Charles Jones Hunter (1894-1966), m. (1st) Rachel Wood
         (1889-1936), m. (2nd) Alice Lee Smith
13314x11  Charles Jones Hunter, Jr. (1920-1939)
13314x2  William B. Hunter
13314x3  Raymond E. Hunter
13314x4  Ruby Hunter
13314x5  Peter James Hunter
13314x6  Aubrey Hunter
13314a  Ida West Jones, m. Oscar Hunter
13314a1  Hubert Hunter
13314a2  Eoline Hunter, m. Richard Snell
```

13314a3 Virginia Hunter, m. William P. Marshall
13314a31 Virginia Hunter Marshall
13315 Olivia Wilcox Jones, m. Culvin Ford
13316 Edward Jones
13317 Amanda Jones
13318 Ella Jones m, George Smith
13319 Pocahontas Bolling Jones
1331x Another child

1332 Elizabeth Bolling West (1812-1885)

134 Lenaeus (Linnaeus) Bolling. Named for heathen God of Wine.
1341 Mary Bolling, m. Dr. James Madison Cobbs, son of John Lewis
      and Susan Hammer Cobbs.

13423 James Lenaus Hubbard. Lt. Col. C.S.A. (44th Regiment,
       Virginia Volunteers).

13424 William Hubbard, C.S.A.

       In SECOND ADDITIONS AND CORRECTIONS 13424 is also
       given for Eugene Hubbard (died at 8 years). To avoid
       confusion, the number of Eugene (born in 1843) should
       be 13424a.

13428 Bolling Hubbard (b. 1845), m. Felitia Chapman, dau. of
       Rueben and Felitia Ann Chilton Pickett Chapman.
134281 Felitia Pickett Hubbard

1344 Robert Bolling (b. 1799)

13443 Robert Bolling, Jr.

135 Powhatan Bolling (b. 1769). Mercurial temper. Fought many
     duels.

14232242 William W. Boykin, m. (1st) Elizabeth B. Rucker; m.
          (2nd) Lynn L.   . 142322415 is not correct.
142322421 William W. Boykin, Jr.
1423224211 Sean Boykin
1423224212 Mirabel Boykin
142322422 Elizabeth Boykin, m. Philip S. Newswanger
1423224221 Caitlin Elizabeth Newswanger

15 Sarah Bolling (b. Chesterfield County-d. Charles City County
    after 8/ /1798), m. John Tazewell (d. Williamsburg), son of
    Littleton and Mary Gray Tazewell.

153 William Tazewell (b. before 1795-d. Richmond), m. Mary Page
     Tanner (b. Amelia County 1784-d. Charles City County
     1877), dau. of Branch and Mary Page Finney Tanner.

153413212 Mary Frances Poteet, m. 7/24/1993, James Martin
           Watkins (4/16/1967-   )
15341322 Francis Leonidas Joyner, Jr., m. Margaret Anne Dulin
1534133 Mary Southall Shelburne, m. (1st) William Reddick
         Crawford

1535 Sally Bolling Tazewell (b. Charles City County 1812-d.
      Richmond 1895), m. before 1842 George Fitzgerald (b.
      Nottoway County 1800-d. Nottoway County 6/29/1864),
      son of Francis and Frances ("Fanny") Jones Fitzgerald.
      She was his third wife. He conducted, in 1834, The Glebe
      Female School, My School for Young Ladies, at the Glebe,
      near Nottoway Court House.
15351 Mary Lou Fitzgerald (3/2/1843-   ), m. before 1872 John
       W. Pierce
153511 Sally Tazewell Pierce (1/26/1873-   )
153512 Mattie Coke Pierce (2/7/1876-   )
153513 Mary Louise Pierce (5/10/1882-   ), m. after 1898
                          Shore
153514 Frances Page Pierce (6/27/1884-   )
15352 William Tazewell Fitzgerald (11/15/1844-   ), m. before
       1876 Pattie G. Doggett (b. before 1861-   ). He
       graduated from Hampden-Sidney College 1862.
       Children born in Virginia:
153521 Imogene Fitzgerald, m.   Walters
153522 Lulie Fitzgerald, m.   Enroughty
153523 Martha G. Fitzgerald, m.   Sutton
153524 Brooke Fitzgerald
153525 David Doggett Fitzgerald (6/29/1877-   )
153526 Tazewell Fitzgerald (10/15/1878-d. after 1927)
153527 John Pierce Fitzgerald (2/7/1880-   )
153528 Gerald Fitzgerald (7/1/1881-   )
15353 Susan Catherine Fitzgerald (12/14/1845-   )
15354 Littleton Fitzgerald (Nottoway County 6/16/1848-Richmond
       9/15/1935), m. 10/13/1875 Alice Eliza Flournoy (11/4/
       1852 in "Haymarket", Prince Edward County-2/18/1926
       Richmond), dau. of William Cabell and Martha Watkins
       Venable Flournoy. Littleton graduated from Hampden-
       Sidney College in 1874. He may have died 2/ /1935.
153541 Littleton Fitzgerald, Jr. (8/14/1876-2/28/1968) (b. and
        d. in Richmond), m. 10/10/   Elie Maury Werth (1878-
        1955), dau. of James R. and Anne Maury Werth (she was
        a granddaughter of Matthew Fontaine Maury).
1535411 Mary Maury Fitzgerald (8/2/1907-   ), m. Newton F.
         Mckeon, Jr. (d. ca. 1985 in Amherst, MA). Mary

graduated from Mount Holyoke College 1931. Residence:
Lexington, MA

15354111 Edith Mckeon (b. ca. 1938-   ), m. Samuel Abbott (b.
            ca. 1936)
153541111 Mathew Fontaine Abbott (3/ /1974-   )
153541112 Frances Abbott (b. ca. 1976-   )
15354112 Maury Mckeon (7/9/1936-   ), m. 7/11/1959 Jean
            Richardson (4/7/1936-   )
153541121 James Maury Mckeon (4/29/1960-   )
153541122 Lyn Elliott Mckeon (7/23/1962-   ), m. 8/12/1989
            Peter Andrew Muszynski (3/9/1961-   )
152541123 Karen Jean Mckeon (2/19/1964-   ), m. 8/20/1994
            Miguel Angel Lopez (6/5/1963-   )
15354113 Lewis Herndon Mckeon (7/26/1949-   ), m. 6/30/1973
            Barbara Stow Twichell (9/21/1949-   )
153541131 Sarah King Mckeon (8/22/1978-   )
153541132 Ryan Edward Mckeon (10/10/1980-   )
15354114 Seamus Rhodes Mckeon (12/3/1950-   ), m. Lydia Gifvert
            (4/26/1957-   )
153541141 Mathew Maury Mckeon (8/8/1986-   )
153541142 Marion Gardner Mckeon (6/17/1988-   )
1535412 Alice Flournoy Fitzgerald (b. Richmond 4/13/1914-   ),
            m. 8/17/1940 Richard David Harfst (b. Detroit 11/5/
            1914-d. Chapel Hill 4/18/1994). The Harfsts moved
            into "Homewoods" in 1970. There they built a house
            on Gaston Lake in Bracey, VA (called "Alegria").
            Moved to Chapel Hill in 1989. Evidence is that Alice
            was born 2/7/1915.
15354121 Richard Herndon Harfst (8/17/1942-   ), m. (1st) 1967
            Helen Spoehr (b. 1946). Div. before 1972. M. (2nd)
            1972 Meade Boswell (b. before 1944). Div. before
            1980. M. (3rd) 1980 Elizabeth Baukages (b. before
            1956). Div. after 1982. His residence Mathews, VA.
        Child by Elizabeth Baukages:
153541211 Richard Frederick Fitzgerald Harfst (11/23/1982-   )
15354122 Dabney Harfst (10/15/1944-   ), m. 4/18/1970 Alfonso
            Narvaez (b. before 1944 in Puerto Rico)
153541221 Alfonso Narvaez, Jr. (b. before 1970)
153541222 Paul Narvaez (b. before 1970)
153541223 Alicia Isabella Narvaez (1971-   )
153541224 David Narvaez (1974-   )
15354123 Martha Venable Harfst (2/ /1947-   ), m. (1st) 1970
            Alfred Alix (b. before 1958). Div. 1985. M. (2nd)
            10/7/1989 George J. Crowdes III
153541231 Erin Alix (Richmond 1978-   )
153541232 Benjamin Alix (Richmond 1980-   )
153541233 Dabney Alice Alix (New Hampshire 1983-   )
15354124 David Littleton Harfst (1950-   ), m. Pat Shae (before
            1965-   )
153542 George Fitzgerald (1/29/1878-ca. 1939) (born and died in
            Richmond. Graduated from Hampden-Sidney College 1899.
            Wrote and illustrated (portraits, snap shots,
            etc.) in 1886 a book, later known as "Uncle
            George's Scrapbook", which has passed through

the family as an heirloom. Nine copies have
been made for cousins.

153543   John Patterson Fitzgerald (b. Richmond 7/ /1881-1881)

153544   Cabell Flournoy Fitzgerald (Richmond 11/16/1882- New York
         after 1918), m. Flora (Florine) Shenton (Shelton) (d.
         after 1918). He graduated from Hampden-Sidney College
         1902.

153545   Alice Elizabeth Fitzgerald (3/10/1884-11/10/1891) (born
         and died in Richmond)

153546   Sallie Tazewell Fitzgerald (Richmond 2/7/1888-Lynchburg
         9/2/1966), m. 3/ /1927 Thomas Flournoy (8/3/1877-7/20/
         1959) of Brunswick County, son of Jacob Morton and
         Mildred Coles Carrington Flournoy. Their bodies were
         interred in Brunswick County. Sallie's will was
         probated in Brunswick County.

1535461 Alice Fitzgerald Flournoy (Richmond 2/7/1928-   ), m.
         6/10/1954, in Lawrenceville, VA, August Frederick
         Schmitthenner (b. India 1924). Residence: Wooster,
         Ohio.

15354611 August Edward Schmitthenner (6/28/1955-   ), m. 1995
         Linda   . Residence: Canton, Ohio.

15354612 Thomas Flournoy Schmitthenner (b. Wooster, Ohio, 8/26/
         1958-   ), m. 10/10/1987 Penny Wagahoff. Residence:
         Delaware, Ohio.

153546121 Matthew Fritz Schmitthenner (1990-   )

153546122 Rebecca Alice Schmitthenner (8/25/1994-   )

1535462 Mildred Carrington Flournoy (b. Brunswick County 2/20/
         1930-   ), m. 5/10/1961 Robert De Marcellus (1/15/
         1930-   ). Residence: Palm Beach

15354621 Roland Flournoy De Marcellus (10/8/1962-dec'd.)

15354622 Henri Venable De Marcellus (10/16/1964-   ), m. 1995
         Sharon Kinikin

15354623 Sarah ("Sally") Tazewell De Marcellus (10/26/1966-   )

15354624 Robert Cabell De Marcellus (9/27/1968-   )

15354625 Paul Carrington De Marcellus (3/7/1972-   )

15354626 Mary Littleton De Marcellus (9/5/1973-   )

1535463 Sally Tazewell Flournoy (b. Homewoods, Charlie Hope,
         Brunswick County 1933-   ), m. 9/10/1955 Earl Alvin
         Gerhardt, Jr. (Lynchburg 10/15/1930-   ), son of
         Earl Alvin and Georgia Winifred Burton Gerhardt.
         Residence: Jonesborough, TN.

15354631 Elizabeth Morton Gerhardt (7/16/1959-   ). Residence:
         Galveston.

15354632 Earl Frederick Gerhardt (9/25/1961-   ). Residence:
         Dartmouth College.

15354633 Thomas Flournoy Gerhardt (10/15/1963-   ). Residence:
         Buzzards Bay.

15354634 Anna Carrington Gerhardt (4/16/1966-   ). Residence:
         St. Louis.

153547   Marion Nantz Fitzgerald (8/4/1892-11/5/1965), m. 12/29/
         1926 Elizabeth Aiken Jennings (9/19/1901-12/15/1981)

1535471 William Cabell Fitzgerald (1/20/1932-   ), m. (1st)
         2/22/1957 Lucie Fitzgerald. Div. 4/ /1990. M. (2nd)

5/6/1990 Pat Altwegg Brown (5/6/1932-   ). Residence
of William: "Mount Pisgah", King William County.
Children by Lucie:
15354711 Virginia Nantz Fitzgerald (9/5/1963-   ). Residence:
Portland, Oregon.
15354712 Tazewell Fitzgerald (4/30/1966-   )
1535472 Elizabeth Fitzgerald (1/12/1939-   ), m. 4/29/1961 Sam
Kneeland Wallace. Div.
15354721 Sam Kneeland Wallace, Jr. (6/20/1963-   ), m. 5/16/
1987 Mary Lewis Thorp. Residence: Williamsburg.
153547211 Sam Kneeland Wallace III (1989-   )
153547212 Tyler Wallace (1991-   )
153547213 Elizabeth Jennings Wallace (12/ /1994-   )
15354722 Cabell Fitzgerald Wallace (9/18/1967-   ). Residence:
Williamsburg.
153548 Martha Venable Fitzgerald (Richmond 4/25/1898-Fort Worth
5/11/1959), m. Flynn Vincent Long (1898-Charlotte 2/7/
1980)
1535481 Flynn Vincent Long, Jr. (Texas 5/9/1928-   ), m. (1st)
before 1970 Carol Calkin, of Bartlesville, Okla. Div.
after 1975. M. (2nd) after 1970 in Waco Gloria Long.
Residence: Big Spring, Texas.
Children by Carol:
15354811 Martha Long
15354812 Flynn Vincent Long III. Residence: Kerrville, Texas
15354813 Sarah ("Sally") Long
1535482 Martha Venable ("Teeka") Long (Texas 5/14/1930-   ), m.
12/27/1952 Pete Baldwin (cira. 1930-   ). Residence:
Dallas.
15354821 Elizabeth Blair Baldwin (Texas 1/30/1954-   ), m.
before 1982 Charles Hudson (before 1966-   ). Div.
after 1987.
153548211 Nora Angell Hudson (8/22/1983-   )
153548212 Martha Caitlyn Hudson (3/1/1985-   )
153548213 Andrew Weldon Hudson (3/18/1987-   )
15354822 George Weldon Baldwin (Texas 8/22/1955-   ), m. before
1981 Mary Roberts (before 1968-   )
153548221 Jennifer Annin Baldwin (9/ /1982-   )
153548222 Peter Roberts Baldwin (1/13/1986-   )
15354823 Samuel Long Baldwin (Texas 5/30/1957-   ), m. Beate
Hintennach (before 1976-   ). Samuel immigrated to
Munich, Germany 1994.
15354824 Thomas Benton Baldwin (10/21/1960-   ), m. before 1989
Felicia Garcia (before 1977-   )
153548241 Taylor Benton Baldwin (2/15/1991-   )
15355 Fanny Page Fitzgerald (4/28/1850-   )

16 Archibald ("Archie") Blair Bolling

16113 Mary Melvina Megginson (6/20/1826-   ), m. 1850, Thomas
Jeter Davidson (8/23/1807-   )
161131 Carrie Patrick Davidson (9/26/1851-   )
161132 Charles Davidson (died at age 7)
161133 Maria Antoniette Davidson (3/20/1856-   )

161134   Frank Elwood Davidson (4/12/1859-   )
161135   Pocahontas Davidson (died in infancy)
161136   Virginia Cabell Davidson (5/18/1865-   ), m. Joseph
          Walker Brightwell (1/30/1860-   ) of Prospect,
          Prince Edward County.
1611361   Charles Edwood Brightwell (2/22/1891-   )
1611362   Mary Lillian Brightwell (10/14/1897-   ), m. Harvie
          deJarnette Coghill (12/13/1884-   ) of Richmond.
16113621 Phyllis Anne Coghill (9/24/1920-12/5/1996), m. 6/14/
          1943, LeRoy Edwards Brown III (11/7/1916-   ), son
          of LeRoy Edwards (Jr.) and Mary Phoebe Cullingsworth
          Brown.
161136211 Susanne Page Brown (9/5/1945-   ), m. Beverly L.
          Crump
1611362111 Cyane Bemis Crump (7/2/1969-   )
1611362112 William Tayloe Crump (6/24/1972-   )
161136212 Maria Randolph Brown (4/22/1951-   ), m. James
          ("Jimmy") Byrd Horner
1611362121 Alexander Brown Horner (11/10/1987-   )
1611362122 Jackson Coghill Horner (5/17/1989-   )
16113622 Mary Louise deJarnette Coghill (5/9/1926-   ), m.
          Robert Waverly Poland of Richmond.
161136221 Leigh Waverly Poland (1948-   ), m. Mary
          Resides in Carmel Valley, CA.
1611362211 Austin Poland (1979-   )
1611362212 Ashleigh Poland (1982-   )
161136222 Lydia deJarnette Poland (1951-1995), m. (1st) Albert
          Selby of Deltaville. Div. M. (2nd) Howard Rock of
          Deltaville.
1611362221 Forest Selby (1973-   )
1611362222 Hillard Rock (1987-   )

161161   William M. Farrar (1867-   ), m. E. L. Watson
1611611   William M. Farrar, Jr. (1893-   ), m. E. C. Righter
16116111 Mary Elizabeth Farrar (1928-   )
16116112 William Ward Farrar (1929-   )
16116113 Katharine Ann Farrar (1931-   )
1611612   Anna V. Farrar, m. H   ?
1611613   Catharine C. Farrar, m. P. R. Lewis
1611614   Benjamin Randolph Farrar, m. C. Osterman
16116141 Elizabeth R. Farrar (1932-   )
16116142 Alice B. Farrar (1935-   )

161172   Boyd Bosworth
161173   Eden Bosworth

161181   Thomas J. Farrar, m. M. Harris

1611x1   Ruth Farrar, m.   ?
1611x2   Benjamin J. Farrar, Jr., m. M. Weisiger
1611x21   Nicholas DeWitt Farrar, m. (1st) Virginia Boxley, m.
          (2nd) Eunice Huffman
1611x211 Mansfield DeWitt Farrar (1934-   )
1611x212 John Nicholas Farrar (1942-   )

1611x22 Pocahontas Virginia Farrar, m. (1st) Carolton L.
         Saunders, m. (2nd) Charles H. (?) Jacobsen

1611a1 William Hunt Horsley (d. age 21)
1611a2 John Rolfe Horsley, m. A. Davidson
1611a3 Annie Horsley (d. infancy)

17 Anne Bolling, m. 4/21/1770, William Alexander Dandridge II
    (d. 1801), b. and d. Hanover County. He was a major in
    1777 and a colonel in 1779-1783. In 1781, as commissary
    for troops at Yorktown, seized 280 gallons of liquor.
    Played minuet with Patrick Henry and Thomas Jefferson at
    "Elsing Green".
171 John Bolling Dandridge (11/14/1780-1843), m. 11/23/1810,
     Mary Underwood (-1846)
1711 Bolling Starke Dandridge (1812-1876), m. (1st) 11/19/1835
      Laura E. Dudley of New Kent County, m. (2nd) 1840,
      Elizabeth Ann Bowles (1814-1908)

172 William Spotswood (Alexander?) ("Dover") Dandridge (b. 8/30/
     1772 Hanover County-9/10/1842 Henry County), m. (1st)
     before 1799 Joanna Stith (b. 1778 in New Kent County), m.
     (2nd) 6/26/1800 Goochland County, Nancy Harris Pulliam
     (3/23/1782 Goochland County-5/9/1835 Henry County), dau.
     of William and Mourning Richardson Pulliam. Both buried
     in Henry County. After 1814, Dandridge moved to Henry
     County.
1721 William Alexander ("Little Dover") Dandridge (5/12/1807
      Hanover County-10/27/1865 Henry County). Settled in
      Henry County, near Martinsville. After 6/ /1847 moved
      to "Locust Grove" near Spencer, Va. M. (1st) 11/7/1832,
      Sarah Virginia Nichols (Nicholds?) (b. Hanover County or
      Goochland County-1845 Henry County), dau. of John F. (or
      Tom?) Nichols, sister of Granberry Nichols. M. (2nd)
      6/1/1847 Mary Jane Hamner (6/15/1817 Brunswick County-4/
      /1879 Tate County), dau. of Nancy House Hamner. Bur.
      Thyatira Cemetery, Tate County. After 1865 moved to
      Tate County, MS.
17211 Thomas West Dandridge, M.D. b. Henry County. Unm.
17212 Robert Bolling Dandridge, b. Henry County-d. 2/13/1907 on
       Chestnut Knob on Ridgewood Road near Horsepasture. On
       3/8/1860 graduated Virginia Medical College (now MCV).
       C.S.A. Co. H, 24th Reg. Va. Inf. ("Nurse"). On 6/3/1862
       discharged and returned to "Locust Grove". Bur. Horse-
       pasture Christian Church, Henry County. M. 12/ 1866
       Susan Webster Rangeley (11/30/1843 in Stuart, VA-9/26/
       1836 Martinsville, VA), dau. of John and Mary Caroline
       Webster Rangeley. Bur. Martinsville in Oakwood Cemetery.
172121 William Rangeley Dandridge (9/10/1867-2/13/1948) b. Henry
        County. Rumored to have been a whisky bootlegger. M.
        5/18/1915 Grace Overton (5/25/1885-2/22/1976)
1721211 Mary Susan Dandridge (4/28/1916-   ), m. 8/12/1943
         Clinton Eugene Main (8/22/1910-5/7/1970). No issue.

1721212   William Frank Dandridge (9/5/1917-   ) b. Martinsville,
          m. (1st) 8/ /1941 Mary Ann Shelton (8/22/1915 Stuart-
          10/7/1994). M. (2nd) 1995 Nell Horton.
17212121 Robert Edward Dandridge (8/19/1943-   ) b. Portsmouth,
          m. 5/28/1977 Carolyn Sue Bates (4/24/1950-   ) b.
          Red Bay, AL. Living as of 10/ /1994 in Guntersville,
          Al.
172121211 Robert Edward Dandridge II (11/8/1980-   )
172121212 Meredith Bates Dandridge (4/19/1983-   )
17212122 Charles Wayne Dandridge (9/16/1947-   ), m. 10/20/1984
          Placerville, CA, Beverley Marlene Blanchfield (2/5/
          1949 Melrose Park, IL-   ), dau. of Daniel J.
          and Florence E. Shipley Blanchfield. Living in CA.
172121221 Karen Ruth Dandridge (10/29/1988-   )
17212123 Carolyn Faye Dandridge (7/22/1953-   ), m. David
          Pointer Nicholls (6/4/1944-   ), b. Buxton,
          Newport News. Living in Newport News.
172121231 David Pointer Nicholls, Jr. (1/20/1982-   )
172121232 Mathew William Nicholls (9/22/1984-   )
1721213   Lucy Virginia Dandridge (6/23/1920-6/11/1996) b. Henry
          County, m. 12/24/1948 Edward Henry Watkins (6/10/1921-
          11/13/1982 in Durham), son of Aubrey Watkins. Bur.
          Oakwood Cemetery, Martinsville.
17212131 Thomas Edward Watkins (9/9/1951-   ), b. Martinsville.
172122   John Robert Dandridge (7/14/1870-2/15/1946) b. Henry
          County, d. Martinsville. Farmer. M. 12/18/1912 Annie
          Delmar Lovell (5/10/1886-5/24/1955) b. Henry County, d.
          Lynchburg, dau. of John Fountain and Mary Lucy A.
          Turner Lovell. Bur. Roselawn Cemetery, Martinsville.
1721221   Robert Jackson Dandridge (9/23/1913-9/23/1978) b.
          Rangeley, Henry County, d. Martinsville, m. 6/3/1944
          Sarah Ruth Anthony (6/23/1921-3/2/1983) b. Stella,
          Patrick County, d. Martinsville, dau. of Arthur Abner
          and Annie Sue Bowles Anthony. Bur. Roselawn Cemetery,
          Martinsville.
17212211 Robert Jackson Dandridge, Jr. (4/30/1945-   ), m.
          (1st) 8/26/1967 Virginia Carolyn Martin (12/3/1943-
) b. Bassett, dau. of Roy Gilbert and Sallie
          W. Martin. M. (2nd) 2/ /1991 Theresa Anne Duffey
          (12/31/1954-   ) b Baltimore, dau. of Maurice
          Jefferson and Lillian Hattie Stuessy Duffey.
172122111 Robert Clay Dandridge (11/28/1969-   ) b. Darnall
          Army Hosp., Ft. Hood, TX
172122112 Sarah Jamison Dandridge (5/16/1974-   ) b. St. Mary's
          Hosp., Henrico County.
  Child of second wife:
172122113 Victoria Theresa Dandridge (2/27/1992-   ) b. Henrico
          Doctors' Hosp., Henrico.
17212212 Martha Ann Dandridge (6/23/1949-   ) b. Stuart, m.
          (1st) 12/27/1969 Gordon Wallace Sofield (11/30/1948-
          7/22/1978). Bur. Roselawn Cemetery. Son of Robert
          Thomas and Phyllis Marion Hefler Sofield. M. (2nd)
          10/27/ 1979 in Raleigh, Charles Jay Overton III

(3/19/1947-   ), son of Charles J. Overton, Jr.
and of his wife Janie Bell Hardy.

172122121   Martha Shannon Sofield Overton (12/30/1972-   ) b.
Raleigh, NC, m. 6/3/1995 Harold Edward Atkins (2/17/
1969-   )

172122122   Kelly Jensen Sofield Overton (5/24/1976-   ) b.
Raleigh

172122123   Susan Ruth Dandridge (9/30/1953-   ) b. Martinsville,
m. 10/6/1984 John Paul McFarland (10/8/1945-   )

1721221231 Abigail Kathleen McFarland (12/30/1990-   ) b.
Falls Church.

17212214   William Rangeley Dandridge (7/24/1960-   ), b.
Martinsville, m. 12/6/1986 Elizabeth Harris Fulghum
(5/30/1964-   ) b. DeKalb County, GA, dau. of Tommy
Alonzo Fulghum, Jr. and his wife Judith Lenanne
Harris.

172122141   Paul Rangeley Dandridge (12/7/1988-   ) b. Richmond.

172122142   Erin Michelle Dandridge (5/6/1992-   ) b. Richmond.

172122143   Adam Harris Dandridge (2/2/1996-   ) b. Richmond.

1721222   Lucille Rangeley Dandridge (6/11/1915-   ) b. Rangeley,
Henry County.

1721223   Iris Elizabeth Dandridge (11/2/1916-   ) b. Rangeley,
Henry County, m. 12/16/1938 Chesley Randolph Yates
(3/31/1911-4/6/1987) b. Pittsylvania County, d.
Danville.

17212231   Iris Jean Yates (6/21/1944-   ) b. Pittsylvania County
m. 6/15/1968 Dale Keith Kennedy (12/22/1944-   )

172122311   Mathew Keith Kennedy (4/11/1971-   ), m. 7/8/1995
Amy Marie Seibel, Westerville, OH, dau. of Richard
J. Seibel.

172122312   Andrew Randolph Kennedy (7/30/1979-   )

17212232   Carolyn Fay Yates (1/27/1948-   ) b. Pittsylvania
County, m. 11/29/1975 Jack L. Raynor (10/2/1941-
)

17212233   Chesley Randolph Yates, Jr. (10/12/1957-   ) b.
Pittsylvania County, m. 6/27/1981 Janet Lynn
McDaniel, b. Pittsylvania County.

172122331   Chealsea Elizabeth Yates (6/1/1990-   ) (twin)

172122332   Jacob Randolph Yates (6/1/1990-   ) (twin)

1721224   Elaine ("Essie") May Dandridge (5/6/1918-   ) b.
Rangeley, Henry County, m. 8/28/1943 Eugene Gregory
Cehan (5/25/1915-   ) b. Chicago.

17212241   Barbara Jean Cehan (1/4/1946-   ) b. Greenville, SC,
m. 12/16/1967 William G. Bell (2/ /1946-   ) b.
Dixon, TN.

172122411   James William Bell (12/16/1976-   ) b. Rancho Santa
Fe, CA.

172122412   Elizabeth Lee Bell (9/27/1978-   ) (twin) b. Rancho
Santa Fe, CA.

172122413   Christine Lee Bell (9/27/1978-   ) (twin) b. Rancho
Santa Fe, CA.

17212242   Francis Elizabeth Cehan (5/15/1949-   ) b. Greenville,
SC, m. Dan Hewlett Owens (7/5/1947-   )

17212243   Eugene Gregory Cehan, Jr. (9/18/1950-   ) b. Green-
           ville, SC, m. Sarah Ann Sennott (b. about 1954-   )
           b. Texas.
1721225   Mary Alice Dandridge (1/16/1920-   ) b. Rangeley,
           Henry County, m. Walter Krawczel (- d. about
           1990)
17212251   Richard Steven Krawczel (2/3/1952-   ), m. Ann
172122511 Kate Krawczel
1721226   Thomas Hugh Dandridge (12/8/1921-   ) b. Rangeley,
           Henry County, m. Martinsville, Va, 8/9/1974 Sallie
           Ruth Ross (7/20/1933-   ) b. Franklin County, dau.
           of LeRoy and Sallie Louvenia Cannaday Ross.
1721227   Harry Neal Dandridge (3/31/1923-   ) b. Rangeley,
           Henry County, m. 9/20/1952 Helen Louise Harmon
           (6/28/1929-   ) b. Henry County.
17212271   Cathy Jeanine Dandridge (4/12/1964-   ) b. Martins-
           ville, m. Jerrard Harrison Draper (10/23/1958-   )
           b. Martinsville.
172122711 Jessica Catherine Draper (5/28/1987-   )
172122712 Joshua Logan Draper (3/26/1990-   )

172123   Harry Clay Dandridge (1/23/1887-5/29/1947) b. Henry
           County, d. Williamson, WV. Moved to WV, owned and
           operated department store "Mingo's" in Kermit, WV.
           M. 6/9/1914 Grace Mildred Barr (4/27/1894-5/29/1964)
           b. Woodstock, d. Huntington, WV. Bur. in KY across
           river from Kermit. Dau. of William Henry and Annie
           Lawrie Yew Barr.
1721231   Harry Clay Dandridge, Jr. (10/20/1915-11/11/1986) b.
           Blackey, d. Mentor, OH, m. 10/26/1940 Mary Belle
           Preece (6/1/1913-   ) Still living in Kermit as of
           7/ /1996. No issue.
1721232   William Robert Dandridge (4/30/1917-6/14/1992) b.
           Grundy, d. Charlottesville. Physician Charlottesville.
           M. 3/3/1944 Hetty Wray Hurd (4/26/1922-   ) b.
           Martinsville, dau. of Muncie Hubbard and Mary Hetty
           Wray Hurd.
17212321   William Robert Dandridge, Jr. (1/2/1945-   ) b.
           Charlottesville. Physician Charlottesville. M.
           (1st) 6/28/1969 Jenny Waller Jeffress, b. Camp Hill,
           PA. M. (2nd) 2/17/1995 Betty Benfer Winston
17212322   James Hurd Dandridge (3/28/1947-   ) b. Charlottes-
           ville. Attorney, living in Charlottesville. M.
           5/ /1984 Jane Mikelski, b. Charlottesville.
172123221 Alice Elizabeth Dandridge (5/15/1986-   ) b.
           Charlottesville
172123222 Julia Peyton Dandridge (10/30/1987-   ) b. Charlottes-
           ville.
17212323   Thomas Clay Dandridge (7/8/1949-   ) b. Charlottes-
           ville, m. 11/26/1976 Nancy Dawn Ward, b. Sandston.
           Living in Orangeburg SC as of 6/ /1996.
17212324   Anne Wray Dandridge (9/22/1950-   ), b. Charlottes-
           ville, m. 10/2/1976 Carter Hunter Conrad, b. Scotts-
           ville. Living in Scottsville as of 6/ /1996.

172123241 Carter Hunter Conrad, Jr. (11/9/1978-   ) b.
           Charlottesville.
172123242 Haden Dandridge Conrad (11/19/1980-   ) b.
           Charlottesville.
1721233 Thomas Rangeley Dandridge (10/25/1918-7/ /1938) b.
         Blackey, d. Matewan, WV. Unm.
1721234 Ellen Katherine Dandridge (7/29/1922-   ) b. Kermit,
         WV. Unm.
1721235 Anna Pearl Dandridge (3/22/1925-   ), m. 10/1/1949
         Harold T. Eastwood (8/13/1924-   ), son of Raymond
         H. and Julia Ann Eastwood.
17212351 Gary Dandridge Eastwood (9/3/1952-   ). B. Hunting-
          ton. M. 6/30/1974 Daninels Marie Ehman of San Diego.
17212352 Dean Raymond Eastwood (4/11/1955-   ). B. Hunting-
          ton. M. 3/6/1982 Linda   of San Diego.
17212353 Beverly Barr Eastwood (5/17/1957-   ). B. Hunting-
          ton. M. (1st) 9/30/1978 Clay A. Fox. M. (2nd) 1988
          Perry L. Smith. Las Vegas.
172123531 Ryan Allen Fox
172123532 Jenne Nicole Fox
172123533 Kaylee Anne Smith
1721236 Janet Lee Dandridge (1/19/1933-   ) b. Kermit, WV, m.
         11/ /1960 Thomas Edward Miller (8/16/1929-   ).
         Charlottesville.
17212361 Thomas Edward Miller, Jr. (8/15/1961-   ) b. Sevilla,
          Spain.
17212362 Katherine Galt Miller (5/30/1963-   ) b. Washington,
          DC, m. 9/1/1990 Frank Stagg Rogers. Milwaukee.
172123621 Anna Mae Miller Rogers (9/27/1994-   ) b. Charlotte,
           NC.
17212363 Susan Dandridge Miller (2/28/1965-   ) b. Washington,
          DC.
172124 Una Denzil Dandridge (3/31/1876-12/18/1959) b. Rangeley,
        Henry County, d. Martinsville. Operated Rooming House
        on Starling Avenue, Martinsville. M. 10/ /1907 Kelsey
        Puckett (2/16/1869-4/ /1924) b. Carooll County, d.
        Martinsville. Both bur. family cemetery at Penn's
        Store, Patrick County.
1721241 Evelyn Spottswood Puckett (1910-1912)
1721242 Virginia Rangeley Puckett (8/20/1913-   ) b. Penn's
         Store, Patrick County, m. 11/23/1935 James Fontaine
         Hodnett (9/26/1907-   ) b. Martinsville. Son of
         Calley Hodnett Minter.
17212421 James Fontaine Hodnett, Jr. (2/8/1937-   ), m. Tiffany
          Ann Kearfort, b. Martinsville.
172124211 Elizabeth Hodnett (4/23/1965-   )
172124212 William Fontaine Hodnett (3/27/1969-   )
17212422 Carolyn Rangeley Hodnett (2/24/1941-   ), m. Charles
          Kelly Wyatt
172124221 David Fontaine Wyatt (10/28/1969-   )
172124222 Virginia Nelson Wyatt (6/14/1973-   )
172125 Annie Dell Dandridge (1/15/1881-4/5/1964) d. Maryland.
        Unm. Taught school Henry County. Worked for U.S.

Dept. of Agriculture in DC . . . "perfect penmanship".
Buried beside mother at Oakwood Cemetery, Martinsville.
172126 Thomas Nicholas Dandridge (10/18/1883-2/29/1964) d.
Martinsville. Unm. Lived in log cabin off old
Danville Road, Martinsville in 1940's. Operated Auto
Service Station with nephew R. J. Dandridge. Loved
fishing and smoking his pipe. Buried beside mother at
Oakwood Cemetery, Martinsville.

17213 Henry Clay Dandridge (8/5/1840-   ) b. Henry County, d.
Missouri(?). M. (2nd) 10/31/1867 Maria ("Mattie") Dodd
(-7/3/1869) d. Stoneville, NC.
   Child by second wife (may have been others):
172131 Nathaniel V. (or W.) Dandridge (b. about 5/ /1869-   )

17214 John Dandridge (about 1843-about 1862) b. Henry County.
17215 Sarah Virginia Dandridge, b. Henry County, d. Darlington,
SC. Educated at Powell's School for Girls in Richmond.
Taught school in Virginia and North Carolina and nursed
during the Civil War. M. Samuel Wall
172151 Thomas Wall
172152 Elizabeth Roseboro Wall
172153 Samuel S. Wall
172154 Nannie Spotswood Wall
172155 Robert Edward Wall
   Child by Mary Jane Hamner:
17216 Nannie Anderson Dandridge, b. "Locust Grove", Henry
County, d. Winston-Salem, NC, attended boarding school
at Penn's Store Community. In 1868 taught school in
Rockingham, NC. M. Peter Washington Dalton, First
Lieutenant Co. H, 1st Virginia Infantry.

172165 Nannie Anderson Dalton, d. infancy.
172166 Hunter Dalton, d. infancy.
172167 Irene Dalton, d. infancy.

17217 Mary Pocahontas Dandridge, b. "Locust Grove". In 1873
moved to Tate County, MS. M. James Thomas Wilborn
6/15/1849-1/24/1940) of Tate County. D. Memphis.
Son of Josiah C. Wilborn, Jr., and his wife Elizabeth
Haley.
172171 William ("Willie") Clark Wilborn (2/26/1875 Tate County-
d. after 1915), m. 12/22/1913 Anna Davis of Carbondale,
IL.
1721711 Marjorie Wilborn
1721712 Willodean Wilborn
172172 James Durward Wilborn, M.D. (12/8/1877 Tate County-
4/14/1936), m. 10/1/1908 Mamie Allen (12/17/1882 Tate
County-5/2/1960), dau. of Harris Ogilvie Allen, Jr.,
and his wife Mattie Leonard Richardson.
1721721 James Harris Wilborn (8/24/1909-10/12/1974), m. 4/15/
1937 Jewel Lipsey (3/14/1910 Sardis, KS-   )

1721722   William Allen Wilborn (5/24/1911 LeFore County, MS-
          2/9/1969 Tate County), m. 11/25/1954 Ruth Hyde
          (2/23/1910-   )
1721723   Marcus Eugene Wilborn (2/11/1918 Tate County-   ), m.
          6/7/1941 Mary Louise Triplett (4/6/1923 Winston
          County, MS, dau. of Raymond and Willie Rose Johnson
          Triplett.
17217231 Sandra Anne Wilborn (7/3/1942 Memphis-   ), m. 7/1/
          1962 Bobby Carl Hunt (11/6/1938 Lee County, MS-   )
172172311 Leslie Susan Hunt (3/20/1964 Tupelo, MS-   )
172172312 Melissa Lynn Hunt (6/22/1967 Tupelo-   )
17217232 Diana Sue Wilborn (10/11/1944-   ), m. Pensacola, FL
          2/4/1967 Joseph Worth Teagarden III (10/9/1943 Palm
          Springs, CA-   )
172172321 Joseph Worth Teagarden IV (12/7/1967 Jacksonville NC-
)
172172322 Rebecca Rush Teagarden (3/7/1970 Pensacola-   )
172172323 Catherine Jean Teagarden (6/13/1971 Pensacola-   )
1721724   Mabel Elizabeth Wilborn (2/11/1918 Tate County-   ),
          m. 6/21/1943 Dr. Michael E. Shaleen (1910-2/23/1988)
1721725   Thomas Henry Wilborn (11/4/1925 Tate County-1/31/1990,
          m. (1st) 12/10/1952 Connie Roe, m. (2nd) 1/24/1965
          Anita Stratten.
172173   Marcus Samuel Wilborn (6/8/1883-2/12/1966), m. (1st)
          8/22/1905 Beatrice Dandridge, dau. of George Gilmer
          and Mattie Norfleet Dandridge. M. (2nd) 3/1/1951 Eva
          Smart Powell.
172174   Bessie V. Wilborn (3/19/1891-after 1915), m. 3/17/1914
          Memphis, Dr. Locke LaFon Welborn.
1721741   LeFon Welborn, m. Bessie Louise Bacon
1721742   Clary Welborn
1721743   Mary Nell Welborn
172175   Ora Wilborn (about 1882-2/8/1888)
172176   Mabel Wilborn (6/8/1883-about 1886)
17218   Louise M. Dandridge (11/19/1857-4/22/1930) b. Henry
          County. Moved with her mother and brother Walter to
          Tate County, MS. Lived in Pontotoc, MS. Unm.
17219   Martha Washington Dandridge (1/2/1859 "Locust Grove",
          Henry County-1/31/1918)

172193   Mary Thornton (d. infancy)
172194   Margaret Thornton
1721x   Elizabeth ("Bessie") Lee Dandridge (9/8/1865 "Locust
          Grove"-   ), m. Walter G. Cumpton
1721x1   Dandridge Cumpton
1721x2   Mary Cumpton
1721x3   Anna Lou Cumpton
1721x4   Walter George Cumpton (-1906)
1721a   James Spotswood Dandridge, b. "Locust Grove", m. 1/4/1881
          Mary Eliza Cathey. About 1872 moved to Tate County, MS.
1721a1   Cathey Spotswood Dandridge (2/15/1891 Tate County-7/25/
          1970). Served in Europe in World War I. M. 2/ /1911
          Ollie May Dupuy, dau. of Joseph S. and Mary Artilla
          Cathey DuPuy.

1721a11 Hayley Cathey Dandridge (4/6/1913-   ).   Served in
        European World War II. M. 3/18/1942 Euphora, MS,
        Marjorie Latham
1721a111 Nancy Dandridge, m. Howard Patterson
1721a12 Edward Ray Dandridge (10/23/1918-   ), m. 7/4/1941
        Grace Griffin (b. Pontotoc)
1721a121 Edward Cathey Dandridge
1721a122 Ralph Marlin Dandridge
1721a13 James Spotswood Dandridge (12/ /1920 Tate County-7/7/
        1948), m. 5/28/1940 Dorothy Hyde (b. Thyatica, MS),
        dau. of J. B. Hyde.
1721a131 Edith Gwendolyn Dandridge
1721a132 James Haley Dandridge (about 1941-about 1963), m.
        12/19/1962 Ellen Marie Patrick
1721a2 Jimmie Ophelia Dandridge (1893-4/ /1979), m. Marvin
        Ingram (d. about 1940 Texas)
1721a3 James Spotswood Dandridge, Jr. (d. 6/31/1894)

1721b Samuel Hamner Dandridge, b. Henry County, d. Thyatira,
        MS (?), m. Nannie Cathey, dau. of Alexander and Sarah
        Olivia Fowler Cathey.
1721b1 Mildred Hamner Dandridge (10/11/1891 Tate County-3/23/
        1957), m. Perrin Lowery
1721b11 Gloria Dandridge, m. John Kelly
1721b2 William Cathey Dandridge (-6/11/1971), m. 4/14/1929
        Velma Dickerson
1721b21 Anne Dandridge (1/22/1920-Tate County-   ), m. George
        Hugh Freeman (-12/6/1952)
1721b211 Carol Diane Freeman (9/24/1946-   )
1721b212 Patricia Freeman (5/ /1948-   )
1721b22 William Cathey Dandridge, Jr. (6/16/1938 Tate County-
        ), m. 8/28/1960 JoAnn Hawkins
1721b23 Lightie Rivers Dandridge (12/9/1942 Tate County-   ),
        m. 3/6/1964 William Maurice Durley
1721b3 Lightie Louise Dandridge. Unm.

1721b5 James Spotswood Dandridge
1721c George Gilmer Dandridge, b. "Locust Grove". In 1872 moved
        to Thyatira, MS. In 1880 moved to Paris, AR

1721c3 Beatrice Dandridge, m. 8/22/1905 Marcus Samuel Wilborn
        (6/8/1883-2/12/1966), son of James Thomas and Mary
        Pocahontas Dandridge Wilborn.
1721c5 George Gilmer Dandridge, Jr.

1721c7 Mattie Dandridge
1721c8 Martha ("Pattie") Washington Dandridge

1721cx James Spotswood Dandridge

1721d Walter Alexander Dandridge (7/24/1862-9/5/1932) b. Henry
        County, m. 6/15/1931 Lucy Cathey (d. 12/23/1953), dau.
        of Alexander Cathey, Jr. and his wife Ann Eliza Haley.
        Lived in Pontotoc, MS.

1722   John Robert Dandridge (5/26/1814 Hanover County-   ),
          m. (1st) 1/12/1836, Martha Washington Pulliam, dau. of
          Thompson W. and Ann Catherine Moore Pulliam of Goochland
          County, m. (2nd) after 1856 Louisa Virginia Perkins of
          Louisa County.
     Children by first wife:
17221 James T. Dandridge (ca. 1837 Hanover County-   ), m.
          2/5/1869, Bettie J.
17222 Anne Catherine ("Aunt Puss") Dandridge (ca. 1841-   ).
          Never married.

17223 Henry Spotswood Dandridge (7/15/1842 Hanover-4/23/1915
          in Laurel, MS), m. Sarah Frances Armstrong (8/20/1844
          Hanover-3/5/1921 Laurel, MS), dau. of Price and Sarah
          Jenkins Armstrong.
172231 Leonard Joseph Dandridge (ca. 1865 Hanover-   ), m.
          Fannie
1722311 James Dandridge (ca. 1887-   ). Lived in Meridian, MS
1722312 Benjamin (Spencer?) Dandridge (ca. 1893-   ). Lived in
          Meridian, MS
1722313 Rena Dandridge (ca. 1895-   )
1722314 Charles Dandridge (ca. 1898-1941), m. Nellie Dewberry
17223141 Leonard Dandridge
17223142 Marvin Mathew Dandridge
17223143 James Dandridge
17223144 Joyce Dandridge
17223145 Barbara Dandridge
1722315 Winnie Dandridge (ca. 1900-   ), m. Francis Scanlan.
          Home: Mobile.
1722316 Lennie Dandridge, m. Frank Leonard. Home: Mobile
1722317 John Dandridge. Lived Stonewall, MS.
172232 Charles L. Dandridge (1871 AL-   )
172233 James Guy Dandridge (3/11/1873 Cuba, AL-11/11/1945
          Purvis, MS), m. (1st) Ada Arrington (1875-1905), m.
          (2nd) Jennie   (1869-1935)
1722331 Willie Newlyn Dandridge (10/14/19__ Laurel-1/29/1973
          Purvis), m. 9/16/1926, Lewis Virgil Murray
17223311 Frances Adrienne Murray (6/13/1927-   )
17223312 Lewis Virgil Murray, Jr. (11/3/1930-   )
1722332 Robert Carey Dandridge (11/10/1910-3/19/1966), m.
          Earnestine Everett (-1939)
17223321 James Everett Dandridge (1-8/1937-   )
17223322 Barbara Jean Dandridge (6/7/1938-   )
172234 Stephen Price Dandridge (11/ /1875 AL-1947 Gulfport), m.
          Martha Ann ("Dolly") Leggett
1722341 Helen Mae Dandridge (1903-1993), m. 6/30/1927, Duncan
          McLaurin
17223411 Mary Martha McLaurin (1930-   ), m. Donald J. Crawford
172234111 Duncan M. Crawford (1956-   ), m. 3/5/1977, Teressa
          Nickleson
172234112 Robin S. Crawford (3/3/1965-   ), m. (1st) Christopher
          Manzone, m. (2nd) Thomas Williams
17223412 Helen Margaret McLaurin (9/6/1934-   ), m. 1/14/1955,
          Walter L. Shirley

172234121 Michael L. Shirley (8/30/1956 Dayton, OH-   ), m.
        11/7/1987, LaTriccia Anderson
172234122 Connie Lynn Shirley (10/14/1960 Dayton-   ), m.
        12/27/1986, Terry Diroff
172234123 John Frederick Shirley (12/20/1965-   )
17223413   Rosa Ann McLaurin (6/10/1936-   ), m. 8/27/1957, James
        H. Cossett
172234131 Elizabeth A. Cossett (12/2/1958 Dayton-   ), m.
        10/8/1982, Steven Phillips
172234132 James D. Cossett (10/29/1961-8/2/1993)

172234133 Patricia J. Cossett (11/5/1962-   ), m. 6/27/1992,
        Michael Horsley
1722342   Clinton Price Dandridge (1909-1920)
1722343   Margaret Dandridge (1915-   ), m. 1934, Frank Holzer.
        They have two adopted children, Frankie Lynn Holzer
        and Stephen Dandridge Holzer.
172235   Martha Roberta ("Burda") Dandridge (8/16/1882 Cuba,
        AL-10/7/1940 Hattiesburg, MS), m. 10/4/1903, Horace
        Greeley Culpepper (6/16/1872-12/25/1958). She was
        reared in Laurel, MS but lived after marriage in
        Forrest County, MS.
1722351   Lillian Aline Culpepper (8/2/1904-1/18/1966), m.10/4/
        1923, Swift McAulay
17223511   James Davidson McAulay (12/24/1925-   )
17223512   Martha Frances McAulay (11/23/1927-   )
1722352   Mary Frances Culpepper (12/30/1906-5/27/1983), m. (1st)
        Jack Hayne, m. (2nd) Harold Samuel Levi
17223521   Harold Samuel Levi, Jr. (4/20/1939-5/14/1978), m. Joyce
172235211 Kelly Levi
1722353   Horace Cohn Culpepper (5/22/1909-5/21/1990), m. Bobbie
        Ridgeway
17223531   Jack Thomas Culpepper (1/30/1945-   )
1722354   Bessie Lee Culpepper (6/3/1911-d. infant)
1722355   Virginia Pearl Culpepper (11/27/1912-8/11/1990), m.
        (1st) J. W. Montgomery, m. (2nd) John Douglas Askew.
        No issue.
1722356   Mable Elizabeth Culpepper (10/20/1916-11/11/1988), m.
        7/31/1941, Reece L. Lewing of LA (1913-12/28/1976)
17223561   Mary Elizabeth Lewing (11/9/1942-   ), m. 6/24/1966,
        Charles Milton Moore (11/14/1946-   )
172235611 Charles Michael Moore (4/1/1967-   )
172235612 Jennifer Leah Moore (6/24/1970-   )
17223562   Reece L. Lewing, Jr. (7/6/1948-   ), m. 6/19/1970,
        Teri Lynn Hunt (2/21/1953-   )
172235621 Reece L. Lewing III (12/8/1970-   )
172235622 Christina Rene Lewing (1/1/1973-11/16/1991)
1722357   Thomas Webber Culpepper (11/22/1921 MS-   ), m. 8/23/
        1952, Marilyn M. Mayer (8/20/1922-   ) of Lansing, MI
1722358   Bobbie Louise Culpepper (7/3/1924 MS-   ), m. 2/2/1945,
        Franklin L. Young
17223581   Robert Young (8/30/1946 MS-   ), m. 12/16/1966, Sue
        Mason. Niceville, FL
172235811 Sherry Young (12/16/1968-   )

172235812 Kelly Young (10/14/1980-   )
17223582   Judith Young (1/26/1946-   ), m. 2/15/1974, Glen
               Palmer
172235821 Joshua Palmer (6/9/1977-   )

17223583   Patricia Young (3/17/1951 England-   ), m. 3/28/1970,
               James Norris
172235831 Shannon Norris (5/9/1971-   )
172235832 Ashley Norris (2/10/1975-   )
17223584   Hendrix Alan Young (4/19/1960 Alaska-   )

1722359   Joseph Henry Culpepper (2/14/1928-10/14/1976), m. (1st)
               12/30/1948, Elizabeth Munson, m. (2nd) after 1949
               Madelyn Gomes of Shreveport.
17223591   Katherine Culpepper (5/23/1950-   )

172236   Henry Armstrong Dandridge (4/9/1886 Laurel, MS-3/27/1953
               Poplarville), m. 7/1/1907, Della Lee Davis (12/19/1886
               Rome, GA-2/18/1960), dau. of William C. and Martha
               Lavina Strickland Davis.
1722361   Virginia Elizabeth Dandridge (4/11/1908-10/21/1989), m.
               Robert Love
1722362   Margaret Rebecca Dandridge (9/27/1909-2/18/1965), m.
               Cortes Rubio
17223621   Amanda Josephine Cortes Rubio (-10/6/1980)
17223622   Nancy Lucille Cortes Rubio (9/27/1937-3/21/1956)
1722363   Anne Katherine Dandridge (7/3/1911-   )
1722364   Samuel Joseph Dandridge (1/19/1913-2/13/1956), m.
               Lucille Denison
1722365   Sarah Henrietta Dandridge (10/13/1914-2/11/1973), m.
               Dillard Durham
1722366   Mable Ruth ("Bootsie") Dandridge (3/3/1920-2/3/1987),
               m. Kenneth Neely
1722367   Mary Frances ("Toodlum") Dandridge (4/4/1922-   ), m.
               11/20/1948, James Byrd
17223671   James Ronald Byrd (1/13/1950-7/4/1972)
17223672   Teresa Anne Byrd (6/29/1954-12/2/1987), m.   Loper
1722368   Henry Davis Dandridge (5/7/1925-1/1/1973), m. Patricia
               Ward
1722369   Charles Keith Dandridge (8/27/1931-1/29/1983), m. Mary
               North
17224   John Dallas Dandridge (3/27/1846-   ), m. (1st) 2/5/1869,
               Elizabeth Jane Atkisson (-   /27/1887) (sometimes
               Atkinson), m. (2nd) 2/6/1889, Susan Catherine Ragland
172241   Martha Elizabeth Dandridge (12/6/1869-3/7/1955, m. 2/6/
               1889, Morgan Jackson Toler (1867-1943)
1722411   Betty Jane Toler (6/18/1890-3/9/1972), m. 1/4/1909,
               Andrew Jackson Atkinson
1722412   Bernice Lee Toler (11/21/1891-2/15/1912), m. 1/5/1911,
               George Washington Brooks
1722413   Ray Davis Toler (6/23/1894-9/14/1975), m. 12/20/1922,
               Allenia Elizabeth Powers
17224131   Myrtle Jewel Toler (9/28/1923-   ), m. 6/25/1943,
               Frank Shelton Leake

17224132 Eugene Brady Toler (3/16/1927-   ), m. 5/1/1948,
          Lucille Catherine Beasley
1722414   Roy Jackson Toler (6/23/1894-12/15/1973), m. 12/20/1927,
          Gracie Lillian Long
1722415   Charles Clay Toler (9/18/1898-12/9/1970), m. 12/20/1924,
          Daisy Estelle Gammon
1722416   Annie Lelia Toler (8/5/1900-2/15/1986), m. 3/20/1917,
          Frank Elery Willis
172242   Clay Arlington Dandridge (6/20/1871-11/27/1947), m. 11/8/
          1911, Nancy Caroline Brooks
1722421   Flora Jane Dandridge (10/18/1912-10/3/1993), m. Joel
          Lester Powers
1722422   James Dallas Dandridge (3/26/1914-   ), m. Virginia
          Payne
1722423   Marian Arlington Dandridge (10/6/1915-d. infancy)

1722424   Hazel Bernice Dandridge (3/7/1917-   ), m. 10/20/1935,
          Bryan Branson Wilson. Richmond.
1722425   Eleanor Myrtle Dandridge (6/4/1919-   ), m. 3/28/1933,
          Emory Alvis
172243   Lelia Celestial Dandridge (10/6/1879-3/11/1966), m. 2/11/
          1903, Landon Cutler Singleton
1722431   Harvey Jackson Singleton (11/11/1903-6/10/1991), m.
          4/26/1928, Lady Rozelle Gammon
1722432   Grace Lee Singleton (3/29/1906-2/29/1968), m. 4/26/1921,
          Waverly Samuel Goode
1722433   Richard Cleveland Singleton (11/11/1908-10/27/1984), m.
          Evelyn Brooking
1722434   Maude May Singleton (5/11/1911-   ), m. Charles Lewis
          Butler
1722435   Nora Gertrude Singleton (12/1/1914-   ), m. Woodrow
          Wilson Fletcher
1722436   Janie Shelton Singleton (3/26/1917-   ), m. Charles
          Herbert Gordon
17225   William B. Dandridge (b. ca. 1848)
17226   Robert Dandridge. b. 5/10/1854)
17227   Charles C. Dandridge (ca. 1856-   ), m. 1/15/1885,
          Elizabeth Carter
      Children of second wife (Louisa Virginia Perkins)
      of John Robert Dandridge:
17228   Rosa Lee Dandridge (1/28/1873-11/23/1876)
17229   Lucy Anderson Dandridge (3/17/1875-1876)
1722x   Eunice Dandridge (8/24/1877-10/11/1931), m. 11/24/1897,
          Benjamin Franklin Amos
1723   Elizabeth B(olling?) Dandridge (8/11/1801-9/22/1804)
1724   William P(ulliam?) Dandridge (12/7/1803-12/22/1803)
1725   Ann L. Dandridge (3/1/1805-5/11/1818)
1726   Sarah T. Dandridge (5/30/1809-5/ 1841), m. 1/12/1831,
          William H. Starling. Henry County.
1727   Robert T. Dandridge (4/22/1811-4/28/1843), m. 7/14/1836,
          Sarah Pulliam, dau. of Thompson W. and Anne Catherine
          Moore Pulliam.
1728   Nathaniel W(est?) Dandridge (4/30/1813-5/5/1813)

1729 Mary Jane Dandridge (12/7/1816-9/5/1820)
172x Spotswood B(olling?) Dandridge (2/7/1820-7/25/1828)
173 Nathaniel West Dandridge, m. Martha H. Fontaine b. Henry
      County, dau. of John and Mary Catherine Henry Fontaine.
      Both are bur. in Pontotoc, MS.

1732 William Fontaine Dandridge, m. Susan C. Stith
1733 Elizabeth Ann Dandridge, m. 4/23/1817 William Hereford
1734 Martha Lightfoot Dandridge (d. 6/3/1850)

1737 Henry (Harry?) Bolling Dandridge (1823 Martinsville, VA-
      after 1885). Practiced in Carroll County, MS. About
      1850 left MS for CA ("Gold Rush"). About 1854 returned
      to Sardis, MS. About 1880 moved to Looahoma, MS. M.
      5/ /1860 Adeline Kenon Wilbourn, dau. of Sanford
      Wilbourn.

17372 Nannie Dandridge
17373 Henry Bolling Dandridge, Jr.

174 Dorothy Ann Dandridge, m. Frederick William James (1781-
      1/25/1825). The James came to AL between 8/ /1817 and
      5/ /1820 when their last child was born.

174a312211 Laura Michelle Giese

175 Jane Butler Dandridge (b. 1783?), m. Rev. Joseph Davies
      Logan (b. 1783)

17511 Joseph Davies Logan (9/16/1855-12/17/1926), m. 5/18/1886,
      Georgine Washington Willis (3/22/1861-11/22/1941), dau.
      of Col. George and Sally Innes Smith Willis.
175111 Fielding Lewis Logan (4/9/1903-10/2/1965), m. 11/17/1934,
      Jean Markley (1/21/1908-2/2/1989)
1751111 Jean Dandridge Logan (12/16/1938-   ), m. 4/18/1970,
      William Kitchell Ince (8/29/1936-   )
17511111 Anna Fielding Ince (2/14/1972-   )
17511112 Charles Kitchell Ince (9/7/1973-   )
17511113 William Logan Ince (12/31/1975-   )
1751112 Fielding Lewis Logan, Jr. (6/16/1939-   ), m. 5/15/
      1971, Diana Gail Graham (2/2/1945-   )
17511121 Fielding Lewis Logan III (1/24/1974-   )
17511122 John Markley Logan (9/7/1975-   )
17511123 Mary Graham Logan (8/18/1979-   )
1751113 Charles Markley Logan (11/3/1941-   ), m. 7/1/1972,
      Jacqulyn Cundiff (7/10/1948-   )
17511131 Charles Markley Logan, Jr. (10/30/1978-   )
17511132 William Cundiff Logan (8/30/1980-   )
175112 Maud Matthews Logan (2/20/1890-11/1/1985), m. 1/8/1916,
      Garland James Hopkins (8/22/1887-1/29/1949)
1751121 Byrd Willis Hopkins (12/18/1917-3/3/1996), m. (1st)
      11/16/1946, Katherine Roseborough (2/28/1925-   ).
      Div. 1964. M. (2nd) 5/21/1966, Harriot Hamilton
      Rutherfoord (12/17/1928-12/28/1994).

```
        Children by first wife:
17511211   Helen Carter Hopkins (5/24/1949-     ), m. 6/22/1979,
             Pierre Greffard (8/29/1939-    )
175112111  Melanie Catherine Greffard (8/27/1980-    )
175112112  Marie-Helene Greffard (3/2/1982-   )
17511212   Lewis Willis Hopkins (5/23/1954-     ), m. 6/15/1996
             Elizabeth Young Cannon
17511213   William Roseborough Hopkins (5/21/1958-     ), m. (1st)
             . M. (2nd) 8/14/1993, Evangeline
             Marie Fisher (5/23/1970-    ).
175112131  Chelsea Marie Hopkins (5/20/1996-     ). Twin.
175112132  William Jacob Hopkins (5/20/1996-     ). Twin.
        Child by second wife:
17511214   Harriot Duval Hopkins (10/5/1970-   )
1751122    Fortescue Whittle Hopkins (2/17/1920-     ), m. (1st)
             2/10/1948, Jean Dixon Talbot (6/30/1926-2/23/1994).
             Div. 11/15/1969. M. (2nd) Lora Crutchfield McWorter
             (4/30/1928-    ).
17511221   James Talbot Hopkins (6/20/1949-     ), m. Shelly Moore
17511222   Janie Ellison Hopkins (9/6/1953-     ), m. (1st)
             6/5/1976, John Beckwith Payne. Div. 1993.
175112221  Beckwith Benjamin Payne (11/15/1985-    )
175112222  Elisha Ellison Payne (1/20/1989-    )
17511223   Susan DuVal Hopkins (6/19/1959-     ), m. 6/18/1983,
             Mark Brent Meyers (12/5/1953-    )
175112231  Mark Brent Meyers, Jr. (7/14/1988-    )
175112232  Jean Holleman Meyers (3/10/1990-    )
175112233  Anna Logan Meyers (3/16/1993-    )
17511224   Jean Talbot Hopkins (6/25/1961-     ), m. 10/15/1994,
             Robert Trudeau
175112241  Jett Talbot Trudeau (1/25/1996-    )
1751123    Nancy Washington Hopkins (10/28/1924-     ), m. 4/24/1954,
             William Mahone IV (12/2/1926-    )
17511231   Nan Overton Mahone (1/11/1956-     ), m. 6/22/1996
             William Revere Wellborn
17511232   William Mahone V (1/21/1958-     ), m. 6/6/1981, Bonnie
             Lynn Pryce (6/10/1956-    )
175112321  William Mahone VI (6/21/1987-    )
175112322  Anna Catherine Mahone (3/23/1989-    )
1751124    Garland James Hopkins, Jr. (4/11/1931-7/30/1989), m.
             2/5/1955, Judith Hale Wilhoit (10/18/1932-    )
17511241   Katharyn Douglass Hopkins (9/5/1958-    )
17511242   Garland James Hopkins III (12/31/1959-     ), m. 6/8/
             1996 Regina Leigh Ferris
17511243   Robert Whittle Hopkins (8/6/1961-     ), m. 6/24/1995,
             Alice Jean Stewart (4/9/1964-    )
175113   Sallie Strother Logan (3/6/1887- / /1952), m. 1928,
             John Lacy Dunlap (1884-1953)
1751131    Sara Logan Dunlap (6/7/1929-12/4/1977), m. 4/28/1951,
             Charles Edward Lukens (3/17/1929-1/24/1972)
17511311   Sallie Lukens (3/28/1952-     ), m. 4/4/1970, Lee Allen
             Ebert (6/23/1951-    )
175113111  Jennifer Sara Ebert (11/25/1970-    )
175113112  Maryam Joan Ebert (9/30/1975-    )
```

175113113 Sara Juliette Ebert (10/10/1982-   )
17511312 William Courtland Lukens (5/19/1955-   ), m. (1st)
          10/18/1975, Jan Gregory (9/1/1954-   ). M. (2nd)
          10/11/1987, Patricia Allen
    Children by first wife:
175113121 Courtland Gregory Lukens (7/30/1979-   )
175113122 William Courtland Lukens III (1/20/1981-   )
    Child by second wife:
175113123 Elizabeth Lukens (7/2/1989-   )
17511313 John Dunlap Lukens (7/27/1957-   ), m. 8/2/1980, Dawn
          Patsell (2/26/1957-   )
175113131 Charles Edward Lukens II (5/29/1984-   )
175113132 Fara Virginia Lukens (2/19/1989-   )
17511314 Mary Wilson Lukens (3/9/1961-   ), m. 6/16/1991, Angus
          Cameron Goodson II (9/2/1950-   )
175113141 Kathryn Lemon Goodson (12/9/1992-   )
175114 Nancy Clayton Logan (7/8/1888-6/23/1978)
175115 John Lee Logan (9/17/1892-9/17/1973), m. 2/23/1918,
          Marjorie Wood (2/20/1892-10/14/1978)
1751151 Marjorie Jean Logan (1/4/1925-   ), m. 9/3/1949,
          Richard Thomas Watts III (3/28/1921-12/18/1981)
17511511 Richard Thomas Watts IV (7/21/1950-   ), m. 6/5/1982,
          Patricia Matthews Stebbins (10/9/1945-   )
17511512 Elizabeth Cushing Watts (12/11/1953-   ), m. 5/26/1984,
          George Randolph Holland (10/25/1950-   )
175115121 Thomas Wilson Holland (5/15/1986-   )
1751152 Joseph Dandridge Logan (12/29/1926-8/29/1995), m.
          6/17/1950, Florence Susanne Kime (9/29/1927-   )
17511521 Susanne Lee Logan (8/17/1951-   ), m. 10/2/1976, John
          Edward Frederick, Jr. (9/25/1953-   )
175115211 Katharine Taylor Frederick (7/26/1987-   )
17511522 Katharine Logan (9/29/1952-   ), m. (1st) 9/5/1976,
          Chris Shiell. Div. M. (2nd) 12/9/1987, Allen Keith
          Hucks (6/22/1956-   )
175115221 Sagen Andrew Shiell (3/26/1976-   )
17511523 Stephen Davies Logan (5/6/1954-11/24/1995), m. (1st)
          Michelle   . Div.
175115231 Jon Davies Logan (11/10/1980-   )
175116 Joseph Dandridge Logan (7/3/1898-7/26/1950), m. 5/28/
          1938, Frances Wilson McNulty (6/10/1907-2/13/1992)
1751161 Joseph Dandridge Logan III (7/22/1940-   ), m. 12/27/
          1967, Laura Oglesby Burks (8/21/1946-   )
17511611 Anna Clayton Logan (3/9/1974-   )
17511612 Beverley Haskins Logan (6/24/1976-   )
17511613 Joseph Dandridge Logan IV (1/24/1978-   )
1751162 Anna Aylett Anderson Logan (5/10/1943-   ), m. 5/14/
          1966, Thomas Towles Lawson (1/8/1938-   )
17511621 Thomas Towles Lawson, Jr. (7/7/1971-   )
17511622 Frances Blair Lawson (6/25/1973-   )
1751163 George Willis Logan (1/2/1945-   ), m. 12/29/1972,
          Helen Harmon Best
17511631 George Willis Logan, Jr. (10/16/1978-   )
175117 Georgine Willis Logan (7/28/1899-4/21/1984), m. 6/25/
          1927, Wallace Wilmer Lawrence (1/27/1898-7/31/1978)

1751171   Josephine Dandridge Logan Lawrence (9/13/1928-6/10/1984)

176   Elizabeth Blair Dandridge (4/21/1774-4/1/1796)
177   Archibald Bolling Dandridge (12/22/1776-   ), m. 9/13/1798
        in Goochland County, Elizabeth M. Underwood, dau. of
        George Underwood.
178   Robert Honeyman Dandridge (10/12/1784-before 12/3/1838 near
        Courtland in Lawrence County, AL), m. 12/6/1808 Goochland
        County, Elizabeth Terrell Dandridge (his first cousin)
        (5/7/1793-1844 or 1845), dau. of Robert Amber and Mildred
        Aylett Allen Dandridge.
1781 Jane Dandridge, m. 4/3/1838 Moulton, AL, Reuben Allen
1782 George Washington Dandridge (1812-8/ /1860) (b. in VA), m.
        1/14/1841 Elizabeth Norwood
1783 Mildred Ann Dandridge (1814 or 1816-ca. 1873) (b. in VA, d.
        Lee County, MS), m. 3/23/1841 in Moulton, Lawrence
        County, AL, Robert H. Creilly (Creely) (ca. 1814-2/ /
        1856) (b. Belfast, Ireland, d. Pontotoc County, MS).
        He came to U.S.A. as an orphan. Worked his passage to
        America on a boat rolling barrels. Naturalization
        declared 10/20/1849. Mildred "was as mean as a snake".
17831 Mary ("Mollie") C. (E.?) Creilly (1842-ca. 1869) (b. in
        AL)
17832 Andrew Jackson Creilly (1844-1862) (b. Pontotoc County,
        d. Bowling Green, KY). C.S.A. May have been pressed
        into service by the Confederates. Home: Mississippi
        Disappeared during Civil War.
17833 Margaret ("Mag") J. B. Creilly (3/16/1845-2/15/1905) (b.
        in AL, d. at Cale, Indian Territory (now Calera, OK).
        M. in Tupelo 11/11/1868, William L. Barton (1835 AL-
        7/18/1898 MS). Moved to Indian Territory around 1896.
        He was an overseer. All children born in Tupelo.
178331 James ("Jim") Robert Barton (b. 2/9/1871-   ), m. 3/10/
        1899 in Bonham, TX, Elizabeth Milner.
1783311 Mildred Barton (11/8/1901-10/16/1905). Bur. Calera.
1783312 Howard Barton (b. 1907). Went to West Texas. Fannin
        County.
178332 Hance H. Barton (9/23/1873-   ), m. (1st) 5/29/1904,
        Bulah Moore (d. 7/14/1909), m. (2nd) Willey Shirley
    Child by first wife:
1783321 Mildred Barton. Graduated from high school at Boynton,
        OK.
178333 Andrew Jackson ("Mac") Barton (9/24/1875-9/10/1903), m.
        12/11/1898, Carrie Heart. It is said that he was
        killed riding a train. Bur. Calera.
178334 Mary N. ("Sis") Barton (1/31/1877-   ), m. 2/24/1909,
        Frank A. Walden. She d. Durant, OK. Both bur. in
        Calera.
1783341 B. F. Walden (b. 8/10/1911), m. (1st) 10/13/1936, Hazel
        Drake, a school teacher, m. (2nd) Freida Howard and
        they reside at Greenville, MS.
    Child by first wife:
17833411 James Franklin Walden (b. 2/11/1940 at Durant), m.
        Carolyn Ann Duckworth (b. 1/1/1943 at Panama City,

FL). Children born at Monroe, LA. A banker in
Monroe.

178334111 Timothy S. Walden (b. 3/20/1961), m. Connie Sue
Johnson
178334112 Mark James Walden (b. 4/7/1962), m. Julia McCullin
178334113 Kristina Rene Walden (b. 12/18/1964)
178334114 Todd F. Walden (b. 5/25/1969)
178335 Sarah ("Sally") Azile Barton (1/28/1878-   ), m. 12/19/
1899 in Bonham, Fannin County, TX, Sam Cline. Last
known address was Talco, TX
1783351 Hazel Cline
1783352 True Lynn Cline
178336 John Dandridge Barton (7/1/1880-5/31/1967) (bur. Calera),
m. 1/14/1914 in Durant, Inez Hightower (1/11/1896 at
Stamps, Arkansas-8/14/1950)
1783361 John Dandridge Barton, Jr.
1783362 Mary Margaret Barton
1783363 Thomas E. Barton
1783364 Infant
1783365 A. L. Barton
178337 Troy Barton (1/7/1884-2/7/1884)
178338 Lelia Barton (1/14/1887-   ), m. Jim Jordan
1783381 Robert Jordan, m. Dessie Roller, a twin, died shortly.
Robert went to West Texas.
1783382 Jimmie Jordan
1783383 Lelia Jordan, m.   Allen
17833831 James Nolen Allen (b. 3/19/1943). Twin.
17833832 Lee Olen Allen (b. 3/19/1943). Twin.
17833833 Margaret Rynie Allen (b. 11/29/1953)
17833834 Susan Lanell Allen (b. 5/5/1956)
17834 George Washington ("Tommy") Creilly (12/ /1847-1930) (b.
Pontotoc County), m. 5/18/1871, Georgia Ann Conant (b.
5/ /1855). Residence: MS.
178341 Lura ("Lov") Creilly, m. 1/1/1886, J. H. Scruggs
178342 Thomas Jefferson ("Bud") Creilly (b. 7/ /1877), m.
Etoile Lessell
1783421 Ola Mae Creilly (b. 12/19/1904), m. Calvert Gault
17834211 Frances Etoile Gault, m. Hugh Kenneth Bell
178342111 James Kenneth Bell (b. 11/28/1941). Twin.
178342112 Gerald Ray Bell (b. 11/28/1941). Twin.
178342113 John Thomas Bell (b. 12/27/1944)
178342114 Mary Jacqueline Bell (b. 8/5/1949)
17834212 Evelyn Gault, m. Harold Trennis Grubbs, a Reverend.
178342121 Harold Trennis Grubbs, Jr.
17834213 Robert Ray Gault (b. 5/27/1936), m. Ruth Brown
178342131 Robert Ray Gault, Jr.
178342132 Phillip Ray Gault
178342133 James David Gault
1783422 Lucille Creilly (b. 1/2/1907), m. Auzie Norris Myatt
17834221 Charleen Myatt, m. Leo Childers
178342211 Christopher Childers
17834222 Auzie Norris Myatt, Jr., m. Joyce Brock
178342221 Norris Myatt
178342222 Cecille Myatt

17834223 Creely Neal Myatt, m. William Wilson, a Reverend.
178342231 William Wilson, Jr.
178342232 Claire Wilson
178342233 Melanie Wilson
17834224 Carl Preston Myatt, m. Karen Liung
178342241 John Myatt
1783423 Preston Creilly, m. Thelma Scott
17834231 George Thomas Creilly (b. 3/10/1928), m. Patsy
178342311 George Roger Creilly (b. 2/28/1956)
178342312 Carl Thomas Creilly (b. 8/8/1958)
178342313 Patsy Georgeanna Creilly (b. 3/10/1960)
17834232 Charles Preston Creilly (b. 7/28/1931), m. (1st) Loyce
           , m. (2nd) Mary   . No issue.
178342321 Michael Charles Creilly (b. 4/10/1956)
178342322 Charlotte Neal Creilly (b. 8/30/1959)
178342323 Van Preston Creilly (b. 9/13/1966)
17834233 Martha Etoile Creilly (deceased)
17834234 Mary Nell Creilly, m. Hopson Dorris
178342341 Lowery David Dorris (b. 2/4/1955)
178342342 Mary Pamela Creilly Dorris (b. 10/21/1956)
178242343 Jeffrey Scott Creilly Dorris (b. 8/9/1958)
178342344 Carol Annette Dorris (b. 11/22/1960)
17834235 Jerald Creilly. Unm.
1783424 Carl Creilly, m. Teddie Deaton. Residence: 438 South
          Main Street, Greenville, MS.
17834241 Carlene Creilly (b. 6/1/1932), m. Victor J. Cefalu
178342411 Rose Octavia Cefalu (b. 1/12/1954)
178342412 Cade Camillo Cefalu (b. 1/28/1958), m. C. Gifford
178342413 Cashew Cefalu (b. 4/4/1959), m. Wm. Jude Frey
178342414 Corese Cefalu (b. 7/22/1960)
178342415 Chana Cefalu (b. 9/12/1961)
1783425 Mildred Creilly, m. Elmo Murff
17834251 Etoil Murff, m. Charles Ferguson
178342511 Phyllis Jean Ferguson
178342512 Charles Ellwood Ferguson
178342513 David Murff Ferguson
17834252 Guy Thomas Murff, m. Ettie Jean Neal
178342521 Daniel Thomas Murff
178342522 Richard Murff
178342523 Michael Murff
178342524 Janet Murff
178342525 Stanley N. Murff
17834253 Betty Jane Murff, m. Joe M. Wright
178342531 Sherribeth Wright
178342532 Joseph ("Jody") Marshall Murff Wright
1783426 Bonnie Laverne Creilly (b. 2/4/1914), m. 4/4/1942,
          Eugene V. Davis (5/27/1912-10/15/1984)
17834261 Eugene Davis II (b. 2/20/1945), m. (1st) Mary McCrea,
           m. (2nd) Donna Micklin. Eugene, a pilot, was
           murdered in a charter plane (shot twice in the
           back).
    Child by first wife:
178342611 Todd McCrea Davis

Child by second wife:
178342612 Brandelyn Davis
17834262 James Milton Davis (b. 10/14/1948), m. (1st) Ruth
              , m. (2nd) Lori Ann Williams of Mattawan,
          MI. James, an accountant, Kalamazoo, MI.
   Children by first wife:
178342621 James Zekharyah Davis (b. 5/30/1979)
178342622 William Dandridge Davis (b. 7/26/1981)
   Children by second wife:
178342623 Robert Eugene Davis (b. 11/25/1982)
178342624 Benjamin Thomas Davis (b. 2/11/1984)
1783427 Lurlyne Creilly (b. 12/24/1916), m. Burwell Wade, Jr.
17834271 Burwell Wade III, m. (1st) Betty McKessick, m. (2nd)
              Brenda Edwards
   Children by first wife:
178342711 Judy Wade
178342712 Burwell Wade IV
178342713 Phil Wade
   Child by second wife:
178342714 Keith Wade
17834272 Martha Ann Wade, m. (1st) William Byrd, m. (2nd) Tom
              Logan
178342721 William Wade Byrd
17834273 Dorothy Jean Wade, m. William Lamar
178342731 Kelly Lamar
178342732 Carrie Lamar
178342733 Kathy Lamar
178342734 Clay Lamar
17834274 Virginia ("Jennie") Wade, m. Eugene O'Callaghan
178342741 Elizabeth S. O'Callaghan
178342742 Michael Wade O'Callaghan
1783428 Troy Edward Creilly (b. 4/26/1918), m. Syble Partridge
17834281 Troy Edward Creilly, Jr., m. Shella Jane Trener
178342811 Chadwick T. Creilly (b. 10/10/1975)
178342812 Heather R. Creilly (b. 4/13/1977)
17834282 James Thomas Creilly (b. 11/24/1952), m. Rhonda Gale
              Card
178342821 James Bradley Creilly (b. 11/2/1974)
178342822 Byron David Creilly (b. 2/9/1976)
178343 Homa Creilly (b. 11/ /1881), m. Joe Bennett
178344 Alma Creilly (b. 10/ /1884), m. 8/22/1900 Jeff Crider
178345 Dessie Creilly (b. 2/ /1888), m. Mitchell Ogilbee
178346 Maude Creilly (b. 3/ /1890), m. Arthur Harrison
17835 Robert Gordon Creilly (5/17/1848-3/1/1924) (b. Pontotoc
          County, d. Sulphur, OK), m. (1st) 2/1/1871), Jennie
          Lynn Brookshire (1851-1881), dau. of Isaac and Mahalia
          Raines Brookshire. M. (2nd) 1/17/1900, Honorra
          Sullivan. Div. No children.
178351 Electra Lynn Creilly (2/2/1872-12/30/1951) (b. Chester-
          ville, MS, d. Sulphur, OK), m. 12/20/1893 in Tupelo,
          MS, John Tillman Alexander (2/2/1867-9/12/1947) (b.
          Chesterville, Armory, MS, d. Sulphur, OK --- Oaklawn
          Cemetery), son of Sam B. and Eliza Sarah Adams
          Alexander.

1783511   Ruth Electra Alexander (11/11/1894-4/8/1973) (b. Armory,
          d. Houston), m. Hannie Fortner
17835111 Child. Shot himself when very young.
1783512   Ethel Donnon Alexander (6/21/1896-1988) (b. Armory, d.
          Houston), m.   Bates
17835121 Jo Ann Bates (b. 6/6/1921), m.   Road
17835122 Betty Low Bates (b. 5/30/1925), m.   Hillman
1783513   Iska Lynn ("Aunt Mickey") Alexander (8/2/1897-3/18/1987)
          (b. Armory, d. Houston), m. Houston, W. P. Inman. No
          children.
1783514   Otto Tillman Alexander (10/25/1899-3/19/1967)(b. Armory,
          d. Drake, OK), m. Leona
1783515   John Gordon Alexander (2/7/1903-9/25/1983) (b. Berwyn,
          OK, d. Sulphur, OK), m. Edna   . No children.
1783516   Edna Bell Alexander (10/16/1905-9/6/1943) (b. Berwyn,
          OK, d. Houston), m. Houston, 12/4/1926, Volly Booth
          Nelson (7/24/1903-11/19/1971) (b. Johnson City, TX,
          d. Houston), son of John Amos and Martha Bell Booth
          Nelson
17835161 Yvonne Nelson (b. 9/23/1931) (b. Houston), m. 11/5/1949
          Michael Maida
17835162 Volly Booth Nelson, Jr. (9/12/1936-8/26/1982) (b.
          Houston, d. Lakeland, FL), m. (1st) Sigrid Schobel;
          m. (2nd) Ida Malone
1783517   Letha Aline Alexander (2/15/1907-4/ /1984) (b. Sulphur,
          d. Houston), m.   Barbough. No children.
1783518   Joe Wheeler Alexander (3/7/1910-2/24/1943) (b. Sulphur)
1783519   Frances Delores Alexander (9/16/1912-8/18/1958) (b.
          Sulphur, d. Dallas - Lakeland Cemetery), m. 5/19/1934,
          Port Arthur, TX, Jared Mann Wilcox (4/7/1899-3/17/
          1960) (b. Galveston, d. Port Arthur), son of Samuel
          Morey II and Carman Virginia Wilcox.
17835191 Virginia Lynn Wilcox (b. 11/15/1936) (b. Port Arthur,
          TX), m. (1st) 7/14/1954, George Scotty Smith (12/6/
          1933-9/8/1988); m. (2nd) 6/19/1976, Alvin R. Penry
          (b. 1/14/1943). No children.
178351911 Elizabeth Dawn Smith (b. 10/18/1956), m. 2/14/1992,
          Port Arthur, TX, Chester Reeves
178351912 Jared Dodd Smith (b. 8/18/1958), m. 8/20/1977, Joni
          Lewis. Address: Nederland, TX
178351913 Dayna Marie Smith (b. 3/9/1960), m. 10/28/1983, Ben A.
          Hyatt, Jr. of Port Arthur
178351x   Paul Wilson Alexander (b. 2/15/1914) (b. Sulphur)
178352   S. A. ("Art") Creilly (b. 1874)
178353   Oscar T. Creilly (b. 1876)
178354   Lulla ("Jossin") Creilly (b. 1878)
178355   Mahalia Delullah Creilly (1881-1946), m. Gentry H.
          Shofner (1877-1937)
1783551   Creilly Shofner
1783552   Otto Shofner
1783553   Ernestine Shofner, m.   Hendrix
1783554   Mary Shofner, m.   Morgan
17836   John Dandridge Creilly (b. 1852, died from burns) (b. MS).
          Unm. Went to Paris, TX, but returned to Lee County

(Tupelo). John got drunk, got too close to a fireplace
and was badly burned. An old black man found him and
took him to the house of his brother Jimmy.

17837   James ("Jimmy") Louis Creilly (now Creely) (5/14/1854-
        10/14/1941) (b. MS, d. Lee County, MS) (Creely-Raines
        Cemetery), m. 2/2/1882, Lee County, Georgeanna Ford
        (1/27/1863-1/27/1943)
178371 Jennie Lee Creely (7/12/1883-11/20/1886)
178372 Alma Gertrude Creely (b. 8/9/1885), m. 5/23/1914, Gaston
        Allen
1783721 Jimmie Lee Allen, m. Grace Malone
17837211 Brenda Allen
1783722 Bernice Allen, m. James McCarter
17837221 Freda McCarter
17837222 Martha McCarter
178373 Andrew Jackson Creely (2/5/1888-12/ /1971), m. 9/9/1908,
        Ollie Mae Baldwin
1783731 Katie Creely, m. Lynn Daugherty. Residence: Tupelo
1783732 Raymond Creely, m. Marietta Moffett
17837321 Georgia Ann Creely
17837322 Betty Ray Creely
17837323 Tommy Creely
1783733 Albert Creely, m. Henryetta Hodges. He was formerly
          a Sheriff.
17837331 Gerald Creely
17837332 Earl Creely
1783734 Jimmy Lee Creely, m. Orin Hamner
1783735 Allen Jones Creely. Lee County Sheriff before 1783733.
1783736 Eunice Creely, m. Buford Brown
17837361 Wayne Brown
17837362 Bobby Brown
178374 Harvey Medford Creely (11/12/1889-2/3/1979), m. 2/16/
        1917, Bessie Pool (3/9/1896-1/13/1974)
1783741 Mavis Creely, m. T. J. McCarter
17837411 Tommy McCarter
178375 Bessie Earl Watson Creely (9/30/1891-9/18/1983), m. 4/13/
        1913, Andy Hamilton
1783751 Bilbo Hamilton
1783752 Dallas Hamilton (deceased)
1783753 Oscar Hamilton
1783754 James Hamilton
1783755 Cleta Hamilton, m. Woody Russell. Residence: Antler, OK
1783756 Pat Hamilton
178376 Eunice Creely (12/11/1893-9/17/1895)
178377 Norman Jones Creely (7/19/1895-9/18/1983), m. 11/19/1921,
        Minnie Bell Lee (11/12/1900-2/4/1983)
1783771 Leon Creely, m. Louise Curry
17837711 Lee Creely
17837712 Ronnie Creely
1783772 Jack Creely (Mayor of Fulton, MS), m. Wilma Comer
17837721 Jackie Marie Creely
17837722 Natalie Creely
17837723 Chris Creely

178378   Allie Azalee Creely (b. 9/27/1898), m. 11/24/1918, Elzie
         Grady Armstrong (3/2/1899-2/24/1985)
1783781 Lorraine Armstrong (b. 8/27/1927 Boynton, OK), m. (1st)
         6/4/1948, John Dillard Davis
17837811 John Armstrong Davis, M.D. (b. 5/4/1950), m. 8/ /1974,
         Linda Evans Hayes
178378111 John Armstrong Davis, Jr. (b. 8/18/1977)
178378112 Jason Hayes Davis (b. 12/23/1979)
178378113 Brittany Anne Davis (b. 1/8/1984)
17837812 Connie Linda Davis (b. 8/20/1952)
17837813 Sandra Elizabeth Davis (b. 1/28/1954), m. 8/10/1975,
         Richard Wayne Pitner
178378131 Richard Nathan Pitner (b. 10/29/1978)
178378132 Jordan Blake Pitner (b. 4/26/1981)
1783782 Mary Lou Armstrong (b. 9/5/1931), m. (1st) Bobby Russell
         Parker (d. 9/29/1966), m. (2nd) 6/5/1971, Harry L.
         O'Neal (d. 4/6/1981)
17837821 Nancy Angela Parker (b. 2/8/1953), m. 9/15/1973, John
         Larry Fruge
178378211 Parrish Hunter Fruge (b. 9/5/1979)
178378212 Andrew Dandridge Fruge (12/27/1984)
17837822 Cythia Marilyn Parker (b. 8/30/1955)
178379   "Sugar Lumps". Still born. No date.
17837x   Sam Barnes Creely (b. 8/13/1905), m. 11/25/1935, Birdie
         Mae Smith
         Adopted son: Paul Barnes Creely (b. 3/13/1952)
17838   Sarah ("Sally") C. Creilly (b. 5/ /1855 or 1860) (b.
         MS), m. 11/24/1881, Daniel Raines. Raines shot and
         killed Sally. It was ruled an accident but the family
         did not believe it.
178381   Minnie Raines, m. Ed Motley
1783811 Bonner Motley, m. Carl Armstrong. No issue.
1783812 Earl Raines Motley. No issue.
178382   Inez Raines, m. Will Pierce
178383   Willie Raines
178384   Boyd Raines
178385   Daniel Raines, Jr.
178386   Babe Raines
178387   John Bell Raines
1784   John T(errell?) Dandridge (1831-3/5/1870) (b. in AL), m.
         4/26/1864 Octavia E. Banhook
1785   Robert Honeyman Dandridge, Jr. (1832-7/ /1884) (b. in AL),
         m. 7/22/1854 Margaret Ann Johnson
179   George Washington Dandridge (2/3/1787-9/27/1794)
17x   Thomas Bolling Dandridge (2/3/1789-5/29/1842), m. Henry
         County 5/29/1819, Caroline Matilda Nichols (1803-   ),
         dau. of John F. (or Tom) Nichols
17a   Martha A. (Anne?) Dandridge (1/21/1790-1/22/1790)
17b   John Marshall Dandridge (5/8/179 -   )
1x   Archibald Blair Bolling (1/26/1729*1730-6/20/1749)

1d   Anne Bolling (-4/2/1743)
1e   Elizabeth Bolling (3/21/1753-   )
1g   Rebecca Bolling (-8/1/1754)

21   Richard Randolph, Jr., m. (1st) ca. 1755 Jane Bolling (1740-
      1756) who was the mother of (216) Jane Randolph. Jane
      Bolling Randolph may have died in childbirth. His second
      wife was Anne ("Nancy") Meade (b. 1732) (he married ca.
      1756).

2114 William Byrd Randolph. Midshipman U.S.N.

2118 Gawin Lane Corbin, Jr., m. (2nd) 8/5/1846, Mary A. Hines

2118125 Miriam Ethel Sowers (d. 5/12/1976), m. William Thomas
         Howard (d. 2/16/1976), son of Oscar Watts and Ella
         Virginia Goodwin Howard.
21181251 Kathrine Howard (11/24/1920-   ), m. Robert Munford
         Biggs, Jr. (7/20/1920-   ), son of Robert Munford
         and Amelia Pfeiffer Biggs.
211812511 Robert Munford Biggs III (11/18/1944-   ), m. 12/19/
         1970, Mercedita Delgado (9/28/1947-   ) (b. in
         Rio Piedras, Puerto Rico, dau. of Reinaldo Rafael
         and America Carrion Delgado.
2118125111 Robert Michael Biggs (3/19/1975-   )
2118125112 Kathryn Michelle Biggs (12/28/1976-   )
211812512 Thomas Howard Biggs (4/10/1949-   ) (b. in Front
         Royal, VA). Unm.
211812513 Kamelia Pfeiffer Biggs (4/16/1952-   ) (b. in Front
         Royal), m. 9/29/1979, William George Crowley (7/1/
         1945-   ) (b. in Auckland, New Zealand), son of
         George Andrew and Florence Sylvie Gibbons Crowley.
2118125131 Amelia Sylvie Crowley (6/11/1985-   )
2118125132 Robert Andrew Crowley (9/15/1986-   )
211812514 Miriam Kathrine Biggs (11/5/1957-   ) (b. in Front
         Royal), m. (1st) 2/10/1979, Kenneth Wayne Campbell
         (6/19/1950-   ), son of Kenneth Glenn and Virginia
         Ritenour Campbell; m. (2nd) Howard Lockhart
2118125141 Matthew Wayne Campbell (4/9/1981-   )
2118125142 Lucas Perry Campbell (12/28/1988-   )
21181252 William Thomas Howard, Jr., m. 6/12/1948, Bessie Vestal
         Hawk (9/19/1927-   ), dau. of Robert Hays and Julia
         Grace Ford Hawk.
211812521 William Thomas Howard III (4/5/1951-   )
211812522 Anne Katherine Howard (7/23/1953-   ), m. 8/2/1975,
         William Bradford Blough, son of Bernard Leo and
         Wilford Frances Yarnall Blough.
2118125221 Jason Howard Blough (2/13/1981-   )
2118125222 Kristen Elizabeth Blough (9/23/1985-   )

21182 Virginia Ann Russell Corbin (11/15/1850-   ), m. 6/15/
         1868 (in Warwick County), John Robert Parker, M.D.
211821 Gawin Lane Parker (5/12/1869-5/13/1869)
211822 John Russell Parker (6/13/1870-8/10/1878)
211823 Waverly Douglas Parker (2/15/1873-11/16/1944)
211824 Joseph Henry Parker (3/19/1875-3/29/1928)
211825 Vernon Clyde Parker (3/19/1878-9/8/1884)

211826   Robert Randolph Parker (12/30/1880-2/14/1942), m.
            6/6/1916 (at Stonega, VA), Margaret Carrier. Lawyer
            State Senator.
2118261   Emily Virginia Parker (8/4/1917-   ), m. 3/22/1941
            (Big Stone Gap, VA), Edwin Lawrence Kendig, Jr.
            (62135121), M.D.   Reside in Richmond.
21182611 Anne Randolph Kendig (1/1/1942-   ), m. 2/23/1963
            (Richmond, VA), Ronald Faris Young
211826111 Margaret Randolph Young (6/30/1964-   ), m. 6/9/1990,
            J. Sargeant Reynolds, Jr. (2/13/1961-   )
2118261111 Virginia Randolph Reynolds (3/8/1993-   )
211826112 Anne Corbin Young (10/20/1973-   )
21182612 Mary Emily Corbin Kendig (6/10/1948-   ), m. 8/15/1983,
            Thomas Taplin Rankin
211826121 John Beverley Rankin (11/29/1984-10/24/1989)
211826122 Thomas Kendig Parker Rankin (5/5/1986-   )
2118262   Anne Corbin Parker (3/16/1923-   ), m. 12/23/1944
            (Richmond, VA), Mason Romaine III, M.D. Jacksonville,
            FL.
21182621 Mason Romaine IV (5/20/1947-   ), m. 9/27/1976, Jean
            Kollen Gillander. Jacksonville, FL.
211826211 Jean Kollen Romaine (5/4/1979-   )
211826212 Mason Romaine V (6/7/1982-   )
21182622 Randolph Parker Romaine (3/22/1950-   )
21182623 Douglas Patteson Romaine (1/17/1952-   ), m. 1/24/1977,
            Jane Williams Collins. Naples, FL.
211826231 Jane Hundley Romaine (4/1/1982-   )
211826232 Anne Mason Romaine (6/28/1985-   )
211826233 Douglas Randolph Romaine (10/15/1986-   )

2135242   Ann Hunley Agee
21352421 Emma Randolph Elebash, m. Brig. Gen. Edward Hunter
            Hurst, USMC
213524211 Ann Randolph Hurst, m. 11/6/1965, Quantico, Col. Myron
            Charles Harrington, Jr., USMC (8/13/1938 Augusta
            County, GA-   ), son of Myron Charles and Stella
            Irene Craig Harrington.
2135242111 Ann Hunley Harrington (1/12/1967 Camp Springs, MD-
)
2135242112 Myron Charles Harrington III, Lt., USMC (9/23/1971
            Canberra, Australia-   )

213524212 Jean Perrin Hurst, m. (1st)   Ireland, m.
            (2nd) 10/4/1986, Annapolis, Thomas Crawford Ramey
            (12/3/1943, Santa Rosa, CA-   ), son of William
            David and Dorothy Ruth Bates Ramey.
213524213 Elizabeth Hunter Hurst (5/25/1950 Pensacola,   ), m.
            7/24/1982 in Alexandria, Victor Kris Biebighauser
            (10/23/1953 Washington, DC-   ), son of Ernest
            Elmer and Myrtice Lucile Shows Biebighauser.
2135242131 John Hunter Biebighauser (4/27/1984 Washington-   )
2135242132 Julia Perrin Biebighauser (5/1/1989 Harrisburg, PA-
)

21352423 Hunley Agee Elebash

215 Susannah Randolph (b. ca. 1764). She may have been the
      third wife of Benjamin Harrison, Jr., who is said to have
      married, second,   Page.

216 Jane Randolph, m. Archibald ("Archie") Blair Bolling

218 Elizabeth ("Betty") Meade Randolph

2192 William Albert Bolling, d. "New Market", Goochland County,
       bur. at his home "Bolling's Retreat", Goochland County.

21924 Susan Christian Bolling (10/29/1850 "Bolling's Retreat"
        12/1/1909 Richmond), m. Washington, D.C., George Henry
        King, Jr. (4/19/1848 Staunton-   ), son of George
        Henry and Olymphia Meredith King of "New Market".
219241 Mary Meredith ("Mamie") King ("Bolling's
         Retreat"-1/9/1908 Greenville, SC), m. Richmond, 5/5/
         1898, J. Newton Johnston
2192411 Mary Bolling Johnston (12/28/1898 Richmond-   )
2192412 Helen Carey Johnston (12/18/1900 Richmond-   )

219242 Richard Bolling King ("Lock Lomond"-6/9/1943
         Pittsburg), m. (1st)   , m.
         (2nd) Mildred
219243 Annie Randolph King (at Miller's or "Loch
         Lomond"-11/30/1955), m. Richmond 6/30/1915, Charles
         Thruston Turner (-8/23/1948, Richmond, age
         72). Bur. Hollywood Cemetery.
219244 Susan Christian King (12/26/1882 at Millers or "Loch
         Lomond"-1/31/1936), m. Ginter Park, Richmond 10/7/
         1908, George Nicholas Skipwith III (11/29/1873-11/4/
         1917), son of Dr. George Nicholas and Maria L. Brooks
         Skipwith.
2192441 Sue Bolling Skipwith (4/10/1909-   ). No heirs
2192442 Helen Brooks Skipwith (3/28/1912-   )
21924421 Daughter
2192443 Anne Randolph Skipwith (9/21/1913-10/14/1914)
2192444 George Nicholas Skipwith IV (5/14/1915-   ). No heirs
219245 George Henry King III ("New Market"-5/10/1907
         Richmond). Never married.
         NOTE: A twin brother of 219245 died a few moments
         after birth.
219246 Robert Skipwith King ("New Market"-11/17/1959),
         m. (1st) Eliza Custis Leatherbury. M. (2nd) Ethel
         Carman
2192461 Robert Skipwith King II (1927-1959), m. 1953, Marilyn
         June Smith
21924611 Robert Skipwith King III (1955-   ), m. 1991, Diane
          Renee Kammler
21924612 Nancy Elizabeth King (1957-   ), m. 1989, Charles
          Hugh Moretz

21924613 Suzanne ("Suzy") Marie King (1963-   ), m. 1988,
          Charles Berschback
219246131 Charlotte Marie Berschback (1991-   )
219246132 Madeline Ann Berschback (1993-   )

21936 Thomas Bolling, Jr., m. 5/27/1878, Sally Bennett Aylett
       Bolling, dau. of Patrick Henry and Emily Aylett
       Rutherford Bolling.
219361 Randolph Bolling (b. 12/2/1879)

21939 Mary Louisa Bolling (1849-1890)

2193x Charles Edward Bolling (b. 9/7/1845), m. (2nd) Parke
       Chamberlayne Bagby

2194 Jane Rolfe Bolling inherited "Bolling Hall"

2195 Mary Randolph Bolling

222 Brett Randolph, Jr. (2/21/1760-after 1833). Born Dursley,
     Gloucestershire, England, m. 5/12/1782, Anne Meade
     Randolph (2/21/1764-1/ /1820)

2221 Richard Kidder Randolph (b. 4/29/1794), change made because
      of cemetery records. D. Greene County, AL. Bur. two
      miles east of Greensboro, AL, on private property.
      Source: HISTORY OF PETER MONTAGUE OF NANSEMOND AND
      LANCASTER COUNTIES, VIRGINIA, AND HIS DESCENDANTS BY
      GEO. WILLIAM MONTAGUE. 1894.

22213 Montague Mickelborough Randolph (b. in 1825 or 1826), m.
       6/2/1853 or 2/16/1859 in Panola County, MS, three miles
       west of Courtland. He and his wife are bur. in Antioch
       Cemetery. Cornelia K. Wright (b. Alabama), dau. of
       Jesse C. and Nancy Watters Wright.
222131 Anna Elizabeth ("Bettie") Randolph (b. 7/17/1857), m.
        (1st) William Wallace Sumerall (5/17/1847-3/20/1882)
        (Sumerall genealogy in book KEAHEY CLANSMEN AND THEIR
        KIN SLAY, SUMMERALL, SMITH), m. (2nd) 11/18/1883
        Julious J. Johnson (2/23/1844-11/29/1924). She, like
        all of her siblings, was b. Robina, Panola County, MS.
2221311 Noel Sumerall (4/21/1875-10/20/1920)
22213111 Clarice Sumerall, m. Dewey Pond
222131111
222131112
22213112 Randolph Bacon Sumerall, m. Selena
222131121 Mary Elizabeth Sumerall
2221312 Arthur Lloyd Sumerall (12/14/1876-11/26/1892)
2221313 Virgie C. Sumerall (10/17/1878-9/10/1907)
2221314 Raleigh Randolph Sumerall (11/10/1880-10/15/1956), m.
         12/27/1908 Helen Christiana Miller (11/15/1885-6/9/
         1968). Both bur. Miller Family Cemetery in Caile, MS,
         Sunflower County.

22213141   Anna Elizabeth Sumerall (1/5/1911-5/10/1993), m. 10/9/
           1932 Henry Alfred Smith (7/27/1908-12/17/1968)
222131411 Robert Alfred Smith (7/20/1933-   ), m. (1st) 8/ /
           1957 Donna Marie Smith, m. (2nd) 7/19/1982 Zoe Ann
           Jansen
2221314111 Quanita Lynn Smith (9/25/1959-   ), m. (1st) Michael
            Ayers, m. (2nd) Rick Brown
22213141111 Joshua Curtis Ayers (6/10/1981-   )
2221314112 Bryan Scott Smith (10/16/1962-   ), m. Catherine
22213141121 Christina Carlene Smith (9/23/1986-   )
22213141122 Zachary Scott Smith (10/6/1994-   )
222131412 Eleanor Miller Smith (9/26/1939-   ), m. (1st) 2/24/
           1958 Steve Morris Kimbrell, m. (2nd) 4/ /1981 Ralph
           Kyte, Jr.
2221314121 Steve Morris Kimbrell, Jr. (1/19/1960-   )
2221314122 Marc Alfred Kimbrell (12/20/1961-   ), m. Andrea
            Brown
22213141221 Elizabeth Marie Kimbrell (11/2/1994-   )
22213141222 Aaron William Kimbrell (10/14/1996-   )
2221314123 Margaret Miller Kimbrell (1/19/1963-   ), m. Tommy
            Poe
22213141231 Thomas Andrew Poe (7/2/1982-   )
22213141232 Matthew Lewis Poe (5/22/1988-   )
2221314124 Robert Dodd Kimbrell (8/6/1964-   ), m. Dena Bennett
22213141241 Marian Caitlin Kimbrell (8/20/1990-   )
22213141242 Robert Aaron Hayden Kimbrell (4/19/1995-   )
222131413 Frances Elizabeth Smith (1/23/1942-   ), m. 12/22/
           1960 Charles Edward Williams (2/18/1940-   )
2221314131 Maria Elizabeth Williams (5/2/1964-   ), m. (1st)
            William Wesley Smith, m. (2nd) Robert Francis
            Duncan, Jr.
22213141311 William Kyle Duncan (6/19/1984-   )
22213141312 Robert Francis Duncan III (9/19/1986-   )
22213141313 Anna Elizabeth Duncan (10/3/1987-   )
2221314132 Paul Albert Williams (3/21/1967-   ), m. Wendy Carol
            Heathman
22213141321 Justin David Williams (8/25/1985-   )
2221314133 Catherine Harrison Williams (12/22/1974-   )
222131414 Randolph William Smith (7/20/1945-   ), m. 4/20/1971
           Carol Austin
2221314141 Henry Alfred Smith II (1/18/1973-   ) (twin)
2221314142 Joseph Anthony Smith (1/18/1973-   ) (twin)
2221314143 Randolph William Smith, Jr. (3/21/1977-   )
22213142 Chloetilda Belle Sumerall (1912-   ), m. H. C. Pearce
222131421
222131422
22213143 Randolph Miller Sumerall (1/13/1920-   ), m. 1948
          Maria Maas
222131431 Randolph Miller Sumerall, Jr. (5/4/1950-5/4/1991)
222131432 Christiana Maria Sumerall (3/ /1951-   )
2221314321
222131433 Paul Maas Sumerall (8/ /1954-   )
2221314331
2221314332

```
222131434  Diane Vera Sumerall (4/15/1956-    )
2221314341
2221314342
22213144  Raleigh Lamar Sumerall (1/13/1920-9/26/1992)
22213145  Lloyd Arthur Sumerall (1922-    ), m. Kay Dodd
222131451
222131452
2221315  Dyer Johnson (7/17/1885-1949)
2221316  Montague Johnson (10/1/1889-1936), m. 9/27/1916 Nella L.
          Lancaster (11/26/1891-1981)
22213161  John J. Johnson (6/29/1917-    )
222131611
22213162  Mary Emily Johnson (2/18/1919-    ).  No issue.

222132  Nancy ("Nannie") W. Randolph, m. Robert Monteith
222133  John Mickelborough Randolph (b. 1861)
222134  Virginia Randolph (1864 or 1866-1934) b. Robina or
          Panola, m. James P. Butts
222135  Richard Montague Randolph (1866 or 1868-    ) b.
          Robina or Panola.
222136  Addie Randolph, b. Panola or Pope & Knights Ferry
          Precinct.
222137  George Washington Randolph, b. Panola or Pope & Knights
          Ferry Precinct.

22215  Thomas E. Randolph, d. in yellow fever epidemic.
22216  Ann E. Randolph (b. Amelia County.  Her earlier siblings
          were born in Powhatan County).
22217  Emily Vaughan Randolph (b. Marengo County, AL)
22218  Lucy A. Randolph (may have d. 1872)
22219  Maria L. Randolph (6/20/1841 or 1842), m. 10/28/1858
          Green Middleton

2223  Patric Henry Randolph (1799-1840).  Twin of 2224 Brett
          Randolph III who died as an infant.  M. 5/23/1821 at
          Chaumiere Farm, KY, Mary Willing Byrd (5/  /1798-5/  /
          1849), dau. of Charles Willing Byrd and Sarah ("Sallie")
          Waters Meade.
22231  Mary Susan Randolph, m. Robert Barnhardt
222311  Cary Lee Barnhardt (        -before 3/  /1916), m. Nannie
          Woodson, dau. of Robert Edward and Carter Woodson.
2223111  Robert E. Barnhardt
2223112  Cara Lee Barnhardt
222312  William Randolph Barnhardt
222313  Mary Olive Barnhardt
222314  Byrd (A?) Barnhardt
222315  Emma (Emmeline?) Barnhardt
222316  Charles Barnhardt
22232  Sarah Anne Randolph, m. George Paxson
222321  Otway Paxson
22233  Evelyn Byrd Randolph (5/3/1832-1884).  Born Jessamine
          County, KY.  M. 10/9/1856, Benjamin Franklin Oxley
          (10/31/1831-4/12/1810) at Weston, Platte County, MD.
          Oxley was born Scott, KY.  Died Ordell Station, Idaho.
```

Buried Morris Hill Cemetery, Boise. He was son of
Clare (d. 1845) and Philadelphia Oliver Oxley (d. 1833).

222331　John Jefferson Oxley (died age 21)

222332　Mary Louise ("Lulu") Oxley (9/21/1869 Louisville-12/20/
1942 Boise). Unm. Buried Morris Hill Cemetery.

222333　Franklin Oxley

222334　Jennie Willing Oxley (4/18/1877 Cincinnati-7/29/1858
Boise). Buried Morris Hill Cemetery. M. Muskogee,
Indian Territory, OK, 8/18/1903, John Finch Lawwill
(4/8/1874 Mayslick, Mason County, KY-11/25/1941 Boise),
son of William Henry and Mary Jane Wells Lawwill.

2223341　John Randolph Finch Lawwill (8/9/1907 Meridian, ID-
6/8/1994 near Riggins, ID). Buried Dry Creek
Cemetery, Boise. M. Grangeville, ID, 7/5/1933, Thelma
Fay Irish (1/9/1909-11/　/1993), dau. of Newton Bailey
and Minnie Elizabeth Jones Irish. Residence: "The
Ranch", Twin Falls, ID.

22233411　Carolyn Louise Lawwill (11/30/1933 Spokane-　　). M.
(1st) 8/31/1955, Orrin Nobel Green (5/16/1930-　　),
son of Norman and Marian Green. Div. (Orrin married
again, Claudine　　). M. (2nd) 5/22/1993,
Donald Gene Dunlap (11/30/1931-　　)

222334111　Mark Randolph Green (1/11/1957-　　)

222334112　Blain Patrick Green (7/21/1958-　　), m. 5/18/1991,
Kathleen Lorraine Perkins, dau. of Robert C. Perkins.

22233412　Leroy Edward Lawwill (3/12/1935 Kellog, ID-　　), m.
6/3/1957, Barbara Enders (1/29/1939-　　), dau. of
Gerald Walter and Violet Eliza ("Lynn") Christenson
Enders. Moved to Perth, Australia 1961.

222334121　Deon Kirk Lawwill (6/7/1958-　　), m. 10/21/1978,
Julie DePiaz (9/30/1960-　　), dau. of Angelo Agusto
and Pierina Coda DePiaz.

2223341211　Glen Robert Lawwill (10/23/1982-　　)

2223341212　Angela Marie Lawwill (10/28/1986-　　)

22233422　Lisa Kay Lawwill (2/6/1960-　　), m. 8/28/1981, Leslie
M. Aquino (9/25/1956 Basine, Burma-　　). He is
Burmese.

2223341221　Ryan Thomas Aquino (2/16/1982-　　)

2223341222　Elton Michael Aquino (3/28/1984-　　)

22233413　Anna Claire Lawwill (11/13/1936 Boise-　　), m. (1st)
6/30/1959, James E. Solomon, son of Ole and Sadie
Solomon. Div. 1978. He divorced Diane Lynn Hart
in 1993. M. (2nd) 6/1/1984, Daniel Douglas Culmer
of Flint, MI, son of Douglas William and Ruth Eleanor
Lewis Culmer. Anna was Daniel's second wife.
Residence: San Jose, CA. Painter.

222334131　Tana Solomon (8/22/1964-　　), m. 6/30/1991, Keith
McKaughan. Residence: Citrus Heights, CA.

2223341311　Kiana Dee McKaughan (12/11/1993-　　)

222334132　Todd Randolph Solomon (10/14/1965-　　)

22233414　Marian Edith Lawwill (10/16/1939 Boise-　　). Moved
to Honolulu. M. (6/24/1967 Honolulu, Arthur Ken
Nakagawa, son of George Kyoshi and Esther Aiko Ogawa
Nakagawa. Div. Marian's residence: Kaniohe, Hawaii.

222334141 Lorena Fay Nakagawa (9/21/1972-   )
222334142 Bryan Kevin Nakagawa (11/25/1975-   )
22233415   Merton Randolph Lawwill (9/26/1940-   ), m. 8/30/1968
           Las Vegas, June Spenger (4/14/1939 Albank, CA-   ),
           dau. of Frank (Jr.) and Evelyn Mae Biana Spenger.
           June was married first to Guy Suchomel and has three
           children by him.
222334151 Joseph Randolph Lawwill (5/20/1970-   )
222334152 Marcella Katherine Lawwill (7/27/1977-   )
22233416   Donna Mae Lawwill (12/27/1942-   ), m. 3/21/1964,
           Chester Leroy Call (1/22/1941-   ), son of Francis
           Chester and Martha Carolina Dockter Call.
222334161 Anna Marie Call (12/27/1964-   ), m. 6/25/1988, Kerry
           William Anderson (2/15/1965 Ravenna, OH-   ), son
           of John William and Katherine Ruth Laney Anderson.
222334162 Eric Osmond Call (4/2/1966-   ), m. 10/22/1993,
           Michelle Renee Macarelli (3/17/1966 Norristown, PA-
           ), dau. of Ronald Francis and Linda Lu
           Galgerud Nacarelli.
222334163 Alex Randolph Call (8/9/1967-   )
22233417   Mary Ella Carrol Lawwill (12/25/1948-   ), m. (1st)
           12/21/1974 Singapore, Michael Robert Tsark, son of
           Richard Y. K. and Ethel Pahio Tsark. No children.
           Div. 9/21/1978. M. (2nd) 6/16/1979 Fort Bragg,
           Donald Eugene Pribble, Jr. (12/21/1951-   ), son
           of Donald Eugene and Eula Elizabeth Pickerel Pribble.
222334171 Jeannie Marie Kristin Pribble (7/26/1981-   )
222334172 Kari Ann Pribble (9/18/1983-   )
           Note: Pribble children born in Munich
2223342   Wells Meade Lawwill (10/30/1909 Caldwell, ID-10/23/1932
           Boise). Buried Morris Hill Cemetery. M. ca. 10/ /
           1928, Verna Evelyn McFarland (ca. 1908 Rome, NY-   ),
           dau. of Walter J. McFarland. Miner in 1930 in Middle-
           ton, ID. After marriage lived in Stibnite, ID. Then
           to Boise. Verna m. (2nd) 9/29/1933, Merle Murray and
           had two children by him; m. (3rd)   Ellis
           and had two children by him.
22233421   Stanley Wells Lawwill (10/12/1930-12/13/1953 Lansing,
           MI), m. Rose Mary   . She met Stanley in
           England while he was in Air Force. Stanley was
           killed in a light airplane crash.
222334211 Robert Lawwill (ca. 1948-   )
222334212 Alan Lawwill (ca. 1953-   )
222335   Anne Page Oxley
22234   Jane Silounce Randolph. Unm. Lived in Jessamine County,
           KY

2232   Heatly Douglas

2234   Archibald Aberdeen Douglas

233   John Randolph of Roanoke. Member of Congress. Minister to
        Russia. Died in Roanoke.

24142x231   Frederick Campbell Stuart Hunter III (d. 1/8/1989)

24142x232   John Morris Hunter (d. 1/10/1984), m. Juliet King
            Lehman (3/14/1922-   ), dau. of William Lawrence
            and Juliet Osborne Peyinghaus Lehman.

24151343   Anne Keim Millholland (8/8/1872-11/28/1932), m. Van
           Lear Perry Shriver (d. 1/8/1953), son of Henry and
           Sarah Van Lear Perry Shriver.
241513431 Van Lear Perry Shriver, Jr. (d. 5/31/1956)
2415134311 Sally Van Lear Shriver, m. 11/28/1959, Nelson B.
           Lee, Jr. (6/12/1932-   ). Div.
24151343111 George Cabot Lee II (7/26/1966-   ), m. 10/25/1996,
            Renate Marina Keyes
2415134312 Van Lear Perry Shriver III, m. 8/8/1953, Mary
           Patricia Roberts (11/1/1934-   )
24151343121 Deborah Adel Shriver (8/6/1954-   )
24151343122 William Michael Shriver (1/23/1957-   )
241513432 Beverley Randolph Shriver (d. 2/1/1973), m. Mary
           Elizabeth Armstrong (d. 9/12/1981), dau. of
           Frederick Searles Armstrong.
2415134321 Beverley Randolph Shriver, Jr., m. 12/4/1954,
           Abigail Alden Smith (6/12/1931-   ), dau. of
           Robert William and Abigail Guthrie Smith.
24151343211 Anne Guthrie Shriver (9/21/1956-   ), m. 3/26/1983,
            Gregory Lee Wagner (11/8/1947-   ), son of Robert
            Howard and Marian Gaertner Wagner.
241513432111 Timothy Michael Wagner (6/29/1985-   )
24151343212 Beverley Randolph Shriver III (8/22/1959-   ), m.
            10/19/1991, Diedra Diane Ryder (12/19/1970-   ),
            dau. of Ray J. and Susan Swadley Ryder.
24151343213 Robert Smith Shriver (11/4/1964-   ), m. 12/19/1987,
            Constance Ann Wyatt (4/26/1964-   ), dau. of
            Charles Edward and JoAnn Huszti Wyatt.
241513432131 Guthrie Marshall Shriver (4/8/1996-   )
2415134322 Frederick Armstrong Shriver (3/27/1933-3/31/1933)

241c1142   Julia Brent Keyser (8/5/1891-3/18/1975), m. Gaylord
           Lee Clark (8/11/1883-2/5/1969)
241c11421 Juliana Gaylord Clark (5/2/1922-   ), m. (1st) George
           Baker Treide. Killed in an airplane accident. M.
           (2nd) Richard Jennings Watts (10/3/1920-6/15/1979).
           Adopted: Thomas Edmund Jennings Watts (10/14/1960-
           ), m. Susan Sunday (8/17/1958-   ) and
           they had a child Julie Alisha Watts (9/4/1986-   ).
241c11422 Letitia Lee Clark (9/11/1923-   ), m. Carlton Lasley
           Sexton (2/18/1925-   )
241c114221 Carlton Clark Sexton (1/1/1952-   ), m. Elizabeth
           Cushing Hoover (7/25/1951-   )
241c1142211 Thomas Clark Sexton (7/13/1981-   )
241c1142212 Joseph Hoover Sexton (6/8/1984-   )
241c114222 Letitia Lee Sexton (3/8/1954-   ), m. Edward Andrew
           Yensho (11/18/1954-   )
241c1142221 Julia Brent Yensho (2/11/1988-   )

241c1142222 Victoria Lee Yensho (5/3/1989-   )
241c114223 Mary Darrington Sexton (5/11/1955-   ), m. William
            Lyle Barlow (5/21/1955-   )
241c1142231 William Nelson Barlow (5/1/1992-   )
241c114224 Jane Corbin Sexton (3/17/1958-   )
241c114225 Jonathan Hager Sexton (7/27/1965-   )
241c11423 Mathilde Keyser Clark (5/25/1925-   ), m. Alexander
            Rutherford Holmes (8/8/1923-   )
241c114231 Gaylord Clark Holmes (7/9/1953-   ), m. Laura Miller
            (10/27/1952-   )
241c1142311 Alexander Rutherford Holmes II (3/10/1984-   )
241c1142312 Gordon McHenry Holmes (5/27/1986-   )
241c1142313 Sarah Carrington Holmes (4/13/1988-   )
241c114232 Anne Rutherford Holmes (1/2/1956-   )
241c114233 Virginia Carrington Holmes (5/13/1958-   ), m.
            William James Price V (10/30/1958-   )
241c1142331 William James Price VI (5/9/1987-   )
241c1142332 Mathilde Brent Price (8/24/1989-   )
241c11424 Gaylord Lee Clark, Jr. (3/27/1928-   ), m. Margery
            Wolfe Clark (5/14/1930-   )
241c114241 Gaylord Lee Clark III (10/4/1957-   ), m. Lee Ann
            Saus (7/23/1959-   )
241c1142411 Madelyn Ruth Clark (10/12/1988-   )
241c1142412 Nina Elizabeth Clark (3/24/1990-   )
241c114242 Margery Levering Clark (6/8/1959-   ), m. Stephen
            Alexander Sheppard (11/12/1958-   )
241c1142421 Jacob McHenry Sheppard (5/7/1990-   )
241c1142422 Isaac Alexander Sheppard (10/23/1992-   )
241c114243 Jane Atkingson Clark (11/21/1961-   ), m. Peter
            Laurenson Worthington (9/2/1961-   )
241c1142431 Peter Laurenson Worthington, Jr. (10/25/1990-   )
241c1142432 Sarah Jane Worthington (9/10/1993-   )
241c114244 Peter Jefferson Clark (11/12/1965-   )
241c11425 Sally Cary Clark (7/9/1929-9/1/1966), m. Stewart
            MacKay Wolff (3/10/1926-   )
241c114251 Stewart MacKay Wolff, Jr. (5/20/1957-   )
241c114252 Robert Brent Keyser Wolff (8/6/1959-   )
241c114253 Edith Gaylord Clark Wolff (5/10/1961-   )

242178231 Mary ("Polly") Boyd Poindexter, m.   Pugh

24222 Mary Skipwith Randolph, m. William Sheets
242221 Elizabeth Lawrence Sheets, m. Archibald Irwin Harrison
        (6/9/1832-12/16/1970 Indianapolis of tuberculosis),
        son of John Scott Harrison (1804-1878), a Congressman
        of Vincennes, Indiana (buried in Harrison tomb in North
        Bend, Indiana).
2422211 Mary Randolph Harrison (-1896), m. Frank Campbell
        Nickels (8/4/1857-1923)
24222111 Harrison Campbell Nickels (12/20/1892-1/6/1912)
24222112 Irwin Harrison Nickels (6/15/1894-   ), m. Jeanette
        Gilbert
242221121 Jean G. Nickels (5/6/1916-3/26/1954), m. John W.
        Beattie

2422211211 Susan Nickels Beattie (1944-   )
2422211212 Carolyn Nickels Beattie (1949-   )
2422212 William Sheets Harrison (-12/17/1890)
2422213 Elizabeth Irwin Harrison (1866-5/6/1946), m. 9/26/1888,
         her cousin, Thornton Lewis (1865-1938), son of John
         Calvin and Alice Fitzhugh (Elizabeth?) Thornton Lewis.
         Elizabeth is buried in Hill Crest Cemetery close to
         the Greenbriar Hotel in White Sulphur Springs, WV
         (note by Shankland's Funeral Home). Alice was a
         granddaughter of President William Henry Harrison.
24222131 William Sheets Harrison Lewis (1890-   ), m. 1917,
         Rema Doris
242221311 Thornton Lewis II (1919-1942)
242221312 William Harrison Lewis (1925-   )
24222132 Alice Thornton Lewis (1894-1974), m. (1st) Franklin
         Attilla Botts (1889-1937), m. (2nd) Hobert Elliott
         Doyle (1889-1966)
242221321 Elizabeth Thornton Botts (1916-1963), m. 1940, William
         Ledwith Paul (1907-1981)
2422213211 Elizabeth Thornton Paul (1941-   ), m. John Edward
         Seykora (1935-   )
24222132111 John Edward Seykora III (1969-   ), m. Christi Ann
         Ganner (1972-   )
2422213212 Mary ("Molly") Ledwith Paul (1945-   ), m. Dr.
         Kimball Ivan Maull (1942-   )
24222132121 Elizabeth Thornton Maull (1963-   ), m. Gary
         Kirchoff (1957-   ). Div. She took back her
         maiden name
242221321211 Lindsey Marie Kirchoff (1989-   )
24222132122 Dr. Christopher Doyle Maul (1968-   ), m. Amy
         Stewart Clarke (1968-   )
242221321221 Mary Stewart Maull (1997-   )
24222132123 Sara Lindsey Maull (1973-   )
2422213213 William Ledwith Paul, Jr. (1953-   )
242221322 Franklin Attilla Botts, Jr. (1918-1921)
24222133 Lawrence Lewis (1895-1954), m. (1st) 1917, Louise
         Clisby Wise (1895-1937), m. (2nd) 1926, Ruby Bigger
         (1903-11/ /1954)
242221331 Lawrence Lewis, Jr. (1918-1995), m. 1940, Janet Keene
         Patton (1920-   )
2422213311 Louise Wise Lewis (1941-   ), m. (1st) Horace Alfred
         Gray III (1937-   ). Div. M. (2nd) John Newton
         Foster, Jr. (1935-   )
24222133111 Horace Alfred Gray IV (1962-   ), m. Carol Diane
         Gordon (1967-   )
242221331111 Hannah Louise Gray (1993-   )
24222133112 Lawrence Lewis Gray (1964-   ), m. Frederica Crane
         Prior (1964-   )
242221331121 Lawrence Lewis Gray, Jr. (1995-   )
24222133113 Catherine Whittet Gray (1967-   ), m. Brantley
         Davis Hathaway (1962-   )
242221331131 Brantley Davis Hathaway, Jr. (1995-   )
24222133114 John Newton Foster III (1973-   )

Note: Louise Wise Lewis Gray Foster adopted (1) Charles
        Baker Foster (1964-   ), who married Kimberly Diane
        Wegner (1962-   ) and (2) Carolyn Ann Foster (1967-
            ), who married Walter Edward Bundy IV (1968-   ).
2422213312 Janet Patton Lewis (1953-   ), m. Bradford Boyd
            Sauer (1950-   )
24222133121 Bradford Boyd Sauer, Jr. (1980-   )
24222133122 Mary Lewis Sauer (1981-   )
24222133123 James Patton Sauer (1985-   )
24222133124 Jessie Lawrence Sauer (1990-   )
24222133125 Savannah Alexander Sauer (1993-   )
2422213313 Jessie Kenan Lewis (1957-   ), m. Benjamin Briscoe
            White III (1957-   )
24222133131 Benjamin Briscoe White IV (1988-   )
24222133132 Elizabeth Harrison White (1991-   )
24222133133 Jesse Kenan White (1994-   )
242221332 Mary Lily Flagler Lewis (1920-   ), m. 1946, Frederick
            Gresham Pollard (1918-   )
        Note: She adopted: Lewis Butler Pollard and
                    Nelson Carter Pollard
2422214 Jean Carter Harrison m. George Evans Davis
24222141 Bettie Harrison Davis, m. (1st) George Edward Darling,
        m. (2nd) Hugh Fleming, Jr.
242221411 Carter Fleming

24244521 Virginia Randolph Bolling Hoge, m. Emidio Marchese
            (born in Arpino, Italy) in San Germano.
242445211 Mary Randolph Marchese

242453b1 John Randolph Harrison (3/15/1904-   ), m. Emily
            Barclay McFadden (7/8/1895-   )
242453b11 Josephine Clement Harrison (9/3/1930-   ), m. Maxwell
            Evarts (1/6/1921-   )
242453b111 James M. Evarts (8/17/1951-   ), m. Rebecca M.
            Martin
242453b1111 William Randolph Evarts (4/30/1984-   )
242453b1112 Mariah S. Evarts (10/3/1985-   )
242453b1113 Susannah D. Evarts (5/14/1989-   )
242453b112 Jane R. Evarts (1/7/1953-   ), m. Dennis T. Grendahl
242453b113 Emily H. Evarts (8/21/1954-   ), m. R. Timothy
            Vaughan
242453b1131 Maxwell Vaughan (8/13/1986-   )
242453b1132 Danielle Vaughan (1/1/1989-   )
242453b1133 Nicholas Vaughan (1/25/1992-   )
242453b114 Thomas Evarts (4/5/1957-   ), m. Victoria Morash
242453b1141 Sophie Evarts (2/24/1990-   )
242453b1142 Alexandra Evarts (6/19/1991-   )
242453b1143 Remi Evarts
242453b115 John R. H. Evarts (2/13/1959-   ), m. Kathleen Keams
242453b1151 Harrison Evarts (3/15/1991-   )
242453b1152 Darragh Evarts (3/14/1993-   )

24248133 Samuel Wilson Blaine (12/29/1912-   ), m. Virginia
            Early

251 Rev. Anthony Walke III, m. (2nd) 5/23/1788, Anne Elizabeth
     Newton (widow Fisher), m. (3rd) 6/27/1811, Anne Livingston
2511 Edwin Walke. There may have been two children named Edwin

2513 John Nelson Walke was child of Anne Elizabeth Newton Fisher

26 Elizabeth Jane Randolph (d. 12/ /1775), m. Col. Richard
    Kidder Meade of "Coggin's Point" in Prince George County.
    After the War he settled in Frederick (now Clarke) County.

31 Col. Thomas Fleming (b. 1727), m.   Randolph. Killed
    in Battle of Princeton 1/21/1777.

32 Col. John Fleming (date of death not correct). Lived at
    "Maiden's Choice", Cumberland County.

3222 John Lewis (-ca. 1770 Gloucester County). A member of
      the Council.

323 Susanna ("Sukey") Fleming (2/5/1752-1820), m. Capt. Addison
     Lewis, son of John and Elizabeth Warner Lewis.

33 Judge William Fleming in 1776-80 was a member of the Virginia
    Conventions, Powhatan County. General Court of Virginia
    beginning in 1780 and President of the Court of Appeals in
    1820-24.
        Source: DAR application. Mary Isham Keith Chapter,
                 Fort Worth. Dated 1915. National Number
                 116518.

3312333 Robert Francis Gribble (d. 1970)

33242 Caroline Wooldridge (d. 1906), m. Edward Cunningham Archer
       (d. 1891)

332425 Mary Bolling Archer (1859-1937), m. 12/21/1887, William
        Phleger Emanuel (1860-1950)
              All four 33242 and 332425 are buried in Manakin
              Episcopal Church in Powhatan, VA
3324251 Virginia ("Jennie") Emanuel
3324252 Frances Stanard Emanuel (10/21/1888-4/ /1931), m.
         10/27/1908, James Milton Graham (5/22/1880-5/ /1952)
33242521 Brownne Caroline Graham (5/24/1923-   ), m. 1/30/1940,
          Edward Carlyle Canada (4/13/1920-   )
332425211 Joan Carolyn Canada
332425212 Frances Stanard Canada (2/25/1943-   ), m. 1961,
           Robert Folger Jessup (7/21/1932-   )
3324252121 Kathryn Elizabeth Jessup (5/19/1962-   ), m. 1989,
            John Guerrant Dickenson, Jr. (10/31/1963-   )
33242521211 Elizabeth Stanard Dickenson (6/18/1995-   )
3324252122 Robert Folger Jessup II (3/14/1965-   )
3324252123 John Darius Jessup II (2/22/1970-   )
332425213 Catherine Carlisle Canada (1/23/1947-   ), m. 1966
           MacArthur Wood (7/25/1945-   )
3324252131 Michael Anderson Wood (10/13/1967-   )
3324252132 Melissa Carolyn Wood (4/8/1969-   ), m. 1995 Keith
            Monroe Barlow (9/10/1971-   )
33242521321 Devin Michael Barlow (7/9/1996-   ). Twin
33242521322 Jonathan Gary Barlow (7/9/1996-   ). Twin
332425214 Anita Graham Canada
332425215 Edward Carlyle Canada, Jr.
332425216 Beverly Ann Canada

3511   Fleming Bolling Evans (12/15/1796-7/15/1861)
35111

35111181   Ann Elizabeth Evans (b. Fort Worth, Tarrant County,
           TX), m.   Henckels

35111183   Alma Evans (b. Sherman, Grayson County, TX), m. William
           P. McLean, Jr.
                Source: DAR Application Rochambeau Chapter of
                     Paris. Dated 1965. National Number 510257

35112   Lucy Ann Evans (3/6/1821-9/9/1876), m. 2/4/1841, Andrew J.
        Cooley (7/4/1812-6/6/1886). She is bur. in Knoxville,
        TN
351121   Mary A. A. Cooley (b. 6/24/1844 in Chattanooga), m. 4/4/
        1864, George T. Fry (3/12/1843-5/29/1897)
3511211   George T. Fry, Jr. (10/15/1872 in Chattanooga-1945), m.
        10/18/1895, Jennie Owen (b. 7/10/1875 in Tennessee-
        d. St. Louis)
35112111   Julia Fry (6/13/1894 in Chattanooga-d. 8/22/1938 in
        St. Louis), m. 1/22/1913, Stanley M. Masters (1/1/
        1878 in Independence, MO-7/14/1954 in St. Louis).
        After her mother remarried McCall, Julia used the
        McCall name. Thus Julia Fry and Julia McCall are
        the same person.
351121111   Jane Masters (b. 10/30/1913 in Springfield, OH), m.
        (1st) John F. Hollenbeck (Div.); m. (2nd) 7/18/1936,
        in Paris, Jean Marie Chaumont. Address: La Gue
        Motte, LaFerte St.Cyr, et Cher, France.

35113   Amelia S. Evans (10/29/1824-   ). Buried Knoxville
35114   Martha F. Evans (9/24/1826-   ), m. 10/2/1855, Robert J.
        Felkner. Buried Lotus Springs, TN
35115   Mary K. Evans (10/11/1828-   ). Buried Knoxville
35116   Elizabeth E. Evans (3/21/1831-5/8/1918 Mt. Pleasant, TX),
        m. 8/28/1851 Knoxville, James Monroe Vaughan.
351161   Jessie Marie Vaughan (6/11/1852-   ), m. 7/19/1869,
        James K. Cummings
351162   Mary Sidney Vaughan (6/14/1855-9/24/1890), m. 8/17/1883,
        Sam Houston Jolly
351163   Laura Vaughan (3/28/1856-1918), m. 1/23/1876, Thomas
        Shook
351164   Elizabeth ("Lizzie") Vaughan (10/8/1859-   ), m. 12/29/
        1881, Daniel C. McCombs
351165   William Leroy Vaughan (11/15/1860-   ), m. Martha
        Merrell
351166   Emma Vaughan (9/25/1861-4/ /1939), m. 12/29/1881, John
        Nichols
351167   Amelia Isabell Vaughan (1/4/1867-4/11/1851), m. 1/11/
        1885, John Ballard Callaway. Born Sulphur Springs,
        TX, died Bonham, TX
3511671   Thomas Lee Callaway (9/30/1886-1966), m. 3/15/1923,
        Lottie Bell Moore
35116711   Frances Geraldine Callaway (b. 4/18/1923)

351167111 Vernon Dale Brown (1/31/1941-   )
351167112 Anita Louise Broadwater (10/24/1943-   ), m. 1/ /
            1966, Jack McCartney
3511671121 David Wayne McCartney (9/14/1965-   )
3511671122 Nancy Ann McCartney (9/8/1966-   ), m. 6/ /1985,
            Glen Mergele
35116711221 Nichole Mergele (10/23/1986-   )
35116712 Alice May Callaway (10/14/1932-   ), m. 3/4/1950,
            Arthur Moore
351167121 Patrick Arthur Moore (3/28/1951-   ), m. 8/30/1985,
            Cynthia Kohler
3511671211 Matthew Hollis Moore (4/5/1988-   )
351167122 Sherri Diane Moore, m. (1st) Kenneth Ray Richardson,
            m. (2nd) Michael Berry Gambill
    Children by first husband:
3511671221 Alicia Francine Richardson (3/24/1970-   )
3511671222 Sonya Kay Richardson (6/5/1971-   )
    Child by second husband:
3511671223 Tracy Michelle Gambill (2/7/1976-   )
351167123 Brandi Kay Moore (8/8/1956-11/4/1994)
351167124 Michael Hollis Moore (10/22/1957-   )

3665 Thomas Jefferson Bernard, m. (1st) 1/9/1823, Mary McConnel
        (d. 2/29/1838), m. (2nd) Mrs. Eliza Atkinson
    Children of first marriage:
36651 William P. Bernard, m. 8/19/1845, Aseneth Johnson
36652 Sarah Bernard, m. William Elliott
36653 Thomas Jefferson Bernard, Jr. (10/12/1834-6/25/1914) (b.
        and d. in OH), m. 10/27/1857, Almeda Young
366531   Sarah Abigail Bernard (b. 4/10/1864 in Clinton County,
        OH), m. 5/4/1884 in Clinton County, OH, Michael Duroc
        Swingley
3665311   Clara Elizabeth Swingley (b. 7/10/1890), m. 1/13/1912,
        Burch Edward Fenner
36653111   Harriet Elizabeth Fenner (b. 10/26/1918 in Wilmington,
        OH), m. 5/24/1941 in Dayton, OH, Robert W. Gaines
366531111 Son
366531112 Son   366533
36653112   366534
36653113   366535
3665312   366536
3665313   366537
3665314   366538
3665315   366539
3665316   36653x
366532   36653a

36654 Nancy Bernard. Unm.

    Children by second wife:
36655
36656
36657
36657

36658
36659
3665x

369 William Bernard (1750-4/27/1776). Lt. Col. in Revolutionary
     War under his cousin, Capt. Charles Fleming. Died in
     service and received a warrant for 2666 acres of land
     which was left to his oldest brother John.

4 Elizabeth ("Betsy") Bolling, m. William ("Will" or "Old Duke")
   Gay, M.D., son of James Gay.
41 Capt. William ("Will") Gay (1749-5/24/1815). Buried in Dog
   Town, VA ("Fairfield" was near "Bolling Hall"). M. (1st)
   Frances Trent, dau. of Judge Alexander and Elizabeth
   Woodson Trent.

4112 Benjamin Franklin Gay

413 Thomas Bolling Gay (1784-2/10/1849)

4133 William Gay, m. Cassandra Desdemona Jackson (second cousin
   to President Andrew Jackson).
41331 Lyria Gay
41332 Page Gay
41333 Fanny Gay, m. 12/8/1878, L. H. Turley. In 1879 moved to
   Spokane County, CA. (Tradition: owns Topaz ring given
   Pocahontas by Capt. John Smith).
41334 Lucy Gay
4135 Powhatan A. Gay. Moved to AL or MS
4136 Virginia F. Gay (owned pistol given by George Washington
   to her great grandfather Archer).

4139 There may have been a brother Henry Gay.

414 Neil Buchanan Gay (9/3/1791-6/25/1864). Born in Powhatan
   County. M. 5/10/1820 Martha Talley (11/27/1795-4/28/
   1864). B. Cumberland County. Dau. of Rev. Elkana and
   Mary Elizabeth Anderson Talley. She was widow Anderson.
   Both buried in Fluvanna County in "Mill Farm" Cemetery.
4141 William Gay (6/20/1823-6/21/1893). C.S.A., m. Sarah Bruce.
   Buried Gay Cemetery, Fluvanna County.

4142 Neil Buchanan ("Uncle Buck") Gay, Jr., M.D. (2/6/1827-
   7/16/1906). Born "Carysbrook", Fluvanna County. Died
   "Dixie", Fluvanna County. Buried "Mill Farm" Cemetery
   in Fluvanna County. M. 11/15/1855, Mary Bunn (8/15/1834-
   5/12/1921), dau. of Nathaniel (Rev.) and Mary Ann Welling
   Bunn. Born and married in Trenton, died in Brooklyn.
   Buried Gay Family Cemetery in Fluvanna County.
41421 Richard Welling Gay (8/15/1856 in Fork Union, Fluvanna
   County-6/4/1858 in Fluvanna Co., at residence of grandfather Gay).
41422 William Bunn Gay (4/2/1858 Mill Farm-12/24/1921 Richmond),
   m. 12/28/1892, Georgie Lee Perkins (11/13/1865-11/4/
   1947), dau. of Constance Osborne and Judith Elizabeth
   Seay Perkins. Buried Fluvanna County.
414221 Constance Mary Gay (2/12/1895-   ), m. 8/19/1922,
   Richard Thomas Morenus
4142211 Constance Gay Morenus (5/14/1926-   ), m. 9/3/1955,
   Herbert Hammerman
41422111 Joseph Richard Hammerman (10/23/1957-   )
41422112 Daniel Aaron Hammerman (8/6/1959-   )

4142212　Richard Cousins Morenus (1/31/1929-　　), m. 10/22/1954,
　　　　　Marjorie Rose Rutherford
41422121　David Rutherford Morenus (1/20/1957-　　)
41422122　Carlyn Gay Morenus (7/25/1960-　　)
41422123　Daniel Hastings Morenus (7/9/1965-　　)
414222　Virginia Lee Gay (4/26/1898-4/27/1985). Buried Fluvanna
　　　　　County.
41423　Neil Buchanan Gay III (4/23/1859 "Mill Farm"-3/11/1926
　　　　　Eunity, AL), m. 6/26/1895, Clara Vaughan near Columbus,
　　　　　MS) her home).
414231　Rebecca Gay, m. John Hem
414232　Wilbur Gay
414233　Neil Buchanan Gay IV
414234　Mary Bunn Gay, m. Middleton Brock
414235　Madison Talley Gay
41424　Charles Wyndham Gay (8/4/1862 "Mill Farm"-10/10/1868 "Mill
　　　　　Farm"). Bur. Gay Family Cemetery Fluvanna County.
41425　Madison Talley Gay (7/29/1864 "Mill Farm"-1/3/1900
　　　　　Adairsville, KY). Dentist. Buried Gay Family Cemetery,
　　　　　Fluvanna County.
41426　Thomas Bolling Gay (9/29/1866 "Mill Farm"-5/16/1929
　　　　　Atlanta), m. 11/2/1892 Atlanta, Susan Eloise Gaston
　　　　　(8/18/1869 Faxima in Brazil-8/15/1950 Atlanta) ("The
　　　　　Great Grand Regulator"), dau. of James McFadden, M.D.
　　　　　and Susannah ("Susan" or "Sue") Greening Brumby
　　　　　McFadden. Buried in Atlanta.
414261　Eloise Gaston Gay (10/16/1893 Atlanta-6/19/1986 Decatur,
　　　　　GA) ("The Second Great Grand Regulator"), m. 9/22/1920,
　　　　　William Foote Brawley (12/23/1892 Chester, SC-7/20/1934
　　　　　Decatur).
4142611　William ("Bill") Gaston Brawley, M.D. (7/1/1922-5/22/
　　　　　1974). Born and died in Atlanta. M. 7/11/1948,
　　　　　Dorothy Lorraine Perry, R.N. (10/6/1927 Savannah-
　　　　　) ("The Third Great Grand Regulator"), dau. of
　　　　　Sumner Whitfield (D. Hum.) and Ruth Ethel Newton
　　　　　Perry.
41426111　Dorothy Elizabeth Brawley, Ph.D. (4/15/1949 Atlanta-
　　　　　). Residence: Decatur.
41426112　Laura Gay Brawley, R.N., M.S., C.S., F.N.P. (7/12/1950
　　　　　Atlanta-　　). Residence: Newport, TN. M. 7/11/
　　　　　1971 Burr Edwin Strader (1/12/1944-8/29/1996) (b. and
　　　　　d. Watertown, NY), son of Henry Alexander and Gladys
　　　　　Hariett Burr Strader. Div.
414261121　Ruth Juliette ("Julie") Strader (9/11/1972-　　)
414261122　Burr Edwin Strader, Jr. (1/12/1974 Atlanta-　　).
　　　　　Associated with Tara Jean Hepburn (12/2/1972-　　),
　　　　　dau. of Charles Anthony and Jeanne Anne Soriano Weil
　　　　　Heimerl.
4142611221　Jessica Alyn Strader (5/9/1992-　　)
414261123　William ("Billy") Alexander Strader (4/7/1977-　　)
414261124　Samantha ("Sammy") Elizabeth Strader (6/13/1985-　　)
41426113　William Gaston Brawley, Jr. (6/13/1952 Augusta, GA-
　　　　　). Residence: Tiger, GA. M. (1st) 6/2/1973,
　　　　　Donna Lynn DeWeese (8/19/1952-　　), dau. of

Richard S. and Margaret (?) DeWeese. Div. 1979.
M. (2nd) 7/15/1989, Ellen Elizabeth Adamczyk, R.N.
(11/1/1955-   ).
   Adpted children: Lee Bolling Brawley (4/24/1984-   ),
     Charles ("Charlie") Stephen Brawley (1/13/1986-   ),
     and Hope Sara Brawley (3/2/1987-   ).
41426114 Bolling Whitfield Brawley, M.D. (7/10/1956-   ), m.
     5/6/1995, Nancy Lynne Graham, dau. of James Rufus
     and Yvonne Ladd Graham.
41426115 Donald Perry Brawley (8/21/1963-   ), m. 9/30/1989,
     Jane Elizabeth Palmer, dau. of Carleton Glen and
     Joan Patricia Gossett Palmer.
4142612 Eloise Gay Brawley (7/31/1923 Atlanta-   ), m. 10/18/
     1952, Donald Malcolm Murray (12/28/1924-   ), son of
     John Hays and Mildred Crocker Murray. Residence:
     Albion, MI.
41426121 Eloise Gay Murray, R.N. (10/29/1953-   ), m. 10/10/
     1981, Donald Eugene Newton, Jr. (9/28/1953-   ), son
     of Donald Eugene and Dorothy Phyllis Primm Newton.
414261211 Lauren Elizabeth Newton (9/29/1983-   )
414261212 Rebecca Lynn Newton (3/1/1985-   )
41426122 Glenn Munro Murray (1/29/1955-   ), m. 3/24/1979,
     Georgianna Cecile Parsell, R.N. (10/16/1954-   ).
414261221 Benjamin John Murray (12/20/1980-   )
414261222 Eric Michael Murray (9/8/1984-   )
41426123 Margaret Thayer Murray (7/19/1957-   )
4142613 Bolling Gay Brawley (12/17/1924-1/24/1979), m. 4/24/
     1954, Helen ("Dee") Wallace Haskins (11/1/1928-   ),
     dau. of Hugh Henry Haskins.
41426131 Douglas Neal Brawley (7/14/1955-   ), m. Lori Margaret
     Lomasito, dau. of Gerardo Egidio and Jacquline
     Nichols Lomasito. Residence: Sunrise, FL.
414261311 Douglas Neal Brawley, Jr. Born Pembroke, FL.
41426132 William Bolling Brawley, R.N. (9/7/1957-   ), m.
     12/27/1987, Wendy Mae Doughterty, dau. of Winston
     Maynard Dougherty.
414261321 Ryan William Brawley (4/12/1989-   )
414261322 Briana Dee Brawley (1/19/1991-   )
41426133 Rebecca ("Becky") Gay Brawley, M.D. (11/11/1965-   ),
     m. 6/8/1991, Thomas Joseph Sawyer (4/22/1961-   ),
     son of Thomas Ellwood and Ellen Kathleen Higgins
     Sawyer.
414261331 Thomas Cabell Sawyer (6/23/1994-   )
414262 Thomas Bolling Gay, Jr., M.D. (3/1/1896-9/15/1982). Born
     and died in Atlanta. M. 6/24/1925, Margaret Elizabeth
     Shaw (11/12/1896-3/5/1976), dau. of Harry M. D. and
     Jane ("Jennie") Bayard Wilson Shaw.
4142621 Margaret ("Peggy") Elizabeth Gay (4/6/1926-   ), m.
     11/14/1947, John ("Jack") Anderson Simmons, Jr.
     (8/8/1924-   ), son of John Anderson Simmons.
41426211 John Anderson Simmons III. Reverend (5/15/1949-   ),
     m. (5/20/1978, Helen Elizabeth Uhl (2/16/1953-   ),
     dau. of Robert Irving and Mary Spencer Uhl.
414262111 Robert John Simmons (12/20/1982-   )

414262112 Elizabeth Gaylen Simmons (5/2/1986-   )
41426212   Margaret Gay Simmons (3/2/1951-   ), m. 5/11/1974,
           Wilkie Schell Colyer (5/12/1949-   )
414262121 Wilkie Schell Colyer, Jr. (1984-   )
414262122 Margaret Elizabeth Colyer (1986-   )
41426213   Richard Sanford ("Sandy") Simmons, M.D. (7/31/1953-
           ), m. 10/20/1984, Deborah ("Debbie") Algrant,
           M.D. (4/24/1957-   )
414262131 Joseph Anderson Simmons (1988-   )
414262132 John Patrick Simmons (1990-   )
414262133 Annabelle Gay Simmons (1992-   )
41426214   Thomas Bolling ("Bo") Simmons (9/22/1964-   ), m.
           1994, Alison Moore (11/7/1962-   ), dau. of B.
           Waldo and Nathalia Lee Vittum Moore.
4142622   Thomas Bolling Gay III (4/28/1928-7/25/1968). Suicide,
           Gunshot. M. 2/23/1952, Elizabeth Dyson Coleman
           (4/21/1929-2/11/1981)
41426221   Sallye Coleman Gay (7/21/1953-   ), m. 8/25/1973,
           Richard Allen Frady (6/28/1952-   )
414262211 Allison Gay Frady (4/16/1980-   )
41426222   Thomas Bolling Gay IV (5/12/1956-   ), m. 10/15/1978,
           Sandy Young (4/30/1957-   ). Div. 1983.
414262221 Caitylyn Elizabeth Gay (7/22/1985-   )
414262222 Lindsey Margaret Gay (2/29/1988-   )
414263   James Gaston Gay, M.D. (10/17/1897-1/21/1951). Born and
           died in Atlanta. M. 10/21/1930, Margaret Fraser
           MacIntyre (6/26/1903-12/28/1978). Buried in Atlanta.
4142631   Margaret MacIntyre Gay (9/25/1931-10/3/1931)
4142632   Julie Gaston Gay (10/8/1933-   ), m. Dominique ("Dom")
           Homan Wyant, son of William Keblinger and Rosemary
           Homan Wyant.
41426321   Margaret Homan Wyant (11/3/1961-   ), m. Gregory
           George Schultz
414263211 Gregory George Schultz, Jr. (12/3/1991-   )
414263212 James Gaston Schultz (4/3/1994-   )
4142633   Elizabeth ("Libby") Bowling (7/16/1937-   ), m. Robert
           Andes Browne, son of Wade Andes and Evelyn Louise
           Belle Isle Browne.
41426331   Robert Andes Browne, Jr. (1/31/1959-   ), m. Kathryn
           Herlong
           Adopted Laura Kathryn (2/5/1993-   )
41426332   James Wade Browne (7/20/1960-   ), m. Anne Fullerton
414263321 Hailey Elizabeth Browne (8/14/1989-   )
414263322 Margaret Fullerton Browne (5/11/1991-   )
414263323 James Wade Browne, Jr. (10/16/1993-   )
41426333   Elizabeth Gay Brown (5/16/1964-   ), m. Shawn Edward
           Reed
414263331 Katherine Elizabeth Reed (6/26/1992-   )
41427   Mary Ann ("Anna", "Annie") Bunn Gay (2/25/1869 "Mill
           Farm"-12/8/1953 Atlanta). Buried Deland, FL.
           Occupation: Missionary China. M. 12/4/1895 Fluvanna
           County, James ("Jayme") McFadden Gaston, Jr., M.D., son
           of James ("Jimmy") McFadden Gaston, M.D., and Susannah
           ("Susan", "Sue") Greening Brumby. No issue.

41428   Martha Gay (6/8/1871 "Mill Farm"-1957 East Orange, NJ.)
        Buried Greenwood Cemetery Brooklyn), m. 2/10/1892,
        Edward McGarvey (8/10/1859-3/25/1920), son of William
        and Jane Closson McGarvey.
414281 Martha Gay McGarvey
414282 Marie Louise McGarvey (3/21/1893 Brooklyn-   ).
        Buried Greenwood Cemetery Brooklyn.
414283 Anna Elizabeth McGarvey (7/31/1893 Brooklyn-6/7/1964
        Northhampton, NC). Buried "Elsing Green", King
        William County. M. John Hannon Gregory (1/ /1886
        King William County-2/23/1960 Rocky Mount, NC). Buried
        "Elsing Green". Son of Deucalion, M.D., and Sallie
        Pendleton Lewis.
4142831 Anna Elizabeth Gregory (1920 Brooklyn-1972), m. 1950,
        Raymond Axel Soderberg in Duke Chapel, Durham.
4142832 Lewis ("Lew") Winston Gregory (8/15/1923 Brooklyn-   ),
        m. 8/3/1951, Dorothy Miller Shields (2/17/1925-   )
        in Scotland Neck, NC.
41428321 Peter Edward Gregory (2/10/1954 Charlotte-   ), m.
        Nancy Rae Hunter (9/21/1955-   )
414283211 Brent Evans Gregory (9/19/1988 Greenville, NC-   )
414283212 Chelsea Elizabeth Gregory (3/7/1993 Greenville-   )
41428322 Barbara Rousseau Gregory, R.N. (6/12/1956 Rocky Mount-
             ), m. Walter Reade Hardin III (2/18/1954-   ),
        son of Walter Reade (Jr.) and Mary Holland Hardin.
414283221 Cary Elizabeth Hardin (4/12/1985 Atlanta-   )
414283222 Catherine Baylor Fields Hardin (10/26/1989 Atlanta-
)
414284 Edward McGarvey, m. Mary Mason
4143   Martha Gay (12/26/1828-12/15/1915). Buried Gay Family
        Cemetery, Fluvanna County. M. Capt. Archelaus ("Archer")
        Perkins, C.S.A. (9/17/1829-4/16/1895). Buried Gay Family
        Cemetery.
41431   Archer Holland Perkins (6/16/1850-1/26/1916). Said to
        have been a genius.
4144   Pocahontas ("Poca") Virginia Gay (9/5/1831-10/14/1922).
        Buried Gay Family Cemetery Fluvanna County.
4145   Caroline Anne ("Aunt Anne") Scott Gay (12/1/1832-5/2/1909).
        Buried Gay Family Cemetery Fluvanna County. Unm.
4146   Mary Elizabeth Gay (6/21/1821-9/4/1827). Buried Gay Family
        Cemetery Fluvanna County.
4147   Judith Scott Gay (6/8/1825-7/15/1945 in VA). Unm.
4148   Richard Anderson Gay (10/23/1835-6/25/1847)
4151   William Gay Strange. Brilliant and eccentric. Died in
        Richmond.

4163   Edward Scott Gay, Jr. (1846 Richmond-ca. 1921 Atlanta).
        Captain C.S.A.

41633   Ewell Gay, m.
416331 Frank L. Gay (lived in New York City 1955)

41634   Dau. m. Inman Sanders
41635   Dau. m. Thomas B. Baine (Raine?)

41636   Dau. m. Philip H. Kunzig

4165   Minnie Wellford Gay, m. Charles Campbell Fleming
41651   Charles Campbell Fleming, Jr.

417   Ann ("Nancy") H. Gay, m. Col. Charles H. Scott
4171   Gay Scott. Died in VA (young man)

4184   Elizabeth ("Lizzie") E. Gay

4186   Agatha Estill Gay. Died after 1928 in Staunton, VA.

419   Sarah ("Sally") Gay

4191   Judith Gay Ferguson (3/9/1810-   ). Born "Fairfield"
4192   Rebecca Pocahontas Ferguson (8/4/1812-   ).   Born
         "Fairfield".
4193   James Boswell Ferguson (8/7/1822-   ). Born "Fairfield".
4194   Mary Frances ("Fanny") Ferguson (7/5/1817-   ). Twin.
         Born "Fairfield".

4196   Robert Bolling Ferguson (11/14/1814-1816). Born "Fairfield"

5 (see page 124 CORRECTIONS AND ADDITIONS). The mother of
Thomas Eldridge, Jr., was Judith Kennon Eldridge.
51 (see page 124 CORRECTIONS AND ADDITIONS). Winifred Jones
Miller was born 1743 and (see page 256 POCAHONTAS'
DESCENDANTS) Thomas Eldridge III's will was not probated
in Madison County, AL, in 1822.
511 Thomas Eldridge IV's Will was probated in Madison County,
AL, in 1822.
5111 John Bolling Eldridge (ca. 1805-   ), m. 2/9/1825
Elizabeth Margaret Browning (ca. 1808-   ), dau. of
James E. and Ann J. Browning.
51111 Sophrona B. Eldridge (8/25/1829 Al-1/30/1893 Limestone
County, AL), m. 12/16/1850, Charles A. Hatchett (8/24/
1821 VA-4/26/1895 Limestone County, AL), son of Edward
and Catherine Crutcher Hatchett. Both bur. Hatchett
Cemetery, Wooley Springs, AL.
511111 Margaret ("Maggie") Catherine Hatchett (10/28/1851
Wooley Springs, Limestone County, AL-5/9/1886 Limestone
County, AL), m. 12/15/1869, Alfred Turner Williamson
(2/10/1839 Richmond, VA-10/12/1923 Athens, AL), son of
Francis Exum and Martha Williamson. Both bur. Hatchett
Cemetery, Wooley Springs, Limestone County, AL.
5111111 Walter Eugene Williamson (9/14/1870 Center Hill, Limestone County, AL-4/2/1950 Sulphur Springs, TX), m.
12/24/1896, Ethel Irene Crutcher (4/27/1875 Limestone
County, AL-12/28/1961 Sulphur Springs, TX), dau. of
William R. and Mary Carter Crutcher. Both bur.
Sulphur Springs City Cemetery.
51111111 Radford Turner Williamson (12/14/1897 Center Hill,
Limestone County, AL-1/5/1973 Richardson, TX), m.
9/1/1918, Hattie McFadden (10/1/1899-   ) (Hattie
still living as of September 1995), dau. of Claud and
Marie Tice McFadden.
511111111 Irene Marie Williamson (6/30/1919 Hatchettville, TX-
        ), m. 8/13/1938, Rose C. Burgin (8/20/1917
Saltillo, TX-6/8/1980 Sulphur Springs, TX), son of
Ernest Edward and Leatha Watts Burgin.
5111111111 Rose C. Burgin, Jr. (9/6/1939 Greenville, TX-   ),
m. 8/24/1961, TX, Norma Kay Attaway (5/26/1942
Sulphur Springs, TX-   ), dau. of Jack and Reba
Watkins Attaway.
51111111111 Susan Kay Burgin (3/23/1963 Greenville, TX-   ),
m. 5/21/1982, Douglas Boydston (12/18/1963 Denton,
TX-   ), son of Danny and Theta Arlene Grissom
Boydston.
511111111111 Joshua Boydston (12/14/1983 Greenville, TX-   )
511111111112 Jeremy Boydston (9/24/1986 Greenville, TX-   )
51111111112 Sharon Michelle Boydston (3/6/1966 Hunt County, TX-
        ), m. 4/6/1991, Kerry Baird (11/4/1965
Herford, TX-   ), son of   and Delores Ann
Sabo Baird.
511111111121 Averie Ann Baird (5/17/1995 Arlington, TX-   )
51111111113 Sheilla Dawn Burgin (11/25/1968 Greenville, TX-   )

5111111112 Joe Bob Burgin (6/28/1944 Sulphur Springs, TX-   ),
            m. 12/29/19   , Linda Norden (10/25/1946 Hopkins
            County, TX-   ), dau. of Elvis and Doris Williams
            Norden.
51111111121 Joel Bradley Burgin (2/16/1970 Bellville, IL-   ),
            m. 8/1/1992, Julie Robb (9/14/1972 Chicago, IL-
            ), dau. of Douglas and Susan Conroy Robb.
51111111122 Corey David Burgin (3/23/1974 Sulphur Springs, TX-
            ), m. 6/3/1995, Teffany Cheri Vanginault
            (3/12/1976 Sulphur Spring, TX-   ), dau. of Ronal
            and Barbara Ward Vanginault.
511111112   Francis Exum Williamson II (11/7/1920 Dike, Hopkins
            County, TX-   ), m. 1/24/1942, Eva Lee Vickers 6/
            7/1921 Dike, TX-   ), dau. of Elmer L. and Katie
            Burkhart Vickers.
5111111121 Carolyn Ann Williamson (12/5/1943 Sulphur Springs,
            TX-   ), m. 7/2/1963, Charles Dennis Hayes. Div.
51111111211 Charles Dennis Hayes, Jr. (9/5/1969 Longview, TX-
)
5111111122 Janet Kay Williamson (7/31/1946 Sulphur Springs, TX-
            ), m. 1/31/1969, Larry Don Vickers (11/14/1945
            Sulphur Springs, TX-   ), son of J. D. and Gracie
            Mae McBride Vickers.
5111111123 Benny Murrell Williamson (4/29/1950 Dallas, TX-   ),
            m. 9/12/1992, Cathy June Paris (10/26/1958 Tulsa,
            OK-   ), dau. of David Lorton and Ruetta June
            Draeger Paris.
5111111124 Debra Elaine Williamson (5/21/1960 Dallas, TX-   )
511111113   Lula Winona Williamson (4/10/1922 Hopkins Co., TX-
            ), m. 4/29/1939, Henry Christopher ("Bill")
            Burgin (1/5/1918 Wood County TX-   ), son of
            John Samuel and Ora Myrtle Mennick Burgin.
5111111131 Linda Joyce Burgin (5/5/1941 Hopkins County, Tx-
            ), m. (1st) Michael Eugene O'Neal. Div. M.
            (2nd) 1/1/1978, Robert Houston Speer (-
            7/20/1995 Webster, TX)
51111111311 Terri Lynn O'Neal (10/5/1957 Texas City, TX-   ),
            m. Paul Zeller
511111113111 Jeremy Scott Zeller (9/24/1982 Texas City, TX-   )
511111113112 Ryan Paul Zeller (10/5/1986 Texas City, TX-   )
511111113113 Jordan Michael Zeller (7/19/1990 Texas City, TX-
)
511111113114 Nicholas O'Neal Zeller (10/29/1991 Texas City, TX-
)
51111111312 Michael Eugene O'Neal II (9/29/1958 Texas City, TX-
)
5111111132 Jo Ann Burgin (12/24/1943 Texas City, TX-   ), m.
            10/14/1982, Terrance Alan Hale (1/9/1948 Alvin, TX-
)
            Adopted children:
              Eric Burgin Hale (2/14/1971-   )
              Kevin Lee Hale (10/17/1973-   )
5111111133 Bobby Gene Burgin (1/21/1947 Sulphur Springs, TX-
            ), m. 7/15/1967, Armelia Nelson. Div.

51111111331 Kimberly Burgin (1/11/1971 Fort Hood, TX-   ),
        m. 10/ /1988, Michael Fernandez (9/2/1966 Texas
        City, TX-   )
511111113311 Danielle Fernandez (5/12/1989 Texas City, TX-   )
511111113312 Damon Fernandez (1/13/1991 Texas City, TX-   )
511111113313 Drew Fernandez (8/19/1993 Texas City, TX-   )
51111111332 Kody Gene Burgin (5/31/1974 Texas City, Tx-   )
511111114 Radford Turner Williamson, Jr. (1/22/1927 Hatchett-
        ville, TX-   ), m. 6/12/1945, Joan Bowden (11/26/
        1926-   ), dau. of Jess V. and Alma Boswell Bowden.
5111111141 Baby girl Williamson (5/13/1956-5/13/1956). A
        memorial to her in the Bowden Family plot, Friend-
        ship Cemetery near Cumby, Hopkins County, TX. Bur.
        Laurel Land Memorial Park, Dallas, TX.
5111111142 Cristi Gail Williamson (11/12/1958-6/30/1992). M.
        (1st) 9/27/1975, Ralph A. Lovegren (4/26/1953-).
        M. (2nd) 8/3/1979, Dennis W. Gray (5/12/1946-)
51111111421 Tamera Gail Lovegren (2/6/1977-). Later adopted
        by Dennis W. Gray.
5111111143 Jana Kay Williamson (5/10/1965-). Adopted a
        daughter on 12/22/1993 - Victoria Gail Williamson
        (1/18/1993-)
511111115 Dennis Wayne Williamson (11/13/1928 Hatchettville, TX-
            ), m. 8/7/1948, Patsy Ruth Trapp (9/5/1930
        Pine Forest, TX-   ), dau. of Dewitt Talmadge and
        Edna Mae Minter Trapp.
5111111151 Vicki Lynn Williamson (7/3/1953 Dallas, TX-   ),
        m. 12/30/1972, Kent Bryan Fulks (11/18/1953 Green-
        ville, TX-   ), son of Paul Morris Fulks, Jr. and
        Doris LaVerne Spradlin Fulks.
51111111511 Kendra Lynn Fulks (1/20/1975 Searcy, AR-   )
51111111512 Ashley Breanne Fulks (3/6/1983 Dallas, TX-   )
51111111513 Megan Elizabeth Fulks (7/15/1986 Dallas, TX-   )
5111111152 Cheryl Denise Williamson (4/22/1955 Dallas, TX-   ),
        m. (1st) 3/24/1972 Michael Wayne Williams. Div.
        4/ /1987. M. (2nd) 6/25/1993, Rusty Lee Boles
        (8/14/1957 Lancaster, CA-   ), son of Alton Lee
        and Joyce Elaine Fisk Boles.
    Children by first husband:
51111111521 Michael Shayne Williams (8/28/1972 Dallas, TX-   )
51111111522 Cory Wayne Williams (2/6/1981 Dallas, TX-   )
5111111153 Gary Wayne Williamson (4/14/1958 Dallas, TX-   ), m.
        12/1/1978, Wanda Gail Davis (2/4/1958 Dallas, TX-
            ), dau. of Cletus and Emma Jean Rucker Davis.
51111111531 Cody Wayne Williamson (6/24/1984 Dallas, Tx-   )
51111111532 Sarah Elizabeth Williamson (6/22/1988 Dallas-   )
5111111154 Larry Don Williamson (8/14/1961 Dallas, TX-   ),
        m. 6/6/1987, Laura Katherine Bradford (7/12/1964
        Sulphur Springs, Tx-   ), dau. of Newman Ray and
        Katherine Margaret Alterman Bradford.
51111111541 Katherine Alexandra Williamson (8/27/1988 Sulphur
        Springs, TX-   )
51111111542 Shelby Penn Williamson (3/20/1992 Mt. Pleasant, TX-
)

511111116   Billy Dean Williamson (8/5/1931 Hatchetville, TX-
            ), m. 9/17/1949, Nellie Alene Hall (2/8/1932
            Sunny Point, TX-   ), dau. of Joseph Leonard and
            Vera Juanita Romans Hall.
5111111161 Terry Dean Williamson (12/22/1951 Dallas, TX-   )
5111111162 Douglas Alan Williamson (8/19/1957 Greenville, TX-
)
511111117   Royal Glynn Williamson (8/5/1931 Dike, TX-   ), m.
            (1st) 5/29/1954, Glada Fay Hall. Div. M. (2nd)
            10/13/1991, Virginia Ann Harrison Griffin.
   Children by first wife:
5111111171 Camey Williamson (3/24/1961 Greenville, TX-   ),
            m. 8/30/1980, Donnie Limbock
51111111711 Joshua Allen Limbock (3/11/1988 Mt. Pleasant, TX-
)
51111111712 Sara Elyce Limbock (10/6/1990 Mt. Pleasant, TX-   )
5111111172 Annette Williamson (3/20/1962 Greenville, TX-   ),
            m. Richard Lewis
51111111721 Meagan Nicole Lewis (9/13/1986 Texarkana, TX-   )
51111111722 Aaron Michael Lewis (6/12/1988 Texarkana, Tx-   )
51111111723 Grant Lee Lewis (2/15/1990 Texarkana, TX-   )
   Child by second wife:
5111111173 Rhonda Williamson (5/25/1963 Greenville, TX-   )
51111111731 Leah Williamson (5/25/1993 Texarkana, TX-   )
51111112   Eugene Maitland Williamson (12/31/1898 Center Hill,
            Limestone County, AL-11/10/1981 Sulphur Springs, TX,
            m. 7/27/1922, Eula Mae Walker (10/30/1900 Itasca, TX-
            11/20/1990 Tyler, TX), dau. of W. D. and Mary Sue
            Woods Walker.
511111121   William Eugene ("Gene") Williamson (6/7/1923 Dike,
            Hopkins Co., TX-   ), m. 2/5/1948, Mary Sue Gibson
            (6/29/1928 Emblem, Hopkins County, TX-   ), dau. of
            Ambers Dotson and Cora Bea Cavitt Gibson.
5111111211 Michael Gene Williamson (11/18/1956 Sulphur Springs,
            TX-5/30/1995 Houston, TX). Bur. Oaklawn Memorial
            Park, Athens, TX.
5111111212 Vicki Ann Williamson (4/8/1959 Athens, TX-   )
511111122   Garland Wendell Williamson (12/29/1929 Sulphur
            Springs, TX-12/21/1971 Portland, TX), m. 8/3/1957,
            Billie Sue Johnson (10/9/1929 Palestine, TX-   ).
            Bur. Sulphur Springs City Cemetery.
5111111221 Mickey Sue Williamson (5/5/1958 Edna, TX-   ), m.
            6/21/1980, Michael Ellis (10/14/1956 WV-   )
51111112211 Christine Michele Ellis (5/4/1990 Houston, TX-   )
51111112212 John Michael Ellis (10/8/1992 Houston, TX-   )
5111111222 Sandra Jean Williamson (9/6/1960-4/21/1965 Houston,
            TX-   ). Bur. Sulphur Springs City Cemetery
51111113   Clarence R. ("Shine") Williamson (6/27/1901 Center
            Hill, Limestone County, AL-1/27/1977 Sulphur Springs,
            TX), m. (1st) late 1920's, Mildred McLarry (-
            died late 1960's). Both bur. Grove Hill Cemetery,
            Dallas, TX. M. (2nd) 1968, Pearl Hargrave (-
            died mid 1980's. No issue.

5111112   Lula Losson ("Lossie") Williamson (7/18/1872 Center
          Hill, Limestone County, AL-11/24/1942 Athens, AL), m.
          12/18/1890, George Calvin Carroll (6/6/1870 AL-1/22/
          1951 Athens, AL), son of Charles Calvin and Amanda
          Jane McKenzie Carroll. Both bur. Hatchett Cemetery,
          Limestone County, AL.
51111121 Charles Carroll (6/9/1893 stillborn)
51111122 Gracie Clara Carroll (8/28/1895 Limestone County, AL-
          9/24/1985 Athens) (bur. Browning Cemetery, Harvest,
          Madison County, AL), m. (1st) 12/10/1912, John
          Clinton Browning (6/13/1890-8/25/1929 Athens, AL),
          son of Melville Biles and Mollie Love Browning. M.
          (2nd) 2/11/1939, Thomas Wesley Hargrove (7/23/1889-
          12/18/1947 Athens, AL).
511111221 Virgia Loretta Browning (10/17/1913 Center Hill, AL-
                    ), m. 4/17/1932, Arnold Hargrove (8/19/1908-
          5/23/1960), son of Thomas Wesley and Dezzie Lee
          Davidson Hargrove.
5111112211 Katie Ruth Hargrove (6/17/1934-   ), m. 12/19/1952,
          Leroy Johnson (12/22/1924-   ), son of Louis and
          Henryetta Johnson.
51111122111 Karen June Johnson (12/7/1955-   ), m. 8/3/1978,
          William Ernest Cunningham
511111221111 Amber Renee Cunningham (3/26/1986-   )
51111122112 Panda Lanice Johnson (9/9/1957-   ), m. 8/12/1977,
          Samuel Patton
511111221121 Wilson Tendl Patton (9/29/1980-   )
511111221122 Jay Collin Patton (6/29/1984-   )
51111122113 Myron Christopher ("Chris") Johnson (9/16/1958-   ),
          m. 8/7/1981 Rhonda Lynn Grisham
511111221131 Daniel Christopher Johnson (3/23/1986-   )
511111221132 Katelyn Susann Johnson (12/23/1991-   )
51111122114 Kevin Jaroy Johnson (5/3/1967-   )
5111112212 Morris Wade Hargrove (3/13/1939-12/28/1984), m.
          10/23/1959, Nancy Gail Tallent, dau. of Charles and
          Nina Durham Tallent.
51111122121 Lisa Renee Hargrove (10/31/1962-   ), m. 10/25/
          1980, David Wayne McNeill
511111221211 Brandon Wayne McNeill (10/25/1984-   )
511111221212 Jeremy Wade McNeill (12/30/1986-   )
511111221213 Sarah Elizabeth McNeill (11/14/1989-   )
5111112213 Doyal Ray Hargrove (10/1/1940-   ), m. (1st) 1/30/
          1969, Joann Nelson. M. (2nd) 7/22/1977, Patricia
          Upton, dau. of Columbus Odie and Oma Dean Lones
          Mullins.
   Child by first wife:
51111122131 Demetrius Deray Hargrove (9/19/1972-   )
511111222 Lula May Catherine Browning (5/9/1915 near Athens, AL-
          4/30/1988 Louisville, KY), m. (1st) 12/19/1931, Fred
          Hagen McGuire (11/5/1912 Ardmore, AL-12/9/1948
          Louisville, KY). M. (2nd) 6/8/1953, Earl Hayes
          (4/30/1934-9/27/1992)
5111112221 Marjorie Frances McGuire (1/23/1933-   ), m. (1st)
          6/10/1950, Stanley Eugene Sattich. Div. M. (2nd)

```
                4/1/1964, Robert Hevern Nugent (9/18/1933 Hawes-
                ville, KY-    )
      Children by first husband:
51111122211  Richard Terry Sattich (6/13/1951 Louisville, KY-
                ), m. (1st) 8/24/1971 Deborah Sue Allen.
                Div.  M. (2nd) 5/18/1987, Michelle DeBoe.
      Child by first wife:
511111222111  James Jason Sattich (12/11/1974-    )
      Child by second wife:
511111222112  Daniel DeBoe Sattich (6/19/1988-    )
51111122212  Ronald Eugene Sattich (3/21/1953-    ), m. 2/16/
                1980, Patricia Darlene Sea
511111222121  Steven Nicholas Sattich (8/11/1984-    )
51111122213  Anthony Wayne Sattich (9/14/1956 Louisville, KY-
                ), m. (1st) 10/29/1977, Kimberley Louise
                Nugent. Div.  M. (2nd) 12/31/1986, Teresa Riley
      Child by first wife:
511111222131  Amanda Brooke Sattich (9/27/1979-    )
   Children by second wife:
511111222132  Gayla Kaye Sattich (2/3/1988-    )
511111222133  Jesse Edward Sattich (11/15/1989-    )
51111122214  Darryl Fredric Sattich-Nugent (7/14/1960-    ).
                Adopted by mother's (5111112221) second huband.
                M. (1st) 9/22/1979, Jerrie Elaine Hibbs.  Div.  M.
                (2nd) 3/18/1989, Becky Lou Vertrees
      Child by first wife:
511111222141  Robert Darryl Nugent (4/6/1980-    )
      Child by second wife:
511111222142  Samantha Nicole Nugent (2/5/1990-    )
51111122215  Sheri Diane Sattich-Nugent (9/6/1961-    ), m. 4/26/
                1980, Michael Allen Byrum.  Adopted by mother's
                (5111112221) second husband.
511111222151  Bradley Allen Byrum (1/25/1983-    )
511111222152  Matthew Scott Byrum (12/12/1986-    )
   Children by second husband (Robert Hevern Nugent):
51111122216  Bobbi Frances Nugent (1/2/1965-    ), m. 1/28/1983,
                Kenneth John Grether
511111222161  David Scott Grether (8/4/1984-    )
511111222162  Layla Michelle Grether (3/11/1987-    )
511111223  Robert Arthur Browning (3/19/1917 Harvest, AL-    ), m.
                12/24/1940, Jossie Ruth Bailey (10/28/1921 Athens,
                AL-    ), dau. of Joseph David and Lillie Mae Conn
                Bailey.
5111112231  Joy Delores Browning (3/20/1942 Athens, AL-    ), m.
                (1st) 9/20/1959, Travis Myrick.  Div. 1966.  M.
                (2nd) 9/12/1972, Ronald Morris, son of Ronald and
                Pauline Morris.
   Children by first husband:
51111122311 Tammy Marie Myrick (6/28/1961- ), m. (1st) 5/ /1979,
                Steve Eck.  Div.  M. (2nd) 6/ /1989, Ben Seikus
      Child by first husband:
511111223111  Stephanie Eck (1/9/1981-    )
      Children by second husband:
511111223112  Justin Seikus (12/12/1989-    )
```

511111223113 Jason Seikus (10/5/1993-   )
51111122312   Beverly Elaine Myrick (7/21/1963-   ), m. 10/21/
              1984, Shaun McCoy. Div.
     Child by second husband (Ronald Morris):
51111122313   Deborah Ann Morris (12/4/1973-   ), m. 8/26/1991,
              Stephen Philburn
511111223131 Stephen Francis Philburn (8/22/1993-   )
5111112232   Judy Lavon Browning (6/4/1943 St. Petersburg, FL-
              ), m. 6/12/1960, Everet S. Myrick (10/24/1941-
              ), son of Clayton and Lois Hudson Myrick.
51111122321   Michael Anthony Myrick (6/7/1962-   ), m. 8/8/1981,
              Linda Faye Thompson. Div.
511111223211 Jason Michael Myrick (4/20/1984-   )
51111122322   Timothy Scott Myrick (1/1/1964-   ), m. (1st) 4/13/
              1982, Margaret Marie Wilkes. Div. M. (2nd) 5/23/
              1992, Karrie Swinehart
     Children by first wife:
511111223221 Cody Austin Myrick (9/12/1984-   )
511111223222 Karli Amber Myrick (5/26/1987-   )
     Child by second wife:
511111223223 Gary Scott Myrick (1/23/1993-   )
51111122323   Randall Curtis Myrick (12/17/1964-   ), m. 10/12/
              1987, Nancy Elizabeth Guzanki
51111122324   Richard David Myrick (3/15/1969-   ), m. 8/20/1989,
              Kristy Ann Bristol
5111112233   Beverly Joan Browning (7/28/1947 St. Petersburg, FL-
              ), m. (1st) 11/13/1965, Otto Joseph Drobny.
              Div. M. (2nd) 10/10/1990, Roy Ware, Son of
              Virginia Gibson. Raised by grandparents.
     Children by first husband:
51111122331   Sherry Arlene Drobny (9/25/1966-   ), m. 8/6/1992,
              Richard Parmley
51111122332   Paula Denise Drobny (5/7/1969-   )
5111112234   Robert Edward Browning (5/28/1955 St. Petersburg,
              FL), m. 3/22/1975, Deborah Kay Whateley, dau. of
              William and Shirley McClure Whateley.
51111122341   Jonathan Adam Browning (10/10/1991 St. Petersburg-
)
5111112235   David Mark Browning (1/14/1958 St. Petersburg, FL-
              ), m. (1st) 12/15/1979, Becky Babbit. Div.
              M. (2nd) 3/20/1985, Carla Gay, dau. of Carl and
              Shirley Cope Gay.
     Child by second wife:
51111122351   Ryan Cory Browning (6/21/1987 St. Petersburg-   )
511111224 Horace Clinton Browning (10/7/1918 Pratt City, AL-
           2/23/1945). Unm. Killed by a sniper in World War II,
           near Pier 1 in Manilla, Luzon Island, Philippines.
           Bur. U.S. Cemetery # 1 a few miles north of Manilla.
511111225 Benton Darby Browning (8/12/1920 Limestone County, AL-
           ), m. 5/7/1943, Annie Irene Willis (12/27/1924-
           ), dau. of Alvie and Melvie Hargrove Willis.
5111112251 Harold Ray Browning (6/30/1945-   ), m. 8/3/1963,
           Ann Brymer (6/20/1945 LImestone County, AL-   ),
           dau. of William and Mary Watkins Brymer.

51111122511   Harold Dewayne Browning (8/3/1964-   ), m. 2/ /
            1985, Donna Scoggins. Div.
511111225111 Christopher Dewayne Browning (6/13/1985-   )
511111225112 Robert Anthony Browning (7/10/1987-   )
51111122512 Gayla Kay Browning (9/16/1966-   ), m. 8/5/1985,
            Randy Collier. Div.
511111225121 Eric Wayne Collier (12/3/1991-   )
5111112252 Rodney Lamar Browning (9/24/1948 Athens, AL-   ), m.
          (1st) in 1966, Patsy Davis. Div. M. (2nd) 6/29/
          1978, Jean Campbell (10/12/1955 Huntsville, AL-
          ), dau. of John and Coy Chandler Campbell.
   Children by first wife:
5111112521 Michael Allen Browning (9/30/1967-   ), m. 1/9/
          1988, Teresa Nails (1/7/1969 Decatur, AL-   ),
          dau. of Bobby Ray and Betty McCafferty Nails.
511111225211 Garrett Benton Browning (2/10/1992 CA-   )
5111112522 Timothy Lamar Browning (11/18/1970-   ), m. 11/23/
          1991, Jenny Williams (7/25/1971 Norfolk, VA-   ),
          dau. of Charles and Ruth Abell Williams.
511111225221 Breanna Lee Browning (1/15/1995-   )
   Child by second wife:
5111112523 John Ryan Browning (10/17/1984-   )
5111112253 Shirley Marie Browning (4/20/1950 Athens, AL-   ),
          m. 5/31/1968, Harold Dilworth (6/9/1947-   ),
          son of C. A. and Loetta Birdsong Dilworth.
5111112531 Kimberly LaDawn Dilworth (8/9/1969 Decatur, AL-
          ), m. 5/9/1991, Patrick Small (5/8/1970-   ),
          son of John Parks and Mary Jane Warden Small.
511111225311 Ashley LaDawn Small (11/15/1991 Limestone County,
          AL-   )
5111112532 Karen Marie Dilworth (12/14/1971 Decatur, AL-   ),
          m. 9/6/1991, Todd Crouch (8/16/1971-   ), son
          of James Earl and Connie Marie Schrimsher Crouch.
511111225321 Gracie Marie Crouch (11/1/1994 Morgan Co., AL-   )
5111112254 Donald Clinton Browning (10/18/1953 Athens, AL-   ),
          m. 6/7/1974, Sally McGee (11/28/1955-   ), dau. of
          John and Audrey Reagan McGee.
51111122541 Nathan Lewis Browning (6/15/1978-   )
51111122542 Brooke Ashley Browning (8/31/1984-   )
511111226 James Juanita Browning (8/71922 Sheffield, Colbert
          County, AL-   ), m. 12/24/1939, John Hollace
          Casteel (12/24/1918 Lauderdale County, AL-5/19/1982
          Athens, AL), son of John Fred and Ethel Hagood
          Casteel.
5111112261 Janice Laverne Casteel (11/2/1940 Athens, AL-   ),
          m. 5/2/1959, William Lee Eaton (6/14/1938-   ),
          son of Noel and Myrtle James Eaton.
51111122611 Gregory Lee Eaton (9/15/1960-   ), m. (1st) Chryel
          Canup. Div. M. (2nd) 11/12/1994, Lisa Ann Pitts
51111122612 Michele Lynn Eaton (6/10/1962-   )
51111122613 Eric Leslie Eaton (4/26/1970-   ), m. Ginger Shields
511111226131 Jerrica Licole Eaton (11/24/1993-   )

82

5111112262 Dorothy Mae Casteel (12/20/1942 Athens, AL-   ), m.
            10/20/1961, Kenneth Dewayne Eaton (11/19/1939-
                   ), son of Noel and Myrtle James Eaton.
51111122621 Teresa Delaine Eaton (10/12/1962-   ), m. 1/17/1979,
            Stanley Riggs
511111226211 Bradley Michel Riggs (8/14/1979-   )
511111226212 Breanna Meaghan Riggs (11/25/1987-   )
51111122622 Timothy Dewayne Eaton (3/29/1965-   ), m. 3/29/1985,
            Paula Ramsey
511111226221 Tiffany Shea Eaton (9/16/1989-   )
511111226222 Tylar Shane Eaton (10/5/1994-   )
51111122623 Troy Daniel Eaton (7/13/1970-   )
5111112263 John Hollace Casteel, Jr. (10/28/1944 Athens, AL-
                   ), m. 8/3/1974, Sandra Kay Butts, dau. of
            Virgil and Lafern Crisco Butts.
51111122631 Jonathan Shane Casteel (3/12/1976-   )
51111122632 Robin Suzanne Casteel (7/21/1977-   )
51111122633 Holly Diane Casteel (12/19/1979-   )
5111112264 Nancy Casteel (8/5/1946 Athens, AL-   ), m. (1st)
            5/29/1965, Hines Thornton. Div. M. (2nd) 6/ /
            1982, Larry Sellers (8/15/1936-   ), son of David
            and Vera News Sellers.
51111122641 Tina Michele Thornton (2/6/1969-   ), m. 8/14/1987,
            Robert Wayne Rouse
5111112265 Wanda Carol Casteel (11/12/1947 Athens, AL-   ), m.
            9/11/1970, Rev. Michel McLemore, son of Dempsey and
            Virginia Dare Christopher McLemore.
51111122651 Brandon Neil McLemore (11/18/1972-   )
51111122652 Bonnie Neisha McLemore (5/25/1979-   )
51111122653 Britney Noelle McLemore (2/20/1981-   )
51111227 Thelma Russell ("Billie") Browning (9/26/1924 Athens,
            AL-11/13/1930 Athens). Killed by a car on second
            day of school.
511111228 Ruthie Etta Browning (12/16/1927 Athens-   ), m.
            7/21/1954, Cecil Everett Simmons (8/5/1913
            Jacksonville, FL-2/11/1973 St. Marys, GA), son
            of William Jasper and Minnie Florence Minton Rawls
            (adopted son of David Franklin and Sarah Beatrice
            Simmons).
5111112281 Pamela Dawn Simmons (6/24/1955 Fernandina Beach, FL-
                   ), m. 3/8/1975, Lawrence Donald Jones, Jr.
            (6/22/1948 Folkston, GA-   ), son of Lawrence
            Donald and Joyce Lane Brown Jones.
51111122811 Jonathan David Jones (4/18/1981 Greenville, SC-   )
51111122812 Sarah Elizabeth Jones (9/17/1982 Greenville, SC-
)
51111122813 Timothy Paul Jones (6/2/1987 Greenville, SC-   )
5111112282 Rhonda Cecile Simmons (4/1/1958 Fernandina Beach, FL
            -    )
51111123 Walter Calvin Carroll (2/1/1897 AL-6/29/1973 St.
            Petersburg, FL), m. (1st) in 1923, Frankie Rebecca
            Hower, dau. of Frank and Flossie Hower. M. (2nd)
            1939, Helen English Feldman. Div.

Children by first wife:
511111231　Harmon Calvin Carroll (6/26/1924 Florence, AL-　　),
　　　　　　　6/26/1948, Dorothy Mae Reagan (2/1/1928 Seymour,
　　　　　　　TN-　　), dau. of Elmer and Cora Lena Cunningham
　　　　　　　Reagan.
5111112311　Robert Harmon Carroll (6/25/1951 St. Petersburg, FL-
　　　　　　　), m. (1st) 3/7/1975, Priscilla Elaine
　　　　　　　Prodger.　Div. 1981.　M. (2nd) 7/5/1984, Ann
　　　　　　　Marie Valeri Laverdure (10/6/1952-　　), dau. of
　　　　　　　Salvatore and Margaret Mary Cataleta Valeri.　Ann
　　　　　　　Marie's children by former marriage:
　　　　　　　　Matthew David Laverdure (10/4/1977-　　)
　　　　　　　　Kristy Lynn Laverdure (5/8/1979-　　)
　　　　　　　　Jeffrey Michael Laverdure (10/19/1980-　　)
　　Child by first wife:
51111123111　Andrew Scott Carroll (10/27/1979-　　)
5111112312　Albert Eugene Carroll (1/9/1953 St. Petersburg, FL-
　　　　　　　　　), m. 12/23/1972, Deborah Ann Martin (7/25/
　　　　　　　1954 Chicago, IL-　　), dau. of William James and
　　　　　　　JoAnn Sowerbrower Martin.
51111123121　Angela Elizabeth Carroll (5/5/1982 St. Petersburg,
　　　　　　　FL-　　)
5111112313　Richard Calvin Carroll (4/18/1954 St. Petersburg,
　　　　　　　FL-　　), m. 1/10/1976, Terri Elaine Sanderlin
　　　　　　　(3/6/1955 Decatur, IL-　　), dau. of Robert
　　　　　　　Eugene and Beverly Joanne Moore Sanderlin.
51111123131　Jennifer Elaine Carroll (2/8/1977 St. Petersburg,
　　　　　　　AL-　　)
511111231311　Jeremy Michael Carroll (8/6/1995 Clearwater, FL-
　　　　　　　)
51111123132　Michael Calvin Carroll (11/22/1979 St. Petersburg,
　　　　　　　FL-　　)
511111232　Frankie Louise Carroll (9/　/19　-lived 6 hours)
511111233　Lettie Jeanette Carroll (1929-lived 11 months)
511111234　Evalyn Inez Carroll (5/13/1932 AL-　　), m. 11/16/
　　　　　　　1950, William Eugene Combee (9/1/1933-　　), son of
　　　　　　　William Hampton and Mildred Elizabeth Messner
　　　　　　　Combee.
5111112341　Curtis Eugene Combee (10/2/1951-　　), m. (1st) 10/2/
　　　　　　　1970, Debrough Lynn Shellnut (12/15/1953-　　).
　　　　　　　Div. in 1980.　M. (2nd) in 1983, Rhonda Elaine
　　　　　　　Hinson.　Div. 1988.　M. (3rd) Patricia Diane
　　　　　　　Mobley.
　　Children by first wife:
51111123411　Christie Lynn Combee (6/11/1975-　　)
51111123412　Mandy Leann Combee (10/28/1977-　　)
　　Child by second wife:
51111123413　Sheena Nicole Combee (5/24/1984-　　)
5111112342　Holly Carroll Combee (12/13/1954-　　), m. (1st)
　　　　　　　10/3/1973, Richard Sheffield.　Div. 3/　/1974.　M.
　　　　　　　(2nd) 2/21/1975, Randy Howard.　Div. 1988.　M.
　　　　　　　(3rd) Jamie Luebcke
　　Child by second wife:
51111123421　Stephanie Carroll Howard (8/18/1978-　　)

5111112343   Cheryl Lynn Combee (10/1/1955-   ), m. 9/10/1977,
          Tony Harnate. Div. 1981. Had maiden name restored.
51111124   Rusha Lenora Carroll (9/22/1898-2/11/1923) (born and
          died Limestone County, AL), m. 9/24/1916, Elmer
          Strange (12/31/1894 Madison Co., AL-9/7/1977 Hunts-
          ville, Al), son of Johnny and Sara Sanderson Strange.
511111241   Maurice Strange (7/24/1917 Toney, AL-   ), m. 12/21/
          1935, Earl Amery Henderson (12/5/1913 Marshall
          County, AL-1/30/1988 Huntsville, AL), son of Walker
          Elmo and Haughty Corrine Gilliland Henderson.
5111112411 David Earl Henderson (5/6/1937 Madison Co., AL-   ),
          m. 2/15/1957, Jan Leota Hudson (11/21/1939-   ),
          dau. of Cecil and Leona Holman Hudson.
51111124111 Donna Lynn Henderson (12/28/1957 Huntsville, AL-
          ), m. 9/13/1980, Richard Austin Smith
511111241111 Scarlett Morgana Smith (4/3/1982 Huntsville, AL-
)
511111241112 Amanda Lynn Smith (6/1/1985 Huntsville, AL-   )
511111241113 Cortney M. Smith (12/17/1986 Huntsville, AL-   )
511111241114 Richard Austin Smith, Jr. (5/13/1992 Huntsville,
          AL-   )
5111112412 William Carroll Henderson, Sr. (6/21/1939 Huntsville,
          AL-   ), m. (1st) Toni Wynell Curles. Div. M.
          (2nd) 10/14/1988, Barbara Allen Garner. Barbara
          had three children.
   Children by first wife:
5111124121 William Carroll Henderson, Jr. (6/9/1961 Albany, GA-
          8/10/1995 Athens, AL), m. 7/11/1981, Katherine
          Grace Jones.
511111241211 William Jesse Henderson (6/1/1982 Chattanooga-   )
511111241212 Walker Aron Henderson (7/2/1985 Chattanooga-   )
5111124122 Wilburn Maurice ("Maury") Henderson (1/20/1968
          Warner Robins, GA-   ), m. (1st) Patricia Joan
          Segrest. Div. 1986. M. (2nd) 6/26/1987, Beth
          Calloway. Div. 1989.
   Child by first wife:
511111241221 Ashley Carroll Henderson (11/2/1985 Montgomery, AL-
)
5111112413 Mary Adeline Henderson (12/15/1942 Huntsville, AL-
          1/19/1943 Huntsville, AL)
5111112414 Martha Jane Henderson (5/11/1944 Huntsville, AL-
          ), m. 6/16/1962, Joseph Franklin Sharp
          (2/5/1941 in Madison County, AL-   ), son of
          George Albert and Rena Pearl Winsett Sharp.
51111124141 Martha Annette Sharp (8/29/1963 Huntsville, AL-
          ), m. (1st) 3/14/1980, Brian McComas. Div.
          M. (2nd) 7/29/1989, remarried Brian McComas
511111241411 Joseph Lee McComas (9/29/1980 Huntsville, AL-   )
511111241412 Brian Jason McComas (1/22/1983 Killeen, TX-   )
51111124142 Cathy Ann Sharp (5/15/1967 Huntsville, AL-   ), m.
          6/15/1985, Ronnie Milligan (3/10/1966 Heidelberg,
          Germany-   ), son of Durwood Milligan and Mary
          Elizabeth Franklin Milligan Mason.
511111241421 Amery Dawn Milligan (1/27/1989 Huntsville, AL-   )

51111124143 Kelli Jo Sharp (9/26/1971 Huntsville, AL-   )
5111112415 Jeanne Ann Henderson (11/29/1952 Huntsville, AL-
          ), m.10/24/1986, Horace Lynn Smith, Jr.
          (7/9/1956 Athens, AL-   ), son of Horace Lynn
          Smith, Sr. and Laura Bell Roberts Smith.
51111124151 Rebecca Jane Smith (3/4/1982 Huntsville, AL-   )
          (Jeanne's dau. and Horace adopted her in 1987).
51111124152 Anna Elizabeth Smith (10/7/1988 Huntsville, AL-   )
511111242 Violet Lowris Strange (10/27/1919 Limestone County,
          AL-   ), m. 9/29/1937, Willie Marvin Henderson,
          Sr. (8/28/1919 Pine Ridge, Morgan County, AL-   ),
          son of Walker Elmo and Haughty Corrine Gilliland
          Henderson.
5111112421 Willie Marvin Henderson, Jr. (2/7/1947 Huntsville,
          AL-   ), m. Sandra Jo Gilbert (2/15/1948-   ),
          dau of Grant and Eulas Gilbert.
51111124211 Micah Dewayne Henderson (10/25/1970 Nurnberg,
          Germany-   )
51111124212 Kyle David Henderson (4/29/1981 Enterprise, AL-   )
511111243 Mary Frances Strange (10/31/1921 Limestone Co., AL-
          ), m. (1st) 9/ /1940, Donnie Alton Locke
          (8/29/1922-   ). Div. 5/19/1947. M. (2nd) 1/7/
          1949, Cecil Edward Balch (9/10/1917 Madison County,
          AL-   ), son of Charley Beverley and Mary Viola
          Brooks Balch.
    Children by first husband:
5111112431 Thomas Wayne Locke (8/18/1942 Madison County, AL-
          ), m. (American Ceremony) 6/ /1963, Germany,
          (German Ceremony was held earlier), Waltraud
          Willand (4/26/1943 Babenhausen, Germany-   ).
51111124311 Melanie Locke (8/14/1963 Babenhausen, Germany-   ),
          m. 1/20/1985, George Wisdom (12/17/1963 Arona, PA-
)
511111243111 Amanda Michelle Wisdom (3/14/1987 Weisbaden,
          Germany-   )
51111124312 John Wayne Locke (12/27/1964 Ft. Sill, TX-   ), m.
          11/21/1987, Melissa Sanders (12/21/1968-   )
5111112432 Joe Alton Locke (4/20/1944 Madison County, AL-   ),
          m. (1st) 2/ /1963, Carlene Worley (4/21/1945-   ).
          Div. 1971. M. (2nd) 1972, Charlene Price (2/5/1949
          Topeka, KS-   ). Charlene Price's daughter
          Melissa Price (6/15/1977 Welsboro, PA-   )
          changed her name to Melissa Locke.
    Children by first wife:
51111124321 David Brent Locke (2/2/1965 Topeka, KS-   ), m.
          12/20/1985, Lisa Shuster (8/3/1967 New Orleans,
          LA-   )
51111124322 Michael Edward Locke (1/31/1967 Topeke, KS-   )
    Child by second wife:
51111124323 Gregory Locke (4/2/1977 Madison County, AL-   )
    Child by second husband:

5111112433 Calvin Edward Balch (10/10/1949 Madison County, AL-
          ), m. (1st) 6/20/1970, Carolyn Diane Aderholt

```
                         (10/25/1951-    ).  Div. 8/  /1985.  M. (2nd) 7/13/
                         1985, Mary Alice White (1/3/1949 VA-      )
     Child by first wife:
51111124331  Carey Edward Balch (1/21/1977 Knoxville, TN-    )
51111125    Earl Williamson Carroll (2/11/1900-2/25/1902)
51111126    Alfred Losson Carroll (2/1/1902 AL-6/5/1982 Athens,
             AL), m. 11/20/1921, Jeanette Hinkle (5/22/1906-3/23/
             1977 Athens, AL), dau. of Benjamin and Minnie Daniel
             Hinkle.
511111261   Clarion Lee Carroll (11/16/1922 Athens, AL-    ), m.
             (1st) 6/12/1943, Laura Watson. Div. M. (2nd)
             8/18/1973, Wilma Bernice Stokes Speake (8/13/1937-
             ), dau. of Barnie McCoy and Fannie Berchie
             Jeffreys Stokes.
     Children by first wife:
5111112611  Martha June Carroll (3/31/1947 Decatur, AL-    ), m.
             (1st) Dale Howard. M. (2nd) Mike Kloster
     Child by first husband:
51111126111 Marisa Dawn Howard (6/30/19  -   ), m. J. Enslinger.
             Div.  M. (2nd) Brandon Herbert
     Child by first husband:
511111261111  Jamie Aaron Enslinger (10/10/1990-     )
     Child by second husband:
511111261112  Sara Elizabeth Herbert (11/2/1995-    )
     Child by second husband:
5111112611112  Amanda Renea Kloster (3/22/1977 Springfield-    )
5111112612  Barbara Fay Carroll (11/27/1949-    ), m. (1st)
             Nelson Tucker. M. (2nd) Mack Fitzgerald
51111126121 Brent Nelson Tucker (4/4/1967-    )
51111126122 April Laurel Tucker (5/16/1969-    )
5111112613  Stephen Lee Carroll (1/20/1951 St. Petersburg, FL-
             ), m. Beverly Price
51111126131 Patty LeNea Carroll (4/14/1979-    )
51111126132 Audra Rose Carroll (4/22/1982-    )
5111112613  Jordan Whitley Carroll (2/14/1984-    )
     Child by second wife:
5111112614  Chella LeeNeece Carroll (7/1/1975 Decatur, AL-    )
511111262   Alfred Burton Carroll (12/5/1924 Toney, AL-2/1/1993
             Placerville, CA), m. (1st) 8/19/1943, Ellen
             Sullivan. Div. 4/14/1964.  M. (2nd) 8/11/1964,
             Marie Amanda Bryant-Collins. Alfred Burton Carroll
             and his second wife Marie raised her two grand-
             children: Richard Joseph Carroll (6/8/1970-   )
             and Roberta Marie ("Bobbi") Carroll (8/25/1971-    )
5111112621  Patricia Joyce Carroll (12/6/1944-    )
5111112622  Suzanne Marie Carroll (12/31/1946-drowned 1958 or
             1959).
5111112623  Garrold Alfred Carroll (died-small child)
5111112624  Glenn Allen Carroll (9/9/1952-    )
5111112625  Karen Teresa Carroll (9/1/1956-    )
511111263   Jeanettie Elnora Carroll (2/25/1927 Florence, AL-
             ), m. 2/14/1947, Odis Morris (4/20/1923 Neel,
             AL-   ), son of Clark Henry and Sally Betty Gray
             Morris.
```

5111112631   Beverly Carroll Morris (7/11/1949 Decatur, AL-   ),
    m. 9/12/1969, Gerald Wayne Cochrane (4/4/1946
    Decatur, AL-   ), son of Bill and Hilda Miller
    Cochrane.

51111126311   Erica Nicole Cochrane (10/19/1974 Baton Rouge, LA-
)

51111126312   Tara Denise Cochrane (7/9/1976 Baton Rouge, LA-   )

51111126313   Gerald Wayne Cochrane, Jr. (12/14/1981 Decatur, AL-
)

5111112632   William ("Billy") Odis Morris (7/20/1953 Decatur, AL-
    ), m. 12/30/1972, Donna Kay Brown (7/11/1955
    Hartselle, AL-   ), dau. of Robert and Nell
    Terrell Brown.

51111126321   Lori Ann Morris (10/21/1976 Decatur, AL-   )

51111126322   Matthew William Morris (4/10/1983 Decatur, AL-   )

51111126323   Leslie Erin Morris (10/2/1985 Decatur, AL-   )

5111112633   Tracey Larue Morris (1/28/1968 Decatur, AL-   ), m.
    3/11/1989, Kelvin Jay Callahan (3/3/1967 Hartsell,
    AL-   ), son of Wendall and Mary Sue Clemons
    Callahan.

51111126331   Kimberly Renae Callahan (3/25/1992 Tuscaloosa, AL-
)

51111126332   Keri Jaye Callahan (8/14/1994 Decatur, AL-   )

511111264   Wilma Jean Carroll (12/12/1929 Athens, AL-   ), m.
    9/21/1946, Alvie Lee Smith, Jr. (9/21/1928 Limestone
    County, AL-   ), son of Alvie Lee Smith, Sr. and
    Zelpha Ruth Tribble Smith.

5111112641   Danny Lee Smith (10/31/1947 Chicago-   ), m. 10/24/
    1969, Elizabeth ("Betsy") Reid Ellis (9/25/1946
    Charlotte, NC-   ), dau. of Joseph Reid and
    Katherine Cox Ellis.

51111126411   Joseph Christopher Smith (5/30/1966 Easton, PA-
    ), m. 10/1/1995, Michelle French (3/6/1969
    Columbus, GA-   ), dau. of George and Billie
    Ballard French.

51111126412   Tracy Shannon Smith (1/23/1971 Long Beach, CA-   ),
    m. 9/11/1993, Eric Todd Hawkins (12/2/1964
    Atlanta, GA-   ), son of Troy and Nevelle
    Kitchen Hawkins.

5111112642   Douglas Michael Smith (6/21/1951 Chicago, IL-   ),
    m. 8/9/1969, Linda Rapinchuk (2/4/1952 Beryn, IL-
    ), dau. of Paul and Betty Fisher Rapinchuk.

51111126421   Leslie Jeanne Smith (3/5/1970 Berwyn, IL-   ), m.
    6/19/1993, William Meldrim Thomson IV (8/22/1970
    Hanover, NH-   ), son of Peter and Glyneta Bonsey
    Thomson.

51111126422   Brandon Michael Smith (4/30/1974 Springfield, IL-
)

5111112643   Teresa ("Terri") Gayle Smith (5/25/1954 Chicago, IL-
    ), m. (1st) 5/25/1974, Kenneth Hodel. Div.
    1975. M. (2nd) 4/14/1979, Wayne Shankle (1/14/1046
    Caddo, Lawrence Co., AL-   ), son of Luther and
    Gertrude Bond Shankle.

51111126431   Jennifer Lynn (Hodel) Smith (5/13/1975 La Grange,
              IL-   ). Jennifer's name was changed legally to
              Smith after her parents div. Teresa took her
              maiden name (Smith) back.
511111265   George Robert ("Bobby") Carroll (4/15/1932 Limestone
              County, AL-   ), m. 8/3/1950, Laquita Joyce Dedmon
              (9/10/1932 Sardis Springs, AL-   ), dau. of Dewey
              Clifford and Ruby Louise Hargrove Dedmon.
5111112651   Marcia Dianne Carroll (3/23/1953 Chicago, IL-   ),
              m. 11/22/1986, James Allen Perry (5/2/1958 Athens,
              AL-   ), son of James Douglas and Juanita Joyce
              Molan Perry.
51111126511   Shane Allen Perry (7/28/1988 Decatur, AL-   )
51111126512   Spencer Andrew Perry (10/21/1989 Decatur, AL-   )
5111112652   Barry Lynn Carroll (8/24/1957 Chicago, IL-   ), m.
              8/18/1979, Teresa Gay Princhard (10/10/1960
              Chattanooga, TN-   ), dau. of Bryson Leonard and
              Mary Louise Childs Prichard.
51111126521   Laura Elizabeth Carroll (5/20/1985 Tuscaloosa, AL-
)
51111126522   Mary Kathryn Carroll (10/20/1988 Tuscaloosa, AL-   )
51111126523   Emily Grace Carroll (11/15/1993 Huntsville, AL-   )
511111266   Gordon Dean Carroll (3/28/1935 Coffee Pot, Limestone
              County, AL-2/17/1970 Decatur, AL), m. 12/24/1956,
              Donna Mae Schrimsher (2/20/1936 Limestone County,
              AL-   ), dau. of Charlie and Gracie Bea McNunn
              Schrimsher.
5111112661   Timothy Dean Carroll (1/14/1958 Chicago. IL-   ),
              m. 5/29/1982, Melissa Tucker (10/13/1963 Morgan
              County, AL-   ), dau. of Roy Clifford Tucker, Jr.
              and Lila Joyce Lentz Tucker.
51111126611   Cassidy Nicole Carroll (4/12/1986 Decatur, AL-   )
51111126612   Madison Callie Carroll (8/14/1991 Decatur, AL-   )
51111126613   Candice Baylee Carroll (5/30/1995 Decatur, AL-   )
5111112662   Susan Charlene Carroll (11/24/1961 Athens, AL-   ),
              m. 2/14/1986, Lonnie Judson Williams (4/13/1954
              Morgan County, AL-   ), son of James Deloin and
              Mary Imogene Johnson Williams.
51111126621   Mary Caitlin Williams (12/14/1988 Decatur, AL-   )
51111126622   Emily Carroll Williams (6/21/1995 Decatur, AL-   )
51111127   Hector Ernest Carroll (8/18/1903 Harvest, AL-7/11/1969
              St. Petersburg, FL), m. (eloped) 8/28/1921, Gladys
              Marie Bowers (5/7/1905 Athens, AL-1/24/1972 St.
              Petersburg, FL), dau. of Franklin Dorsey and Elsie
              Murtella Conn Bowers.
511111271   Alene Marie Carroll (5/9/1925 Athens, AL-   ), m.
              2/1/1947, Philip Gilbert Rizzo (9/16/1924 San Jose,
              CA-   ), son of Philip Aloysius and Frances Margaret
              Larocca Rizzo.
5111112711   Paul Thomas Rizzo (6/25/1949 San Jose, CA-   ), m.
              3/8/1980, Nancy Jean Finley (11/6/1956 Portland,
              OR-   ), dau. of Robert Wally and Arlene Jean
              Ledine Finley.
51111127111   Lisa Marie Rizzo (10/12/1984 Portland, OR-   )

51111127112 Brian Thomas Rizzo (9/28/1987 Portland, OR-)
5111112712 Carol Marie Rizzo (6/20/1950 San Jose, CA-), m.
 (1st) 9/3/1971, Kenneth D. Barney. Div. 12/9/
 1987. M. (2nd) 11/9/1989, John William Scherer
 (2/14/1952 London, England-)
51111127121 Justin Kenneth Barney (10/23/1976 Springfield, MO-
)
51111127122 Nathan Philip Barney (7/15/1979 Jacksonville, FL-
)
5111112713 Thomas Peter Rizzo (3/4/1952 San Jose, CA-), m.
 8/11/1973, Rosemary Helfrich (9/4/1953 Houston, TX-
 ), dau. of Carland Ella Rita Pinney Helfrich
51111127131 Christopher Michael Rizzo (12/8/1979 Houston, TX-
)
51111127132 Dustin Thomas Rizzo (4/1/1981 Houston, TX-)
5111112714 Ricci William Rizzo (4/17/1954 San Jose, TX-), m.
 5/17/1980, Katherine Sue Cunningham. Div. 4/ /1985
5111112715 Rion Christopher Rizzo (12/25/1958 Alameda, Oakland,
 CA-), m. 5/31/1980, Yvonne Marie Carvalho
 (6/11/1958 Yonkers, NY-), dau. of Antone V. and
 Maria Gloria Fernandes Carvalho. Rion Rizzo and
 his wife adopted at birth, Danielle Katherine Rizzo
 (1/14/1994 Atlanta, GA-).
5111112716 Darren Joseph Rizzo (5/26/1965 Montrel, Que. Canada-
)
511111272 Vera Lee Carroll (11/28/1928 Athens, AL-), m.
 8/15/1947, James Donald Jordan (7/27/1925 St.
 Petersburg, FL-), son of George Washington and
 Rose Lee Newberry Jordan.
5111112721 Gaye Kathleen Jordon (5/30/1952- Burderop Park,
 Chisledon, Highworth, England-), m. 10/ /1980,
 Alan Best. Div. 1983.
5111112722 James Donald Jordan, Jr. (6/8/1957 Barstow, CA-),
 m. 3/15/1980, Susan Lorraine Loomis (11/27/1957
 Bowling Green, OH-), dau. of Horace and Peggy
 Loomis.
51111127221 Levi Benjamin Jordan (7/9/1976 Bowling Green, OH-)
51111127222 Rebekah Brianne Jordan (6/5/1981 Largo, FL-)
51111127223 Sarah Rose Jordan (9/9/1986-1/24/1987 Largo, FL-)
5111112723 Victoria ("Vikki") Leigh Jordan (12/19/1965 Fort
 Richardson, AK-), m. 12/6/1986, John Costello
 (2/16/1958-), son of John and Doris Costello.
51111127231 David Joseph Costello (3/20/1987 Dunedin, FL-)
511111273 Doris Mae Carroll (4/13/1931 Athens, AL-), m.
 2/14/1950, Rev. Thomas Black (6/14/1926 Closkelt,
 County Down, North Ireland-), son of William
 John and Bella Jane Cochran Black.
5111112731 Patricia Ann Black (1/5/1951 Rockville Center, Long
 Island, NY-), m. (1st) 8/ /1971, Joseph
 Bishop. Div. 1980. M. (2nd) 7/28/1984, Rev. Cary
 William Boggs (2/7/1952 Columbus, OH-), son of
 Donald Harold and Irene Bishop Boggs.

5111112732 Jackie Lynne Black (7/21/1955 St. Petersburg, FL-
        ), m. (1st) 6/14/1980, Ricky Paul Beechner
        (7/27/1955-1/14/1984). M. (2nd) 8/8/1987, Terry
        Charles Curtis (2/6/1959 New Orleans, LA-   ),
        son of Clarence Charles and M. Aline Livaudais
        Curtis.

51111127321 Christian Charles Curtis (11/10/1993 Slidell, LA-
)

51111127322 Lauren Elizabeth Curtis (3/25/1995 Slidell, LA-   )

5111112733 Sandra Kaye Black (11/5/1959 St. Petersburg, FL-
        ), m. 11/29/1980, George Edward Spohn
        (5/26/1956 Columbus, OH-   ), son of James
        William and Marvene May Myers Spohn.

51111127331 James Thomas Spohn (11/19/1985 Westerville, OH-   )
51111127332 Jacob Michael Spohn (9/27/1989 Westerville, OH-   )

5111112734 Thomas William Black (4/27/1963 St. Petersburg, FL-
        ), m. 5/11/1985, Cristol Lee Dubey (7/22/1063
        Charlevoix, MI-   ), dau. of Leonard Junior and
        Jeanne Carol Drury Dubey.

5111112735 Sharon Beth Black (8/31/1964 St. Petersburg, FL-
        ), m. 5/10/1986, Danny Foster Mason (12/31/
        1963 Columbus, OH-   ), son of Gilbert Russell
        and Florence Gussler Mason.

51111127351 Eli Daniel Mason (12/29/1990 Westerville, OH-   )

511111274 James Richard Carroll (1/25/1935 Athens, AL-   ), m.
        3/14/1952, Ruth Ann Watson (12/29/1934 Dayton, OH-
        ), dau. of Robert William and Alberta Florence
        Cook Watson.

5111112741 Janie Lynn Carroll (1/14/1954 Dayton, OH-   ), m.
        8/28/1981, Tommie Richard Bozich (11/1/1951 St.
        Petersburg, FL-   ), son of Carl Z. and Anna M.
        Bozich.

51111127411 Tommie Carl Bozich (5/3/1983 St. Petersburg, FL-   )
51111127412 Kenneth Ryan Bozich (3/12/1989 St. Petersburg, FL-
)

5111112742 James Timothy Carroll (6/2/1958 Dayton, OH-   ), m.
        (1st) 7/21/1977, Vicky Lynn Moore. Div. 1/20/1984.
        M. (2nd) 3/30/1985, Kathleen ("Kathy") Laura
        Brumbelow. Kathy's children: Christopher Lewis
        Templer (5/2/1983 Clearwater, FL-   ) and Monica
        Monica Nicole Templer (10/21/1984 Largo, FL-   ).
    Children by first wife:
51111127421 Heidi Lynn Carroll (3/3/1979 St. Petersburg-   )
51111127422 James Eric Carroll (4/22/1981 St. Petersburg-   )
    Child by second wife:
51111127423 Shayla Beth Carroll (11/3/1988 Clearwater, FL-   )

5111112743 Mark Daniel Carroll (1/29/1960 Dayton, OH-   ), m.
        (1st) 11/27/1982, Tammy Jo Dew (9/21/1963 MA-   ).
        Div. 8/29/1986. M. (2nd) 11/25/1987, Teresa
        ("Tess") Lynn Lewis (7/21/1956-   ), dau. of
        Larry Keith and Judith Eileen Burton Lewis.
    Children by first wife:
51111127431 Stephen Jeffrey Carroll (11/3/1983 St. Petersburg-
)

51111127432 Scott Daniel Carroll (1/13/1985 St. Petersburg, FL-
)
     Children by second wife:
51111127433 Adam Burton Carroll (2/13/1986 St. Petersburg, FL-
)
51111127434 Avery Nicole Carroll (5/22/1990 St. Petersburg, FL-
)
5111112744 Jeffrey Scott Carroll (2/20/1964 St. Petersburg, FL-
               ), m. (1st) 3/24/1984, Tammie Lynn Hicks.
               Div. 11/2/1986. M. (2nd) 5/13/1989, Kathryn
               Wanda Penney (11/6/1964 Clearwater, FL-   ),
               dau. of Jimmy Ted and Wanda Geraldine Owens Lewis
               Penney.
511111275 Frederick Allen Carroll (12/28/1938 St. Petersburg,
               FL-1/8/1956 St. Petersburg, FL) (killed when a
               train hit his car). Bur. Memorial Park Cemetery,
               St. Petersburg, FL next to his parents, Hector
               Ernest and Gladys Marie Bowers Carroll.
51111128 Jessie Rudolph Carroll (11/18/1914 Madison County, AL-
               7/7/1969 Cleveland, OH), m. 11/18/1933, Ruth Orlene
               Hargrove (4/6/1915 Elkmont, AL-11/8/1990 Brooklyn
               Heights, OH), dau. of Thomas Wesley and Dezzie Lee
               Davidson Hargrove.
511111281 Sarah Ann Carroll (1/7/1935 Athens, AL-   ), m. 11/27/
               1960, Freddie Mounts (11/23/1926 Shivley, WV-12/12/
               1977 Cleveland, OH), son of Hereford Mounts and
               Katie Bryant Mounts Stone.
5111112811 Jeffery Alan Mounts (6/9/1960 Cleveland, OH-5/2/1970
               Cleveland, OH)
511111282 Marilyn Rose Carroll (10/11/1947 Athens, AL-   ), m.
               10/11/1966, Roscoe Ellis (10/9/1943 Switzer, WV-
               ), son of Wilson and Annie Workman Ellis.
5111112821 Steven Lee Ellis (6/29/1967 Cleveland, OH-   ), m.
               6/10/1989, Denise Rae Koltas (12/20/1966 Lorain,
               OH-   ), dau. of Dennis and Elizabeth Moldovan
               Koltas.
51111128211 Joshua Lee Ellis (8/30/1985 Lorain, OH-   )
51111128212 Jessica Rae Ellis (7/24/1986 Lorain, OH-   )
51111128213 Jennifer Elizabeth Ellis (4/23/1990 Lorain, OH-   )
5111112822 Anthony Douglas Ellis (6/20/1968 Cleveland, OH-   ),
               m. 9/8/1990, Catherine Marie Wysocki. Adopted:
               Brianna Marie Ellis (2/26/1991 Bogota, Col., South
               America-   ) and Jacob Anthony Ellis (7/9/1991
               Bogota, Col. South America-   ).
51111128221 Meagan Nicole Ellis (10/17/1994 Lorain, OH-   )
511111283 Phillip Anthony Carroll (11/29/1949 Athens, AL-   ),
               (2nd) on 5/1/1977, Patricia Ann Balog (10/17/1954
               Cleveland, OH-   ), dau. of George and Rita
               Filicko Balog.
     Child by first wife:
5111112831 Scott Alan Carroll (12/8/1972 Cleveland, OH-   )
     Child by second wife:
5111112832 Jay Phillip Carroll (12/21/1979 Cleveland, OH-   )

511111284　Janet Ruth Carroll (1/13/1954 Cleveland, OH-　　), m.
　　　　　1/8/1977, Gary Wayne Coleman (10/2/1953 Cleveland
　　　　　Heights, OH-　　), son of Oscar Lee and Ruth
　　　　　Imogene Geren Coleman. Adopted the following
　　　　　children:
　　　　　　　Brandon Elias Coleman (2/9/1976 San Salvador,
　　　　　　　　El Salvador-　　). Adopted 10/20/1983.
　　　　　　　Benton Wayne Coleman (7/14/1978 Santa Tecla, El
　　　　　　　　Salvador-　　). Adopted 7/4/1984.
　　　　　　　Brittany Ruth Coleman (4/1/1985 Bogota, Col.,
　　　　　　　　South America-　　). Adopted 8/29/1992.

5111113　Charles Franklin Williamson (7/24/1874 Center Hill,
　　　　　Limestone County, AL-8/20/1965 Ardmore, OK), m. 12/14/
　　　　　1893, Sue Ella Love (7/16/1874 Madison County, AL-
　　　　　5/16/1959 Ardmore, OK), dau. of Thomas O. and Lucy
　　　　　Love.
51111131　Lucretia Magdalene Williamson (4/13/1899 AL-1/10/1985
　　　　　Odessa, TX), m. 4/14/1916, Dave Abner Pusley, Sr.
　　　　　(3/11/1894 Hartshorne, OK-　　)
511111311　David Abner Pusley, Jr. (6/26/1921-　　), m. Betty
　　　　　Helen Kilgore. Div.
511111311　David Randolph Pusley (1/29/1954-　　). Adopted
　　　　　when Betty remarried and took the name Frye.
511111312　Ella Maxine Pusley (9/1/1924 Ardmore, OK-　　), m.
　　　　　Jack Sebering Johnson (11/19/1918 Giles, TX-　　)
5111113121　Jacky Wayne Johnson
511111313　Jerry Wayne Pusley (2/17/1930-　　), m. (1st) Joann
　　　　　. M. (2nd) Betty
5111113131　Verna Pusley
5111113132　Susan Pusley
511111314　Shirley Ann Pusley (6/22/1935-　　), m. Jimmie Glynn
　　　　　Keen
5111113141　Linda Lou Keen
5111113142　Tricia Keen
5111113143　Kaylinn Keen
5111113144　Dianna Keen
5111113145　Sharon Keen
511111315　Linda Sue Pusley (4/30/1938 Wirt, Ok-9/7/1991 Glen
　　　　　Rose, TX), m. (1st) Edward Pete Story. M. (2nd)
　　　　　Billy Wayne Coppedge
5111113151　Sara Beth Story, m. Clay Moore, son of Tom W. Moore.
　　　　　Sara Beth Story was adopted by her grandparents,
　　　　　Lucretia and Dave Pusley (51111131) and took the
　　　　　name Pusley.
51111131511　Melony Moore
51111132　Alfred Thomas Williamson (8/4/1904 Sulphur Springs,
　　　　　TX-1/28/1990 Ardmore, OK), m. 8/15/1936, Ruth E.
　　　　　Taylor. M. (2nd) Margaret Ruth Hefner. Div. 10/30/
　　　　　1962.
511111321　Donald Neal Williamson (3/18/1929-11/18/1963 Ardmore,
　　　　　OK), m. (1st) Gwendolyn Willetta Bray (11/23/1934-
　　　　　　　), dau. of Orby Edward and Gertrude Adams
　　　　　Bray. M. (2nd) Leta Jo Robison

       Child by first wife:
5111113211 Donna Yvette Williamson (5/24/1949-   ), m. (1st)
            3/1/1966, James Russell McElvain. M. (2nd) 12/28/
            1973, Donald Ray Barber
       Child by first husband:
51111132111 Gina Michelle McElvain (6/16/1965-   ), m. Gary
            Allen Houston. Adopted: Justin Ray Houston and
            Joshua William Houston.
       Children by second husband:
51111132112 Chad Lynn Barber (5/18/1979-   ) (twin)
51111132113 Brad Alan Barber (5/18/1979-   ) (twin)
       Child by second wife:
5111113212 Beth Ann Williamson
511111322 Kenneth Lloyd Williamson (4/25/1942 Ardmore, OK-10/13/
            1985 Ardmore, OK), m. Earline Sartin
5111113221 Teresa Lynn Williamson (8/ 1962-   ), m. 5/24/1990
            Michael Grider
5111113222 Melissa Williamson (1/ /1971-   )
511111323 Gary Thomas Williamson (6/21/1944 Ardmore, OK-2/22/
            (1964), m. 7/ /1963, Ruby Ann Baxter (1/24/1949
            Ardmore, OK-   ), dau. of James John Henry and
            Dora Alice Roberts Baxter.
511111324 Odis Keith Williamson (4/26/1946 Ardmore, OK-   ),
            m. Mary Alice Baxter (10/21/1945 Ardmore, OK-
            ), dau. of James John Henry and Dora Alice
            Roberts Baxter.
5111113241 Garrie Dawn Williamson (6/11/1964 Ardmore, OK-   ),
            m. (1st) 8/15/1982, Kevin Horn. M. (2nd) 5/30/
            1987, Harlan Labers
       Children by first husband:
51111132411 Geoffrey Garth Horn (12/29/1982 Ardmore, OK-   )
51111132412 Valarie Mitchell Horn (4/4/1985 Ardmore, OK-   )
       Child by second husband:
51111132413 Evan Blake Labers (9/25/1990 Ardmore, OK-   )
5111113242 Jason Keith Williamson (1/16/1966 Ardmore, OK-
            ), m. 4/ /1985, Lucia Fatina Hartsill (Azore
            Islands, Portugal) adopted.
51111132421 Joshua Keith Williamson (12/6/1985 Ardmore, OK-   )
5111113243 Mary Margaret ("Margie") Williamson (6/11/1967
            Ardmore, OK-   ), m. 3/15/1986, Michael Glen King
            son of Luther Dale and Ruth Tibbs King.
51111132431 Emily Jill King (5/25/1990 Ardmore, OK-   )
5111113244 Gabriel Kirk Williamson (5/14/1971 Richardson, TX-
)
51111133 Charles Ersel Williamson (12/17/1907 Sulphur Springs,
            TX 11/24/1957 Ardmore, OK) (bur. Andrews, Texas
            Cemetery), m. Velma Derotha Kirkland
511111331 Howard Dale Williamson
511111332 Gene Yvonne Williamson (female)
511111333 Glen Ray Williamson (6/27/1942-   )
5111134 Reubin Murrell Williamson (3/10/1910-5/5/1972) (bur.
            KS), m. Audrey Mae Dowdy
511111341 Carolyn Ann Williamson (1/4/1935 Wilson, OK-   ),
            m. 12/14/1952, David Lee Brunson

5111113411 David Michael Brunson (9/15/1953-   )
5111113412 Michelle Diane Brunson (3/24/1957-   ), m. Major
       John Manning
5111134121 Ryan Manning
5111134122 Matthew Manning
511111342 Danny Murrell Williamson (7/2/1937 Frederick, OK-
       ), m. Betty Lorraine Phillips
5111113421 Danny Murrell Williamson, Jr. (10/9/1962-   )
5111113422 Keri Lane Williamson (6/1/1964-   ), m. Mark
       Richard
51111134221 Kasandra Lynn Richard (1/24/1991-   )
511111343 Darrell Gene Williamson (1/29/1939 Wilson, OK-   ),
       m. Pauletta Jean Collins
5111113431 Keli Vonne Williamson (4/28/1963-   )
5111113432 Darrell Gene Williamson, Jr.
5111113433 Jason Dane Williamson
511111344 Sharon Kay Williamson (3/16/1945 Wichita, KS-   ),
       m. James Dean Ohl. Adopted child:
         Jamie Kay Ohl (6/5/1969-   ), m.   Pistorius
         Harmony Kay Pistorius (1/31/1991-   )
5111113441 Joshua Dathon Ohl (9/6/1974-   )
5111113442 Justin Tyler Ohl (10/1/1982-   )
51111135 Wanda Lou Williamson (3/12/1920 Pirtle, OK-   ), m.
       4/23/1939, Overton Orndle Teague (6/19/1918 Lebenon,
       OK-7/9/1972 Ardmore, OK) (bur. Rose Hill Cemetery),
       son of Walter Dolphord and Altie Mae Carroll Teague.
511111351 Charles Dean Teague (10/20/1940 Ardmore, OK-   ), m.
       6/23/1960, Linda Carolyn Green (4/26/1942-   ),
       dau. of Herman Vernon and Elizabeth Caroline Green.
5111113511 Elizabeth Ann Teague (10/7/1961 Stillwater, OK-   ),
       m. 7/30/1988, Mark Allen McKinnis
51111135111 Joseph Ian McKinnis (3/30/1995-   )
5111113512 Charla DeAnn Teague (5/27/1963 Ardmore, OK-   ), m.
       11/23/1993, Justin Kelly Knight
511111352 Terry Arnold Teague (3/17/1947 Ardmore, OK-   ), m.
       6/5/1971, Barbara Ann Wade (12/6/1953-   ), dau.
       of Bobbie Jean and Margaret Ann Hackney Wade.
5111113521 Brent Christopher Teague (6/16/1976 Dallas, TX-   )
5111113522 Anthony David Teague (11/29/1977 Dallas, TX-   )
5111113523 Crystal Danielle Teague (1/9/1981 Dallas, TX-   )
511111353 Patsy Lawan Teague (9/15/1955 Ardmore, OK-   ), m.
       6/1/1973, Stephen Erl Harman (8/8/1951 Ardmore, OK-
       ), son of Erl Ludlow Stanley and Margaret Ann
       Parker Harman.
5111113531 Charity Christa Harman (12/14/1975 Denison, TX-   )
5111113532 Austin Stanley Harman (3/19/1980 Enid, OK-   )
5111113533 Samuel Elias Harman (11/19/1984 Durant, OK-   )
5111113534 Seth Elisha Harman (10/5/1987 Durant, OK-   )
5111114 Katie Mae Williamson (5/13/1876 Wooley Springs, Lime-
       stone County, AL-7/23/1939 Pratt City, AL), m. 2/27/
       1896, Percy J. Warren (10/30/1870 Petersburg, TN-
       3/14/1951 Pratt City, AL), son of Andrew Jackson
       and Mary Jane Brown Warren. Both bur. Fraternal
       Cemetery Pratt City, AL.

51111141 Ruth Estelle Warren (7/22/1897 Dan, Madison County,
          AL-6/20/1986 Jefferson County, AL) (bur. Elmwood
          Cemetery, Jefferson County, AL, m. 1/29/1921, Norman
          Ellis Ponder (10/3/1892 Campbell, AL-4/23/1958 Pratt
          City, AL.
511111411 Norman Ellis Ponder, Jr. (5/6/1922 Birmingham, AL-
                    ), m. 12/15/1945, Mildred Oldacker (8/28/19 -
          ), dau. of Thomas and   Oldacker.
5111114111 Norman Ellis Ponder III (2/17/1948-   ), m. Colorado
              Springs, CO, Carol Lawrence. Div.
5111114112 Patricia Kay Ponder (2/12/1952-   )
5111114113 Jon Howard Ponder (8/15/1953-   )
511111412 Marion Colleen Ponder (12/8/1924 Birmingham, AL-   ),
          m. Macon, GA, Milton Forrest Samples
5111114121 Sandra Diane Samples (4/20/1948-   ), m. Wayne
          Hammer. Div.
5111114122 Donna Susan Samples (1/27/1951 Birmingham, AL-   ),
          m. Homestead, PA, James Thomas Pintsak
51111141221 James Christopher Pintsak (9/16/1976 Orange County,
          CA-   )
511111413 Forrest Marion Samples (7/12/1954 Birmingham, AL-   ),
          m. Janet Anne Preston (b. Neptune, NJ-   )
5111114131 Amanda Nicole Samples (7/17/1990-   )
5111114132 Katelyn Elaine Samples (4/21/1992-   )
511111414 Steven Mark Samples (5/6/1957 Birmingham, AL-   ),
          m. Patricia Mary Langford (b. Pittsburg, PA-   )
5111114141 Mark Patrick Samples (11/27/1992-   )
51111142 Rainey Davis Warren (3/27/1899 Center Hill, Limestone
          County, AL-2/19/1987), m. 7/1/1919, Zelma Elizabeth
          Bates (12/22/1902 Clifton, TN-4/10/1992), dau. of
          James R. and Ida Berry Bates. Both bur. Elmwood
          Cemetery, Jefferson County, AL.
511111421 Mary Elizabeth Warren (7/30/1920 Pratt City, AL-   ),
          m. (1st) 3/25/1938, Arthur David Williams (2/23/1916
          Birmingham, AL-4/11/1981) (bur. Elmwood Cemetery,
          Jefferson County, AL), son of Arthur and Maggie
          Smith Williams. M. (2nd) 1/21/1984, Edward Earl
          Munn (7 or 8/20/1916 Jefferson County-11/24/1991)
          (bur. Elmwood Cemetery), son of James and Lannie Lee
          Lokey Munn. (Edward Earl Munn was married first to
          Catherine Virginia Warren (511111431).
5111114211 Patricia Ann Williams (2/2/1939 Fairfield, AL-   ),
          m. (1st) 1/ /1956, Freddie Gary Aderhold 4/4/1939-
). Div. M. (2nd) 3/10/1960, James Herman
          Johnson (7/8/1938 Marion County, AL-   ). Div.
     Child by first husband:
51111142111 Rainey William Aderhold (12/26/1956 Fairfield, AL-
                    ), m. 11/19/1977, Patricia Marie Metcalf
          (9/15/1955 Sylacauga, AL-   )
511111421111 Courtney Lane Aderhold (12/20/1979 Birmingham, AL-
)
511111421112 Robert Rainey Aderhold (12/12/1981 Willingham, NC-
)

Child by second husband:
51111142112 Dee Ann Johnson (7/23/1965 Birmingham, AL-   ), m.
             5/30/1986, Frank D'Amico (8/23/1962 Birmingham,
             AL-   ), son of Anthony and Annette D'Amico.
511111421121 Elizabeth D'Amico (3/30/1991-   )
511111422 Jack Davis Warren (1/14/1922 Jefferson County, AL-
             ), m. 5/25/1942, Margaret Marshall (3/27/1925
             Jefferson County, AL-   ), dau. of William B. and
             Pearl Huston Marshall.
5111114221 William Rainey Warren (1/27/1944 Birmingham, AL-),
             m. 7/ /1976, Diane Miller (/ /1944 Woodstock,
             VA-   ), dau. of S. E. and Elizabeth Miller.
5111114222 James Davis Warren (11/4/1946 Birmingham, AL-   ),
             m. 8/6/1969, Lindsey Lee (11/ /1948 Lindsey, OK-
             ), dau. of Bill and Martha Forte Lee.
51111142221 Christopher F. Warren (6/ /1973 Ft. Sill, OK-   )
51111142222 Jarrod P. Warren (11/13/1976 Jefferson County, AL-
)
5111114223 Robert Steven Warren (10/14/1954 Birmingham, AL-   ),
             m. 10/8/1977, Susan Kelly (/ /1954-   ), dau.
             of Tom and Helen Kelly.
51111142231 Robert Steven Warren, Jr. (12/7/1991-   )
51111143 Oscar Cosmo Warren 7/25/1901 Center Hill, Limestone
             County, AL / /1963), m. (1st) Rose Findley (6/12/
             1905 Paint Rock, AL-   ). Div in 1930. M. (2nd)
             Freida Champion. Bur. Elmwood Cemetery, Birmingham,
             AL.
     Children by first wife:
511111431 Catherine Virginia Warren (12/21/1922 Birmingham, AL-
             11/2/1981, bur. Elmwood Cemetery, Birmingham, AL),
             m. 6/16/1942, Edward Earl Munn (7 or 8/20/1916
             Birmingham, AL- 11/24/1991), son of James and
             Lannie Lee Lokey Munn. Edward Earl Munn's second
             wife was Mary Elizabeth Warren (511111421).
5111114311 Edward Earl Munn, Jr. (3/20/1947 Birmingham, AL-   ),
             m. 3/28/1969, Patricia Arnold (3/22/1950 Jefferson
             County, AL-   ), dau. of Walter and Ludie Millican
             Arnold.
51111143111 Scott Munn (1/1/1977-   )
51111143112 Tracy Munn (2/11/1981-   )
511111432 Augusta Rose Warren (9/5/1926 Birmingham, AL-   ), m.
             1/18/1952, James Van Bost (9/21/1927 Birmingham, AL-
             ), son of Dillon Paul and Lydia Belle McVay Bost.
5111114321 Terry Lynne Bost (7/14/1955 Birmingham, AL-   ), m.
             3/31/1978, Donald Thomas Dennis
5111114322 Catherine Elaine Bost (9/8/1959 Birmingham, AL-   ),
             m. Danny M. Moore
51111143221 Amanda Catherine Moore (3/28/1992-   )
     Child by second wife:
511111433 Ronald Edward Warren (12/2/1948-   ), m. Irene
             Brinkman. Div. in 1981
5111114331 Brent Allyn Warren (2/6/1974-   )
51111144 Alfred Percy Warren (3/14/1905 Pratt City, AL-3/5/1986)
             (bur. Elmwood Cemetery, Jefferson County, AL), m.

```
            3/23/1925, Jewel Geraldine Lawless (5/18/1906
            Sandusky, AL-    )
511111441  William Merrill Warren (1/16/1926 Pratt City, AL-   ),
            m. 11/22/19  , Helen Marie Hooper
5111114411  William Merrill Warren, Jr. (1/17/1956-     ), m.
            Linda Gail Dye
51111144111  William Merrill Warren III
51111144112  Allison Marie Warren (12/2/1987-    )
5111114412  Dawn Marie Warren (8/2/1961-     ), m. 10/3/1986,
            Stephen Lee Ousley, son of Bobby G. and    Ousley.
511111442  Dorothy Jean Warren (7/25/1928 Pratt City, AL-    ),
            m. 7/18/1947, Gene Wesley Garst (12/31/1925-    )
5111114421  Linda Diane Garst (9/23/1949-     ), m. James Edge
51111144211  Kimberly Germaine Edge (1/29/1975-    )
5111114422  John Wesley Garst (7/16/1951-    ), m. Sharon
51111144221  Amy Melissa Garst (7/8/1974-    )
51111144222  Ian Wesley Garst (1/30/1980-    )
5111114423  Sarah Catherine Garst (12/14/1952-    ), m. David
            McCoy
51111144231  Brandon Nicholus McCoy (6/25/1981-    )
5111114424  Alfred Glenn Garst (7/30/1954-    )
5111114425  Cynthia Lee Garst (11/29/1958-    ), m. Jeff Drummond
51111144251  Kristen Danielle Drummond (12/29/1983-    )
51111144252  Emily Rebecca Drummond (3/16/1988-    )
51111145  Mary Margaret Warren (5/19/1909 Pratt City, AL-    ),
            m. 6/18/1927, William Larimore Toney 6/28/1904-11/16/
            1969)
511111451  Warren Larimore Toney (3/13/1929 Tarrant City, AL-
            6/13/1981) (bur. at sea), m. Betty Jane        .
            Div. 1951.
5111114511  Warren Alan Toney (7/10/1959-    ), m. Jeanine Marie
            Lasslett
51111145111  Timothy John Toney (12/13/1974-    )
51111145112  Karina Marie Toney (5/1/1977-    )
511111452  Betty Ruth Toney (5/4/1931-1/22/1993)
511111453  Margaret Eloise Toney (5/5/1932 Pratt City, AL-    ),
            m. 3/4/1951, Harry Hooper, Jr.
5111114531  Daniel Paul Hooper (1/3/1952 Glendale, CA-    ), m.
            4/20/1973, Holly Ann Smith (10/20/1955 Phoenix, AZ
51111145311  Paul Jeffrey Hooper (6/5/19  -    )
51111145312  Scott William Hooper (2/24/1983-    )
5111114532  Judith Lynn Hooper (2/20/1953-    ), m. David Morgan
            Meadows (1/3/1953-    )
51111145321  Michael David Meadows (4/2/1978-    )
51111146  Roy Vernon Warren (7/11/1911 Pratt City, AL-12/3/1978)
            (bur. Fraternal Cemetery, Pratt City, AL), m. Mary
            Lucille Hilyer (3/8/1919 Birmingham, AL-    )
511111461  Marion Gail Warren (2/9/1938 Birmingham, AL-    ), m.
            5/23/1959, William Robert Harville (4/23/1938
            Retton, AL-    ), son of Elmer Ellis and Edna
            Zellers Harville.
5111114611  Steven Robert Harville (1/24/1960-    )
5111114612  Tracey Lynn Harville (4/25/1962-    )
5111114613  William Scott Harville
```

51111147   Nell Katherine Warren (7/10/1917 Pratt City, AL-   ),
           m. 4/10/1937, Ernest Elmore Alexander (1/4/1916
           Republic, AL-5/1/1983) (bur. Forest Crest Cemetery,
           Jefferson County, AL), son of David Hamilton and
           Jeanette Kerr Alexander.
511111471 Hugh Howard Alexander (8/4/1938 Jefferson County-   ),
           m. 2/23/1963, Dianne Ruth Piazza (8/29/1942 New
           Orleans, LA-   )
5111114711 Kevin Michael Alexander (11/1/1964-   )
5111114712 Keith Ernest Alexander (10/16/1965-   ), m. (1st)
           4/22/1989, Cheryl Leigh Miller. Div. No children.
           M. (2nd) Anna
    Child by second wife:
51111147121 Taylor Lee Alexander (8/25/1993-   )
5111114713 David Brian Alexander (5/4/1970-3/22/1989) (bur.
           Shenandoah Memorial Park, Winchester, VA).
511111472 Kenneth Warren Alexander (5/24/1942 Jefferson County,
           AL-   ), m. (1st) 1963, Virginia Meeks. Div. M.
           (2nd) 6/15/1973, Patricia Ware McGriff Halcomb
           (2/4/1946-   ), dau. of J. C. and Sadie Lou
           DeLoache Ware.
    Children by first wife:
5111114721 JoLynn Alexander (1/4/1965 Jefferson County, AL-),
           m. Robert W. Streip, Jr., son of Robert W. Streip,
           Sr. and Mary Streip.
51111147211 Dannika Ray Streip (7/9/1987-   )
51111147212 Peighton Streip (3/22/1994-   )
5111114722 Samuel David Alexander (9/17/1969-   ), m. 4/13/
           1990, Jeannie Jordan (4/4/1970-   )
51111147221 Alan Blake Alexander (9/22/1991-   )
51111147222 Andrew Jordan Alexander (1/4/1995-   )
    Child by second wife:
5111114723 Sharon Amalie Alexander (10/28/1977-   )
511111473 Michael Ernest Alexander (12/14/1946 Jefferson County,
           AL-   ), m. (1st) 2/18/1966, Beleita Acyenith
           Vincent (12/30/1946-   ). Div. M (2nd) 9/18/
           1982, Sally Maxine Swartz Burden. Div.
    Children by first wife:
5111114731 Staci Michele Alexander (6/27/1969-   ), m. 12/3/
           1988, Michael Scott Sulhoff
5111114732 Jason Scott Alexander (10/26/1972-10/27/1972) (bur.
           Forest Crest Cemetery, Birmingham, AL
5111114733 Michael Scott Alexander (8/1/1974-   )
5111115   Thomas Leroy Williamson (9/13/1877-3/9/1878) (b. and d.
           AL)
5111116   Williamson Frederick Williamson (4/1/1879-8/29/1879) (b.
           and d. AL)
5111117   Jeff Davis Williamson (6/9/1880 Wooley Springs, Lime-
           stone County, Al-10/25/1945 San Angelo, TX), m. 12/31/
           1905, Fannie Frankie Wilson (1/3/1886 GA-9/1/1983 TX),
           dau. of George Lee and Mary Emma Baines Wilson. Both
           bur. Belvedere Cemetery, San Angelo, TX.

51111171   Mary Malva Williamson (8/22/1907 Fannin County, TX-
                 ), m. (eloped) 10/9/1926, Curtis Clyde Morris
           (8/26/1903 Shirley Community, Hopkins County, Tx-
           bur. Shirley Cemetery, Hopkins County, TX), son of
           Edmond Lee and Fannie Jane Vaughn Morris.
511111711 Rosemary Morris (6/19/1929 Hopkins County, TX near
           Sulphur Springs, TX-   ), m. 3/18/1949, Phillip
           Dwight Baker (2/7/1929 south of Sulphur Springs, TX-
                 ), son of Henry Hastings and Sally Dea
           Causey Baker.
5111117111 Mary Catherine ("Cathey") Baker (8/20/1951 Grand
           Prairie, TX-   ), m. (1st) 7/5/1972, Charles
           Albert Thomas (2/2/1942 Orange County, CA-   ),
           son of Lynn Charles and Mary Delany Thomas. Div.
           M. (2nd) 10/10/1989, William ("Bill") Hugh Lee, Jr.
           (7/14/1955 Bartlesville, OK-   ), son of William
           Hugh Lee, Sr. and Norma Jean Hipp Lee.
   Children by first wife:
51111171111 Aransas Rose Thomas (3/13/1975 Port Aransas, TX-
)
51111171112 Charles ("Chas") Sloceum Thomas (4/27/1977 Commerce,
           TX-   )
5111117112 Anna Laurie Baker (2/16/1953 Grand Prairie, TX-   ),
           m. 7/27/1979, Steven Cash. Div.
5111117113 Phillip Samuel Baker (10/11/1954 Irving, TX-   ), m.
           5/10/1978, Donna Jean Moncrief (2/23/1960 Grand
           Prairie, TX-   ), dau. of George Herbert and
           Nelda Evelyn Wise Moncrief.
51111171131 Phillip Samuel ("Bo") Baker (8/20/1979 Irving, TX-
)
5111117114 Dwight Daniel ("Danny") Baker (5/26/1957 Irving, TX-
                 ), m. 1/30/1981, Pamela Ann Sanders (5/12/
           1960 Denton, TX-   ), dau. of Bobby Jack and
           Hersel Lee McAnally Sanders.
51111171141 Jason Daniel Baker (8/17/1982 Irving, TX-   )
51111171142 Jacob Dwight Baker (6/9/1984 Irving, TX-   )
511111712 Joy Ann Morris (2/15/1936 in Vernon, TX-6/22/1954
           Paris, TX). Bur. Shirley Cemetery, Hopkins County,
           TX.
511111713 Curtis Ray Morris (2/24/1943 Sulphur Springs, TX-
                 ), m. 6/27/1964 Carrollton, TX, Cloe Marie
           Lawrence (9/4/1945 Commerce, TX-   ), dau. of
           John G. and Ida Self Lawrence.
5111117131 Lawrence Craig Morris (9/30/1966 Lubbock, TX-   ),
           m. 4/22/1995, Donna Lea Hines (9/28/1966 Sulphur
           Springs, TX-   ), dau. of Donald Eugene and
           Lillian Colleen Lewis Hines.
51111172   Era Lee Williamson (9/29/1909 Leonard, Fanning County,
           TX-   ), m. (1st) 8/30/1933, Ernest Sheffield
           (5/15/1902 Miles, TX-12/9/1939 San Angelo, TX). M.
           (2nd) 9/3/1942, William Ovid Coltrane (10/8/1909
           Aberdeen, MS-7/17/1985 Amarillo, TX). Div. 10/5/
           1960. M. (3rd) 11/24/1965, Ira Houston Bryant
           (11/14/1910 Honey Grove, TX-2/27/1974 Lubbock, TX).

Child by first husband:
511111721 Donald Gene Sheffield (10/ /1934-died at birth)
Children by second husband:
511111722 William Lee Coltrane (2/16/1946 San Angelo, Tx-   )
511111723 Robert Round Coltrane (10/17/1947 San Angelo, TX-   )
51111173 Oran Odis Williamson (7/30/1912 Hopkins County, TX-
                    ), m. 4/ /1962, Nellie Jane Renfro (11/17/
                    1925 Emhouse, TX-7/27/1995 Tyler, TX) (bur. Memorial
                    Park Cemetery West, Tyler, TX), dau. of Roy Reuben
                    and Berttie Lee Baygent Renfro. Div. 1/ /1977.
511111731 Tammy Nell Williamson (5/1/1960 San Angelo, TX-   ),
                    m. (1st) in 1977, Randy Dale Beasley. Div. 1982.
                    M. (2nd) 8/2/1986, Michael Martin
Children by first husband:
5111117311 Brandi Michelle Beasley (3/10/1978 Tyler, TX-   )
5111117312 Joshua Dale Beasley (11/5/1979 Tyler, TX-   )
Child by second husband:
5111117313 Megan Martin (11/9/1988 Tyler, TX-   )
511111732 Lana Jo Williamson (7/18/1962 San Angelo, TX-   ), m.
                    (1st) 6/20/1981, Michael W. Kilgore. Div. 5/ /1986.
                    M. (2nd) 9/18/1988, Kent Lee Lawson (11/25/1963
                    Anderson, IN-   ), son of Virgil Glen and Mary Lou
                    Wood Lawson.
Children by first husband:
5111117321 Nathan Oran Kilgore (7/5/1982 Tyler, TX-   )
5111117322 Misty Jane Kilgore (11/16/1983 Lindale, TX-   )
5111117323 Amanda Leigh Kilgore (2/25/1986 Tyler, TX-   )
511111733 Christopher Odis Williamson (5/2/1965 Tyler, TX-   ),
                    m. 6/23/1992, Mary Lou Nicholson (9/13/1948 Tyler,
                    TX-   ), dau. of J. T. Nicholson, Jr. and Pauline
                    Doris Lewis Nicholson.
51111174 Marcie Williamson (3/21/1915 Hopkins County, TX-3/11/
                    1991 San Angelo, TX). Unm.
51111175 Percy Jeff Williamson (8/15/1916 Hopkins County, TX-
                    ), m. 2/5/1945, Katherine Vaughn (6/25/1917
                    Vernon, TX-   ), dau. of Edgar D. and Mary Elizabeth
                    Owen Vaughn.
511111751 Gary Wayne Williamson (8/14/1946 San Angelo, TX-   ),
                    m. 8/16/1968, Glenna Ree Carpenter (1/4/1947
                    Commerce, TX-   ), dau. of Glenn Weldon and
                    Oweneola Bethana Pickett Carpenter. Adopted at age
                    3 days: Robert Wayne Williamson (12/6/1972 Corpus
                    Christi, TX-   ).
511111752 Richard Kyle Williamson (10/21/1947 Dallas, TX-   ),
                    m. 11/28/1974, Essie Pudwill (1/26/1949 Minneapolis,
                    MN-   ), dau. of Clayton and Lorena Heib Pudwill.
                    Div.
5111117521 Kevin Glenn Williamson (6/12/1978 San Diego, CA-   )
5111117522 Scott Allen Williamson (11/1/1979 San Diego, CA-   )
511111753 Mary Helen Williamson (10/30/1951 Monahans, TX-   ),
                    m. 1/19/1974, Ralph Berwanger (8/10/1952 Kingsport,
                    TN-   ), son of Ralph Olaysenaw and Ada Mae Tittle
                    Berwanger. Adopted at age 7: David Bryan Berwanger
                    (11/30/1977 Jacksonville, FL-   ).

5111117531 Rebecca Ann Berwanger (2/12/1976 Okinawa, Japan-   )
5111117532 Nicole Marie Berwanger (2/11/1980 Fairbanks, AK-   )
51111176   Walter Clyde ("W.C.") Williamson (1/2/1919 Dyke,
           Hopkins County, TX-   ), m. 6/5/1942, Bessie
           Cochran (9/18/1924 Houston, TX-2/22/1991 Hemphill,
           TX), dau. of Fred Moore Cochran (he was adopted-born
           1896 as Fritz Yohle) and Nannie Lee Elliot Cochran.
511111761 Don Lee Williamson (8/20/1943 San Angelo, TX-   ), m.
           6/12/1965, Cheryl Ann Glaw (6/14/1944 Blanchard, LA-
           ), dau. of Wilbur Henry and Marion Hennington
           Glaw.
5111117611 Julie Rae Williamson (10/2/1969 Seattle, WA-   )
5111117612 Trevor Alan Williamson (3/15/1975 Chapel Hill, NC-)
511111762 Terry Neal Williamson (12/31/1945 Houston, TX-   ),
           m. 8/12/1978, Kathleen Dynel Hughes (9/8/1954 Texas
           City, TX-   ), dau. of Michael Kerwin and Selma
           Mildred Krenz Hughes.
5111117621 Brett Alan Williamson (7/24/1980 Houston, TX-   )
5111117622 Rachel Dynel Williamson (1/25/1985 Houston, TX-   )
511111763 Dianna Gayle Williamson (3/16/1947 Monahans, TX-   ),
           m. 2/2/1967, John Olen Burns (12/14/1947 Houston,
           TX-   ), son of Chester Thomas and Martha Corinne
           Brown Burns.
5111117631 Kevin Darrell Burns (9/24/1967 Nashville, TN-   , m.
           7/30/1994, Julie Kay Garrison (5/9/1968 Garland,
           TX-   ), dau. of Donald Rae and Pattie Nell
           Watkins Garrison.
5111117632 Robin Denise Burns (6/2/1972 New Orleans, LA-   )
5111117633 Russell Chet Burns (6/26/1977 Garland, TX-   )
511111764 Nancy Louise Williamson (3/6/1949 Monahans, TX-   ),
           m. 2/10/1979, Ersa Ray ("Pete") Newton 10/8/1945
           Kirbyville, TX-   ), son of Ersa Ray Newton, Sr.
           and Mary Ruth West Newton.
5111117641 Travis Ray Newton (8/3/1982 Pasadena, TX-   )
5111117642 Corina Louise Newton (5/18/1987 Pasadena, TX-   )
511111765 Laurel Elaine Williamson (3/24/1958 Pasadena, TX-
           ), m. 6/29/1985, Ari Ariel (7/16/1963 Harvey,
           IL-   ), son of Leo and   Ariel. Div.
5111117651 Joshua Ari Ariel (9/27/1987 Bethesda, MD-   )
51111177   Emma Margaret Williamson (12/4/1921 Hopkins County, TX-
           ), m. (1st) 2/25/1946, Elbert S.("Speck") Hill
           (11/10/1916 Jasper, AL-3/30/1966 San Angelo, TX). M.
           (2nd) 5/7/1978, Thomas S. Henderson (b. Colorado
           City, TX-1/31/1991 San Angelo, TX).
      Children by first husband:
511111771 Jane Sharon Hill (6/28/1947 Jasper, AL-   ), m. (1st)
           3/15/1969, Glyn Jameson. Div. M. (2nd) 10/30/1981,
           Tom Duke (3/25/1948 Snyder, TX-   ), son of Thomas
           Junior and Jeanne Miller Duke.
5111117711 Jonathan Glyn Jameson (9/3/1971 San Angelo, TX-   )
5111117712 Jarod Matthew Jameson (9/26/1973 San Angelo, TX-   )
511111772 Rodger Garren Hill (8/12/1949 Jasper, AL-   ), m.
           (1st) 12/29/1967, Brenda Smith. Div. 1975. M. (2nd)

2/6/1985, Connie Compton (9/10/1948 Sweetwater, TX-
), dau. of Allen Gates and Betty Jo Porter
Compton.
Child by first wife:
5111117721 Rodger Garren Hill II (4/29/1969 White Settlement,
Ft. Worth, TX-   )
511111773 Paul Kelly Hill (12/21/1950 San Angelo, TX-   ), m.
9/5/1976, Leora Ann Agnew (3/26/1950 Big Springs,
TX-   ), dau. of Olvis Agnew and Mildred Janet
Bryant Agnew Holder.
5111117731 Kelley Margaret Hill (10/23/1978 Odessa, TX-   )
5111117732 Kyla Marie Hill (2/3/1982 Hobbs, NM-   )
5111117733 Karissa Michelle Hill (7/30/1985 Hobbs, NM-   )
511111774 Steven Gregg Hill (4/10/1954 San Angelo, TX-   ),
m. 2/11/1985, Doris Whetstone (2/18/1957
Fredericksburg, TX-   ), dau. of Martha Peeper
Whetstone Ellebracht (stepfather - Chester
Ellebracht).
5111117741 Wendy Nicole Hill (11/6/1985 San Angelo, TX-   )
5111117742 Tracy Ann Hill (8/19/1988 San Angelo, TX-   )
511111775 Alan Craig Hill (11/7/1956 San Angelo, TX-   ), m.
4/6/1979, Lisa Godwin (12/8/1958 Odessa, TX-   ),
dau. of Max Everett and Betty Jean Sisk Godwin.
Adopted:
Amanda Jane Hill (10/8/1986-   ) (adopted
12/12/1986 San Angelo, TX)
Alana Kay Hill (1/23/1993 San Angelo, TX-   )
51111178 Roxie Vernell Williamson (8/10/1923 Dike County, TX-
3/14/1987 Richmond, VA), m. 2/3/1944, Grayson Arnold
("Tuck") Melton (1/5/1919 Glen Allen, VA-7/6/1989
San Angelo, TX), son of Grover Grayson and Ora
Leonard Tate Melton. Both bur. Fairmont Cemetery
San Angelo, TX.
511111781 Charlotte Ann Melton (8/20/1947 Richmond, VA-   ), m.
12/24/1965, Cliff Caffey (10/14/1941 Rowena, TX-
), son of Hugh Dalton and Mildred Preidecker
Caffey. Div. 6/ /1986.
5111117811 Angela Charlane Caffey (5/12/1967 San Angelo, TX-
), m. 1/6/1986, David Scott Goddard (11/14/
1963 Provo, UT-   ) son of David Corwin and
Barbara Gay Bagwell Goddard.
51111178111 Tyler Scott Goddard (12/6/1993 Edwards Air Force
Base, Washington, D.C.-   )
5111117812 Kimberly Ann Caffey (3/20/1970 San Angelo, TX-   )
511111782 Susan Lynn Melton (4/30/1947 Richmond, VA-   ), m.
8/16/1969, Robert Thomas Brown. Div.
5111117821 Michele Lynn Brown (3/21/1970 San Angelo, TX-   ),
m. 5/30/1992, Bruce Alexander
5111117822 Misty Leigh Brown (5/18/1976 San Angelo, TX-   )
511111783 Brenda Jean Melton (5/22/1952 Richmond, VA-   ), m.
6/13/1969, Barry Neal Dougan (11/2/1949 Houston, TX-
), son of Clinton Curtis and Willie Mayree
Killebrew Dougan.
5111117831 Joshua Bradley Dougan (10/13/1973 Dallas, TX-   )

5111117832 Joseph Cole Dougan (6/9/1977 San Angelo, TX-   )
51111179 Kenneth Dean Williamson (1/16/1926 Hopkins County, TX-
          ), m. 7/23/1947, Betty Little (8/28/1930
          Taylor County, near Abilene, TX-   )
511111791 Daniel Bruce Williamson (2/28/1951 Odessa, TX-   ),
          m. 4/16/1988, Laura Elizabeth Fox (12/3/1954 Dallas,
          TX-   )
5111117911 Sarah Shawn Williamson (3/29/1991 Denver, CO-   )
511111792 Sandra Sue Williamson (7/28/1953 San Angelo, TX-   ),
          m. 11/17/1973, William McNatt (2/2/1948-   )
5111117921 Gabrial William McNatt (10/13/1980 San Angelo, TX-
)
5111117922 Adam Kenneth McNatt (10/9/1984 San Angelo, TX-   )
5111117x Fannie Lou Williamson (12/24/1927 Hopkins County, TX-
          ), m. 10/20/1948, Grover Leslie ("Kin") Melton
          (10/6/1928 Henrico Co., VA-   ), son of Grover
          Grayson and Ora Tate Melton.
5111117x1 Frankie Nell Melton (4/25/1952 Richmond, VA-   ), m.
          (1st) 6/ /1974, Kenneth Wayne Harvey. Div. 1076.
          M. (2nd) 12/25/1991, Sheldon Eugene Wade (1/9/1962
          Richmond, VA-   )
    Child by first husband:
5111117x11 Shari Dawn Harvey (6/24/1976 Richmond, VA-   )
5111117x2 Robert Leslie Melton (5/27/1956 Richmond, VA-   )
5111118 Benjamin Roland Williamson (7/6/1882 Limestone County,
          AL-8/30/1950 Mangum, OK), m. 4/17/1904, Tressie Jane
          Warren (10/24/1877 Grundy County, TN-2/6/1957 Mangum,
          OK). Both bur. Reed, OK.
51111181 Willie Beatrice Williamson (5/9/1905 Leonard, Fannin
          County, TX-10/31/1975 Pampa, TX), m. (1st) Joe
          Gordon. M. (2nd) William Gordon ("Pat") Darby
          (1/7/1899-1/8/1974 Pampa, TX)
    Child by first husband:
511111811 Joe Gene Gordon (2/20/1923 Silverton, TX-   ), m.
          Richard Patrick McBride (3/24/1925-   ).
          Adopted:
              Royce Gene Staggs Murrah (12/31/1940 Borger, TX-
) (known as Royce Gene Murrah - his adopted
              name), m. 6/29/1963, Josephine Marie Lopez (-
              1/17/1992)
                  Christy Maxine Murrah (7/9/1964 Pampa, TX-   )
                      Tierrie Marie Murrah (12/5/1987 Las Vegas,
                      NV-   )
                  Frank Roland Murrah (9/15/1965 Canadian, TX-
)
                  Terrie Ann Murrah (8/11/1970 Canadian, TX-
                  ), m. Ricky R. Cortez
    Children by second husband:
511111812 Benjamin Roland Darby (4/23/1927-5/18/1941). Bur.
          Shamrock, TX.
511111813 William Junior Darby (7/31/1929 Cheyenne, OK-   ),
          m. Lena Pearl Dick (12/27/1927 Chelsea, OK-   ),
          dau. of David Lee and Lucinda Catherine Mauk Dick.

5111118131 William Lee Darby (3/5/1951 Pampa, TX-   ), m.
           8/26/1982, Krista Lynne Ingerson Sanders (3/11/
           1951-   ). Div. 7/12/1993.
5111118132 Robert Eugene Darby (8/31/1953 Pampa, TX-   ), m.
           Robin Lynn James (3/1/1962 Vinita, OK-   )
51111181321 Megan Elizabeth Darby (12/24/1978 Canadian, TX-   )
51111181322 Catherine Pauline Darby (12/8/1982 Anchorage, AK-
)
51111181323 Matthew Scott Darby (6/24/1984 Pampa, TX-   )
511111814 Leon Cecil Darby (1/22/1931 Strong City, OK-8/18/
           1994). Bur. Hobbs, NM. M. (1st)   .
           M. (2nd) Wanda May Pool (6/2/1933-   ), dau. of
           Joseph Otho and Jewel Smith Pool.
    Child by first wife:
5111118141 Andrea Joyce Darby (b. Pampa, TX-   ), m.
                     Shipley
51111181411 Donnie Shipley (b. Pampa, TX-   )
51111181412 Carolyn Shipley (b. Pampa, TX-   )
    Children by second wife:
5111118142 Gregory Leon Darby (6/27/1959 Ventura, CA-   )
5111118143 Tina Denise Darby (12/28/1960 Boyger, TX-   ),
           m. (1st) Steven Gray Bush. Div. M. (2nd) Brent
           Layman
    Children by first husband:
51111181431 Latisha Dawn Bush (12/8/1981 Carlsbad, NM-   )
51111181432 Lacey Jo Bush (12/14/1983 Carlsbad, NM-   )
    Child by second husband:
51111181433 Bradley Lynn Layman (7/2/1992 Woodward, OK-   )
5111118144 Rhonda Gay Darby (8/7/1963 Dumas, TX-   ), m.
           6/15/1984, Ronald Jay Simon (1/29/1963-   )
51111181441 Brittney LaSha Simon (1/31/1985 Hobbs, NM-   )
51111181442 Darby Breann Simon (1/18/1989 Hobbs, NM-   )
51111181443 Bridget Elizabeth Jo Simon (7/27/1993 Hobbs. NM-
)
511111815 Geraldean May Darby (11/16/1933 Norman, OK-   ), m.
           1/1/1950, Francis Ray Christian (12/23/1930 Fargo,
           OK-   )
5111118151 David Leon Christian (9/23/1951 Pampa, TX-   ), m.
           (2nd) 2/3/1973, Della Rene Worthen. Div. 12/15/
           1984. M. (4th) 11/15/1986, Teresa Ruth Purcell
           (4/29/1960 Boyger, TX-   ), dau. of Doyle Wayne
           and Loyce Marie Shannon Purcell.
           Teresa Christian's children:
              Nathan Todd Vaughn (6/20/1979 Borger, TX-   )
              Megan Rose Vaughn (8/12/1982 Fritch, TX-   )
    Children by second wife:
51111181511 Brandy Rene Christian (12/5/1975 Borger, TX-   ),
            m. 11/5/1994, Shad Eugene White (7/2/1972 OKeene,
            OK-   )
51111181512 Lacey Lene Christian (7/6/1979 Borger, TX-   )
    Children by fourth wife:
51111181513 Kassie Marie Christian (12/6/1988 Amarillo, TX-   )
51111181514 Kadee Mae Christian (1/9/1994 Amarillo, TX-   )

5111118152 Linda Gean Christian (3/29/1954 Pampa, TX-   ), m.
            6/3/1977, Melvin Joe Vick (8/1/1950 Wellington, TX-
                  ), son of Clyde and Mary Lillian Thompson
            Vick.
51111181521 Mary Frances Vick (10/29/1971 Pampa, TX-   )
511111815211 Brittany Nichole Vick (6/18/1992 Amarillo, TX-   )
511111815212 Joleen NaShay Pittman (6/18/1994 Amarillo, TX-   )
51111181522 Jerald Clyde Vick (8/24/1973 Kingsville, TX-   ),
            m. 8/ /1992, Tonya Hester. Div.
5111118153 Bobby Ray Christian (1/3/1956 Pampa, TX-   ), m.
            Rhonda Jean Mitchell (1/11/1957 Borger, TX-   ),
            dau. of Charlie Lee and Wanda Lou Fields Mitchell.
51111181531 Shannon Rachelle Christian (3/24/1976 Borger, TX-
)
51111181532 Kelli Michelle Christian (4/21/1978 Borger, TX-   )
5111118154 Theresa Jane Christian (6/2/1964 Pampa, TX-   ), m.
            Marvin Clay Wells (2/10/1964 Pampa, TX-   ), son
            of Benjamin Clay and Mary Louise Maxey Wells.
511111816 Mildred Fay Darby (4/27/1936-   ), m. Frank Kingham.
            Div. Adopted:
                  Robert Lee Kingham (4/9/1963 Groom, TX-   )
                  Melodie Ann Kingham (3/13/1968 Reno, NV-   ),
                  m. Gary Jobe (6/22/1970-   ). Children:
                        Ashley Faye Jobe (9/12/1988 Las Vegas, NV-
)
                        Allen Joseph Jobe (5/18/1990 Las Vegas. NV-
)
51111182 J. B. Williamson (4/5/1909 Leonard, TX-10/29/1978), m.
            (1st) Edith Melliment. M. (2nd) Faye Bounder
51111183 Golia V. Williamson (6/30/1918 Trenton, Fannin County,
            TX-   ), m. (2nd) 5/28/1976, Liston Wayne Lowe
            (9/14/1924-7/11/1989), son of Will and Gertrude
            Sogers Lowe.
51111184 Ethel Lee Williamson (2/12/1922 Silverton, Briscoe
            County, TX-   ), m. (1st) 3/4/1938 Roy Lee Adams
            (7/15/1912 in Mangum, OK-   ). Div. 1/9/1981.
            M. (2nd) 12/11/1994, Jesse McCord (7/10/1915 Allen,
            OK-   ), son of Willie Fieldman McCord and Clemmie
            Doortine Rhodes McCord.
   Children by first husband:
511111841 Ethellen Adams (10/24/1938-stillborn)
511111842 Kenneth Lee Adams (7/17/1943 Oklahoma City, OK-   ),
            m. Janet Elaine Bennett
5111118421 Kenneth Lee Adams, Jr. (6/3/1969-   )
5111118422 Ashley Lane Adams (3/5/1987-   )
511111843 Ronnie Gene Adams (1/6/1946 Oklahoma City, OK-   ),
            m. Patrice Ann Crane
511111844 Gary Wayne Adams (7/6/1952 Oklahoma City, OK-   ),
            m. Lisa Jeffers
5111118441 Michelle Lee Adams (7/24/1970-   )
51111184411 Geneva Christian Adams
5111118442 Natali Necole Adams (7/10/1986-   )
511111845 Tommy Dale Adams (9/22/1961 Oklahoma City, OK-   ),
            m. (2nd) Kelly Deann Reid

```
5111118451  Crystal Denise Adams (4/24/1978-    )
5111118452  LaTisha Ann Adams (4/27/1982-    )
5111118453  Thomas Dewayne Adams (10/19/1987-    )
5111118454  Devin Mitchell Adams (6/14/1988-    )
5111119  E. Clint Williamson (8/15/1884 Limestone County, AL-
              ), m. Mable Connor
51111191  Ray Williamson
51111192  Fay Williamson
51111193  Buck Williamson, m. Janie
511112  William H. Hatchett (9/15/1853-2/14/1891), m. Sallie W.
          Groomes
511113  James T. Hatchett (5/27/1855-    )
511114  Mary Jane Hatchett (2/12/1857-5/2/1896), m. Alpheus
          Alcuin Poole. Both bur. Hatchett Cemetery along with
          following sons.
5111141  Alvan D. Poole (d. infancy)
5111142  Alpheus A.B. Poole (d. age 23)
511115  Martha E. Hatchett (3/9/1860-2/17/1861)
511116  Jeff Davison Hatchett (11/15/1861 Limestone County, AL-
          7/ /1936), m. 12/12/1881, Lura Mary Williamson
          (10/2/1861-10/2/1895), dau. of William ("Billy") Turner
          and Martha E.              Williamson.
5111161  Roston Hatchett, m. Mollie Gatlin of Limestone County,
          AL
51111611  Lila Hatchett (b. Limestone County, AL-    )
51111612  Lara Hatchett (b. Limestone County, AL-    )
51111613  Reed Hatchett (b. Limestone County, AL-    )
5111162  Holden Hatchett, m. Ann Buckner
51111621  Edna Hatchett (raised in OK)
51111622  Bulah Hatchett, m.              Bull. OK
51111623  Chamoa Hatchett. Lives in OK
51111624  Lillie Bell Hatchett (         -d. CA)
5111163  Fortune Hatchett, m. (1st) Maggie ("Mag") Williamson
          (12/30/1882-3/8/1912) (bur. Hatchett Cemetery,
          Limestone County, AL). M. (2nd) Mary Coggins. Both
          killed in auto accident in OK.
    Children by first wife:
5111631  Ava Hatchett. OK
51111632  Loyal Hatchett (10/12/1911-2/28/1912) (bur. Hatchett
          Cemetery, Limestone County, AL
    Children by second wife:
5111633  Charles Hatchett, m. OK
51111634  Gertrue Hatchett
51111635  Frances Hatchett
5111636  Jerrell Hatchett (Killed in same auto accident as
          parents in OK).
5111164  Illene Hatchett, m. Louis Medlock. Lived near Fayetts-
          ville, TN
51111641  Verna Medlock (b. Limestone County, AL-    ). Lives
          in TX
51111642  Layeuna Medlock (d. infancy Athens, AL)
51111643  Woodard Medlock (was in TN)
51111644  Mary Medlock (b. TN-    ). Lives in TN
51111645  Roberta Medlock, m.              Dunnian
```

51111646 Frank Medlock (b. TN-   )
51111647 Lois Medlock (-d. Cullman, AL)
5111165   Emmett Earl Hatchett (1/23/1880-2/ /1976), m. 11/24/
          1910, Effie Lee Renegar (6/13/1893-12/16/1984), dau.
          of Benton and Louella Sheriff Renegar.
51111651 Geneva Luraleen Hatchett (7/24/1918 Harvest, Madison
          County, AL-   ), m. 12/25/1937, J. B. Raby (3/22/
          1917-10/28/1963 (b. and d. Limestone County, AL),
          son of Tommy Morris and Myrtle Cook Raby.
511116511 Tommy Raby, Sr. (8/23/1940 Madison County, AL-   ),
          m. Patsy Sharp (3/3/1942 Hazel Green, Madison
          County, AL-   ), dau. of Herby E. and Edna League
          Sharp.
5111165111 Tommy Raby, Jr. (7/8/1962 Madison County, AL-   ), m.
          Paula Franklin (8/20/1962 Madison County, AL-   ),
          dau. of Wayne and Shirley White Franklin.
51111651111 Ben Raby (1/31/1987 Madison County, AL-   )
51111651112 Kayla Brook Raby (11/10/1989 Madison County, AL-   )
)
511116512 Johnny Raby (11/5/1948 Madison County, AL-   ), m.
          Barbara Young (12/14/1952 Toney, Madison County,
          AL-   ), dau. of Howard and Linnie May Goodson
          Young.
5111165121 Angie Raby (8/22/1973 Madison County, AL-   )
5111165122 Beth Raby (6/13/1976 Madison County, AL-   )
51111652 Edsel E. Hatchett (9/15/1926 Madison County, AL-   ),
          m. 6/17/1950, Margie Barnett (2/12/1929 Lexington,
          AL-   ), dau. of Audie and Minnie Barnett.
511116521 Dennis Hatchett (1/22/1954 Decatur, AL-   ), m.
          Libby Melvin (2/1/1954-   ), dau. of John K. and
          Thelma   Melvin.
5111165211 Wesley Hatchett (2/6/1982-   )
5111165212 Daryl Hatchett (8/14/1984-   )
511116522 Randy Hatchett (7/29/1955 Decatur, AL-   ) (twin), m.
          5/20/1977, Sherry Bryson
5111165221 Robbie Hatchett (11/30/1981-   )
5111165222 Stephen Hatchett (11/25/1985-   )
511116523 Ronnie Hatchett (7/29/1955 Decatur, AL-   ) (twin), m.
          8/17/1974, Stephenie Cantrell, dau. of Eddie and
          Nancy   Cantrell.
5111165231 Katy Hatchett (11/1/1979-   )
5111165232 Claire Hatchett (6/12/1985-   )
511116524 Jan Hatchett (11/5/1959 Decatur, AL-   ), m. 8/18/
          1979 Byran King (3/7/1957-   ), son of Redmon and
          Beverly   King.
5111165241 Charla King (7/26/1982 TN-   )
5111165242 Kevin King (1/11/1986 TN-   )
5111165243 Rachel King (6/18/1988 TN-   )
5111165244 Jason King (4/9/1991 TN-   )
5111166   Owen Jefferson Hatchett (7/24/1884-   ), m. Margie
          McKee (5/13/1890-   )
51111661 Virginia Hatchett (12/8/1917 Limestone County, AL-
          8/9/1995), m. Andie Michael
511116611 Joyce Michael (9/5/1939-   ), m. Elma Heard

511116612 Bobby Michael (8/19/1940- / /1992 Limestone County, AL)

511116613 Reba Michael (9/2/1941-   )

511116614 Billy Michael (11/7/1946 Limestone County, AL-   )

51111662 O. J. Hatchett, m. Elizabeth Pettigue

511116621 Kathy Hatchett (b. Huntsville, AL-   )

511116622 Lisa Hatchett (b. Huntsville, AL-   )

511116623 Sametha Hatchett (b. Huntsville, AL-   )

51111663 Dillard Hatchett, m. Avis Hovis

511116631 Debby Hatchett (b. Huntsville, AL-   )

511116632 Ginger Hatchett, m.   Bandarnt

511116633 J. D. Hatchett. Lives Huntsville, AL

511116634 Keth Hatchett (b. Madison County, AL)

5111167 Clifton Hatchett, m. Limestone County, AL, Minnie Johnson

51111671 Kathleen Hatchett, m. Johnson Wyatte. Lives in Huntsville, AL.

51111672 Billie Hatchett, m. William Cloud

5111168 John Oscar Hatchett (10/16/1891-7/2/1892)

5111169 Louie Hatchett (9/23/1895-10/6/1895). He died just two weeks after his mother Lura Mary Williamson Hatchett died.

511117 Elmiry A. Hatchett (9/18/1863-   )

511118 Amanda Susan Hatchett (4/25/1865-3/23/1907) (bur. Hatchett Cemetery), m. C. T. Newby

5111181 Lilla Odessa Newby (9/28/1899-5/9/1901). Bur. Hatchett Cemetery.

511119 Edward Lee Hatchett (9/1/1897 Wooley Springs, Limestone County, AL-9/13/1939 Sulphur Springs, TX), m. (1st) 9/8/1884, Mary Susan Bridges (7/1/1868 Limestone County, AL-3/29/1927 Sulphur Springs, TX), dau. of Russell and Mary Elizabeth Poston Bridges. M. (2nd) 1/29/1928, Mrs. Mary Arnold (-1944). Edward Lee and Mary Susan Hatchett are bur. City Cemetery, Sulphur Springs, TX.

   Children by first wife:

5111191 Mary Alice Hatchett (8/31/1885-10/27/1943), m. 8/16/1909, Clyde Sharp

51111911 Ralph Cleburn Sharp

51111912 Child (died infancy)

5111192 Ethel Sophrona Hatchett (10/19/1887 AL-8/25/1984 Sulphur Springs, TX), m. (1st) 12/18/1907, Marvin Kavanaw Norris (11/15/1881 KY-1912 or 1913 Sulphur Springs, TX). M. (2nd) 12/15/1919, Macon Oscar Williamson (b. AL-2/11/1971 Sulphur Springs, TX)

51111921 Velma Odell Norris (3/19/1909 Independence Community, Hopkins County, TX-   ), m. 9/22/1928, Delbert Riley Spencer (11/1/1907 Birthright, TX-2/13/1978 Sulphur Springs, TX), son of Arthur B. and Pearl Ellen McCauley Spencer.

511119211 Donald Gene Spencer (10/15/1932 Sulphur Springs, TX-   ), m. 6/22/1958, Martha Jo Walker (5/25/1938 Greenview, TX-   ), dau. of Wilbur Truitt and Bessie May Boren Walker.

5111192111   Donna Kay Spencer (6/29/1958 Sulphur Springs, TX-
             ), m. 10/10/1976, Ronald Gene McQueen (12/17/
             1955 Sulphur Springs, TX-   ), son of Luther
             and Effie Juanita Moore McQueen.
51111921111 Chandra Kay McQueen (12/23/1981 Sulphur Springs, TX-
)
51111921112 Spencer Gene McQueen (11/12/1987 Sulphur Springs,
             TX-   )
5111192112   Sharon Denise Spencer (6/26/1962 Sulphur Springs,
             TX-   ), m. 4/21/1979, Gregory Scott Ferguson
             (12/6/1961 Cancel Grove, KS-   ), son of Scott
             Clinton and Ella Mae Stanford Ferguson.
51111921121 Candace Michelle Ferguson (11/21/1979 Sulphur
             Springs, TX-   )
51111921122 Logan Zachary Ferguson (4/29/1987 Sulphur Springs,
             TX-   )
511119212   Grace Evelyn Spencer (9/8/1939 Sulphur Springs, TX-
             ), m. 5/8/1959, Charles Wilford Murray
             (11/10/1937 Peerless, TX-   ), son of Wilford
             Earl and Bonnie Eugene Bain Murray.
5111192121   Lana Elaine Murray (3/8/1963 Sulphur Springs, TX-
             ), m. 11/21/1981, Jeffery Frank Caldwell (7/8/
             1961 Houston, TX-   ), son of Howard Franklin
             and Jo Ann Dotson Caldwell.
51111921211 Brandon Jeff Caldwell (7/6/1983 Sulphur Springs,
             TX-   )
51111921212 Blake Lane Caldwell (7/3/1986 Sulphur Springs, TX-
)
51111921213 Kayla Elaine Caldwell (7/21/1988 Sulphur Springs,
             TX-   )
5111192122   Larry Charles Murray (11/16/1965 Sulphur Springs,
             TX-   )
5111193   Thomas Russell Hatchett (12/31/1888-12/10/1918, m. 7/4/
             1909, Gay Sharp
51111931   Austin Hatchett
51111932   Alvin Hatchett
51111933   Dau. (died infancy)
5111194   Amanda Lenora Hatchett (10/13/1890-1/19/1985), m. 12/13/
             1908, Curg Sharp (-6/6/1974)
51111941   Elvin Leon Sharp
51111942   Marlin Wilson Sharp
51111943   Carl Wallace Sharp
51111944   Mildred Jauhnita Sharp
51111945   Mary Ruth Sharp
51111946   Fana Roberta Sharp
5111195   John Edwin Hatchett (12/1/1892-12/20/1980), m. 11/12/
             1912, Bamma Chaney
51111951   John Edwin Hatchett, Jr.
51111952   Olita Farice Hatchett
51111953   Modena Estelle Hatchett
51111954   Helen Frances Hatchett
51111955   Neva Beth Hatchett
5111196   Lillian Lee Hatchett (8/16/1894-3/25/1895)
5111197   Charley Sanford Hatchett (2/13/1896-10/30/1900)

5111198 Elbert Lee Hatchett (1/28/1898-11/7/1969), m. 10/13/
        1918, Rosa Hargrave (-11/20/1961)
51111981 Sophrona Nadine Hatchett
51111982 Harlin Oswald Hatchett
51111983 Child (d. infancy)
5111199 Lester Dillard Hatchett (5/14/1900-3/11/1916)
511119x Clarence Earl Hatchett (1/26/1902-4/21/1985), m. (1st)
        1/3/1923, Pauline Felton. M. (2nd) 8/31/1924, Thelma
        Scarborough (-10/ /1990)
511119x1 Mildred Louise Hatchett
511119x2 Gerald Wayne Hatchett
511119a Morris Clinton Hatchett (2/26/1904-4/10/1975), m. (1st)
        1/1/1922, Geraldine Henry. M. (2nd) Dorothy Grace
        Marion. M. (3rd) 6/4/1961, Lera Faye Jackson
511119a1 Ladelle Mary Hatchett
511119a2 Morris Clinton Hatchett, Jr.
511119b Velma Nelcine Hatchett (4/2/1907-1/7/1908)
511119c Arvie Alsy Hatchett (7/9/1911-   ), m. 9/10/1960,
        Erna Agusta Augh
51111x John C. Hatchett (3/22/1881-10/9/1939)
51112 Thomas Eldridge (b. AL was 18 in 12/10/1850 Census)
51113 James Eldridge (b. AL was 16 in 12/10/1850 Census)
51114 John Eldridge (b. AL was 10 in 12/10/1850 Census)

514   John Rolfe Bolling Eldridge. In about 1808, as a pioneer,
      he moved to Madison County, Alabama as did John Peyton
      Powell.
5141   William Heathe Eldridge (b. 1809) b. Huntsville, d.
      Nashville, probably lived in Aiken, S.C. at one point.
      Trained as a doctor in Philadelphia. M. in about 1845
      Mary Jay, the dau. of a U.S. Navy Admiral. William is
      buried in Annapolis.
51411 Bogardus Eldridge (d. 1899). Captain in U.S. Army and
      died in action in the Philippean Islands.
514111 W. Heathe Eldridge (b. 1880), m. Millicent Harris. He
      lived in Nutley, NJ in 1940.
5142   John Miller Eldridge (6/10/1810-3/19/1901) b. Powhatan
      County, d. Huntsville, AL, m. Alabama 2/4/1835, Frances
      M. A. C. Powell (2/14/1808-7/23/1887), b. Powhatan
      County, d. Madison County, AL.
51421 John Rolfe Eldridge (1839-3/25/1862). CSA 4th Alabama
      Infantry. Died of disease in Fredericksburg, VA.
51422 Sarah J. Eldridge (b. about 2/ /1840) b. and d. in
      Huntsville, m. 4/3/1861 Albert Jones (b. about 10/ /
      1836 in Virginia)
51423 Mary ("Mattie") J. Eldridge (b. about 12/ /1843) b. and
      d. in Huntsville, m. 4/12/1877 G. Newman Jones (d.
      before 1900)
         Adopted Florence Jones (1880-   )
51424 William Benjamin Eldridge (7/1/1844-7/11/1900) b. and d.
      in Huntsville, m. 3/10/1870 Sallie L. Wilburn (5/9/1849
      Texas-3/24/1922). CSA Alabama Cavalry 1862-1864 where
      he was captured.

514241   Fannie May Eldridge (1/24/1871-d. about 1945) b. and d.
          in Huntsville, m. about 1895 William Powers Darwin
          (about 1865-about 1945) b. and d. in Huntsville.
5142411 Sallie May Darwin (b. about 1900) b. Huntsville, m.
          about 1923 Charles Tannock Landman (b. about 9/ /
          1892)
51424111 Sara Landman (b. 3/18/1926 in Huntsville), m. Thomas
           Jerome Whitworth
514241111 Thomas Jerome Whitworth, Jr. (b. about 1952)
514241112 Charles Darwin Whitworth (5/7/1955), m. (1st) Atlanta
           3/15/1980 Kimberly Leigh Allen (6/11/1957-   ).
           Div. M. (2nd) Huntsville 11/14/1993 Sherry Lynn
           Sampson (3/17/1964-   )
5142411121 Alison Lynn Whitworth (4/29/1981-   ) b. Nashville
5142411122 Chase Allen Whitworth (12/8/1982-   ) b. Huntsville
5142411123 Mark Thomas Whitworth (10/29/1984-   ) b. Huntsville
5142411124 Chad Clayton Whitworth (11/18/1986-   ) b. Hunts-
            ville
     Child by second wife:
5142411125 Taylor Elizabeth Whitworth (5/25/1995-   ) b. Hunts-
            ville
514242   George Wilburn Eldridge (8/17/1873-6/29/1949) b. Hunts-
          ville, d. Oklahoma City, m. Huntsville about 1898 Helen
          Merle Moore (12/24/1875-1/14/1961)

5142421 Eva Merle Eldridge (11/24/1899-1/4/1924) b. Huntsville,
          d. Oklahoma City, m. Howard Paul Harrison
51424211 Howard William Harrison (9/10/1923-   ) b. Oklahoma
           City
5142422 William B. Eldridge (2/18/1902-3/26/1979) b. Huntsville,
          d. Luther, OK, m. (1st) Oklahoma City about 1926 Ruby
          Evelyn Drawver (10/10/1904-3/20/1969) d. Luther, OK,
          m. (2nd) Dorsie Cox
51424221 Dexter Charles Eldridge (3/24/1930-2/3/1960) b. Luther,
           OK, m. Oklahoma City about 1956 Margaret Jones (about
           1931-   )
514242211 William Brandt Eldridge (5/26/1957-   ), m. 5/21/1976
            Seree Sims (7/8/1958-   ). Oklahoma City
     Children born in Oklahoma City:
5142422111 William Erik Eldridge (11/30/1976-   )
5142422112 Emily Ann Eldridge (3/12/1978-   )
5142422113 Charles Ryan Eldridge (10/4/1984-   )
514242212 Stuart Reid Eldridge, m. 8/23/1991 Lori Sanders (4/17/
            1972-   ). Div. He, an Oklahoma City fireman,
            helped remove the living and retrieve the dead from
            the Oklahoma City bombing.
5142422121 Mitchell Reid Eldridge (4/6/1992-   )
514242421 Irene Agatha Eldridge (2/5/1904-11/24/1983) b. Hunts-
          ville, d. Oklahoma City, m. Edward Kenney
51424231 Edward F. Kenney, Jr. (about 1924-   ), m. 1948
           Barbara Jean Rowland (1928-   ) b. Kansas City
514242311 Michael Edward Kenney (1951-1993) b. Oklahoma City, d.
            Dallas
514242312 Stephen O'Neal Kenney (1953-   ) b. Oklahoma City

514242313   Susan Lee Kenney (1956-   ) b. Denver
5142424   Helen Eldridge (8/20/1908-3/23/1987) b. Huntsville, d.
          Norman, OK, m. Robert Steele
51424241   Robert Steele, Jr. (7/4/1936-   ), m. Oklahoma City
          9/10/1960 Sharon Cox McGhee
514242411   Tracy Lynn Steele (1961-   )
514242412   Randall Scott Steele (1966-   )
51424242   James Steele (12/29/1938-3/7/1978) b. Oklahoma City, d.
          Dayton, m. Andarko, OK 6/2/1963 Kathryn Elizabeth
          ("Betsy") Duford (1941-   )
514242421   Patricia Elise Steele (1969-   )
514242422   David O'Neal Steele (1972-   )
5142425   George Wilburn Eldridge (9/13/1906-3/6/1940) b. Hunts-
          ville, d. Oklahoma City
5142426   Henry O'Neal Eldridge (10/12/1914-1/6/1984) b. and d.
          Oklahoma City, m. 6/8/1938 Beatrice Spivey (4/13/1918-
) b. Oklahoma City
514243   Annie Irene Eldridge (1/1/1875-6/5/1908) b. Huntsville,
          d. Memphis, m. Huntsville about 1897 Thomas Forsey
          Lansden (1867-   )
5142431   Lucien Eldridge Lansden (6/22/1899-10/4/1965) b. Hunts-
          ville, d. Oklahoma City, m. Oklahoma City about 1922
          Ella Mae Leach (about 1902-12/4/1945) b. Spencer, OK,
          d. Oklahoma City
51424311   Lucien Eldridge Lansden, Jr. (4/5/1926-   ) b.
          Oklahoma City, m. Oklahoma City 8/ /1947 Beverly
          Williams (9/3/1928-1/3/1996) d. Wetumka, OK
          Adopted:
              Christopher Lansden (3/7/1954-   )
              Jill Lansden (7/7/1955-   ), m. 11/7/1983
              Lee Wilson (11/13/1957-   ) b. Tulsa
514243111   Mary Lansden (5/3/1957-   ) b. Oklahoma City, m.
          Oklahoma City 8/4/1978 David Swafford (4/2/1957-
)
5142431111   Shannon Leigh Swafford (8/2/1983-   )
5142431112   Sally Jane Swafford (2/26/1986-   )
514243112   Sara Eldridge Lansden (10/10/1962-   ) b. Oklahoma
          City, m. Alhambra, CA 6/28/1992 Timothy Gurley
          (12/25/1956-   )
5142431121   Samuel Eldridge Gurley (1/14/1993-   ) b. Alhambra,
          CA
514243113   Martha Ann Lansden (2/25/1969-   ) b. Oklahoma City,
          m. 1/18/1992 Robert Davidson (10/26/1957-   )
5142431131   Patrick Ryan Davidson (1/4/1995-   ) b. Columbia,
          MO
51424312   Catherine Lansden (6/18/1930-   ) b. Oklahoma City,
          m. Dallas 7/12/1952 Clarence Travis Rattan (11/7/
          1930-   )
514243121   Carol Rattan (9/7/1953-   ) b. Salzburg, Austria, m.
          Dallas 8/25/1973 Kenneth Ray Green (1949-   ). Div.
5142431211   Kendra Michelle Green (9/13/1976-   ) b. Denton, TX
5142431212   Christopher Scott Green (8/11/1978-   ) b. Denton, TX
514243122   Cynthia Rattan (10/7/1955-   ) b. Dallas

514243123 Constance Rattan (10/23/1960-   ) b. Anniston, AL
           m. Arlington, VA 3/1/1986 Terry Ashton Hunter (8/ /
           1955-   )
5142432 Thomas Forsey Lansden, Jr. (10/5/1900-about 1976) b.
         Tuscumbia, AL, d. Enid, OK, m. 1927 Gladys Campbell
         (3/11/1904-7/21/1956) b. Holdenville, OK, d. Enid, OK
51424321 Louise Lansden (11/26/1935-2/14/1967), m. Lyle Dill
          b. Albuquerque, NM
514243211 Thomas Lyle Dill (1965-   )
51424322 Dorothy Jane Lansden (11/8/1938-   ) b. Oklahoma City,
          m. Lakewood, CO 7/8/1961 Kenneth Richard Dinkel
          (4/21/1937-   ) b. Ellis, KS
514243221 Kent Douglas Dinkel (4/6/1962-   ) b. Denver, m.
           Vicky Moore (4/7/1972-   )
514243222 Beverly Marie Dinkel (4/16/1965-   ) b. Denver, m.
           Lakewood, CO 8/9/1985 Collins Frank Sanders
5142432221 Alexandra Marie Sanders (8/11/1986-   ) b. Modesto,
            CA
5142432222 Dillon Christopher Sanders (6/24/1988-   ) b.
            Modesto, CA
5142432223 Evangella Louise Sanders (2/2/1990-   ) b. Modesto,
            CA
51424323 Thomas John Lansden (3/19/1941-   ) b. Wichita Falls,
          TX, m. Wichita Falls, TX 3/19/1965 Patricia Ann Bates
          (12/12/1944-   ). Div.
514243231 Natalie Paige Lansden (4/17/1967-   ) b. Wichita
           Falls, TX, m. Brent Kutach b. Franklin, TN
514243232 Jennifer Jill Lansden (4/30/1973-   ) b. Wichita
           Falls, TX
5142433 Wyche Wilburn Lansden (4/18/1907-1970) b. and d. Hunts-
         ville, AL
514244 John Rolfe Eldridge (11/11/1879-3/31/1959) b. Huntsville,
        d. Oklahoma City, m. Eufala, OK 9/9/1905 Maude Elvira
        Lindbloom (10/10/1885-1/3/1962) b. McPherson, KS, d.
        Bethany, OK, dau. of David Edward and Charotta Johanna
        Lindbloom
5142441 Juanita Eldridge (8/8/1906-2/14/1982) b. Oklahoma City,
         d. San Antonio
5142442 Edwin David Eldridge (1/18/1913-   ) b. Oklahoma City,
         m. Wewoka, OK 6/10/1933 LaVenia Mozelle Tarlton (12/
         12/1914-   ) b. Sentinel, OK
51424421 Billie Neal Eldridge (5/15/1934-   ) b. Oklahoma City,
          m. (1st) Bethany, OK 6/18/1952 Richard Riddell Riggs
          (1/21/1934-1/7/1987) b. and d. Bethany, OK. M. (2nd)
          Bethany, OK 9/22/1990 Bobby Joe Haxell (2/14/1933-
) b. Purcell, OK
514244211 Julie Annette Riggs (9/18/1954-   ) b. Oklahoma City,
           m. Oklahoma City 11/22/1975 Jackie Ray Jackson
           (8/7/1952-   )
5142442111 Bennett Riddell Jackson (7/4/1979-   ) b. Bartles-
            ville, OK
5142442112 Brandon Ray Jackson (8/14/1981-   ) b. Bartlesville,
            OK
5142442113 Brett Russell Jackson (6/13/1985-   )

514244212 Richard Dale Riggs (10/25/1956-   ) b. Oklahoma City,
           m. (1st) Bethany, OK 8/1/1958 Kelly Bullard (8/ /
           1958-   ) b. Bethany, OK. Div. M. (2nd) Bethany,
           OK 5/16/1995 Denise Annette Sillivan (12/10/1956-
) b. Albuquerque
    Children by first wife:
5142442121 Cory Elizabeth Riggs (7/7/1985-   )
5142442122 Rachel Alison Riggs (7/26/1987-   )
514244213 Kris Alan Riggs (7/2/1962-   ) b. Oklahoma City, m.
           Bethany, OK 7/16/1989 Shelley Elaine Douglas (8/12/
           1969-   )
514244214 Carla Dell Riggs (7/22/1965-   ) b. Oklahoma City, m.
           Bethany, OK 9/10/1983 Donald Keith Owens (1/24/1963-
) b. Oklahoma City
5142442141 Janae Dawn Owens (10/10/1980-   )
5142442142 Joey Dell Owens (4/22/1989-   ) b. Bethany, OK
5142442143 Jill Dean Owens (8/26/1993-   )
51424422 Edwin David Eldridge, Jr. (7/29/1943-   ) b. Oklahoma
          City, m. (1st) Waureka, OK 2/4/1964 Deotta Pool
          (5/23/1947-   ) b. Oklahoma. Div. M. (2nd) 9/4/
          1976 Charlette ("Schatzie") Hale (1947-   )
514244221 Maribeth Eldridge (10/23/1965-   ) b. Wichita Falls,
           TX, m.   Cook
5142442211 Taylor Cook (about 1990-   )
514244222 Lauri Dee Eldridge (4/6/1967-   ) b. Fort Worth, TX,
           m.   Tillinghast
5142442221 Cameron Tillinghast (about 1991-   )
5142442222 Tanner Tillinghast (about 1992-   )
    Adopted (by 51424422):
      David Cameron Eldridge (7/4/1970-   ) b. Fort Worth
5142443 John Rolfe Eldridge, Jr. (3/29/1925-   ) b. Oklahoma
         City, m. (1st) Oklahoma City 9/1/1945 Georgia Afton
         Hurt Kinzy (about 1926-   ). Div. M. (2nd) Orinda,
         CA 5/23/1953 Janice Carolyn Wickersham (7/1/1930-
         10/8/1990) b. Long Beach, CA, d. Arlington, VA. Div.
         M. (3rd) Silver Spring, MD 10/8/1989 Sandra Faye
         (4/22/1937-   ) b. Bronx, NY
    Children by second wife:
51424431 Jane Eldridge (9/15/1958-   ) b. Washington, DC, m.
          Alexandria, VA 9/29/1984 Christopher Ralph Brewster
          (6/30/1950-   ) b. Passaic, NJ
514244311 William Eldridge Brewster (6/6/1987-   ) b. Washing-
           ton, DC
514244312 Kathryn Barrett Brewster (9/30/1991-   ) b. Washing-
           ton, DC
51424432 Laura Eldridge (3/12/1961-   ) b. Washington, DC
51425 Pocahontas Eldridge (1845-5/3/1875) b. and d. in
       Huntsville
51426 Powell Eldridge (5/27/1853-6/13/1853) b. and d. Meridian-
       ville, AL

54 Judith Bolling Eldridge, m. James Boswell Ferguson
541 Maj. James Boswell Ferguson, Jr. (8/6/1780-1810?). Born
     at Osbornes, Chesterfield County. M. (1st) 6/10/1805

(by Rev. John Todd), Jane B. Payne Bolling (d. 2/12/1807
at "Fairfield"). M. (2nd) 8/18/1808 (by Rev. Conrad
Speece), Sarah ("Sally") Gay at "Dungeness", Goochland
County.
Note: Jane's sister married James Madison (Dolly Madison).
5411 Jane Elvira Bolling Ferguson (4/6/1806-9/8/1898), m. 1827,
        Peachy Ridgeway Gilmor Grattan (11/7/1801-9/8/1881).
        Reporter of the Court of Appeals ("The Grattan Report").

54112 Sallie Gay Grattan. Twin of 54113. M. 6/24/1874 Otho G.
        Kean
541121 Elvira Grattan Kean (7/8/1875-8/24/1895). No issue
541122 William Gilmer Kean (9/20/1877-8/18/1943)
54113 Lucy Gilmer Grattan (d. 10/14/1899). Twin of 54112. M.
        1/6/1863, William Felix Alexander (5/7/1832-8/17/1907),
        son of Dr. Adam Leopold and Sarah Hillhouse Gilbert
        Alexander (10/23/1805-   ). Home: Augusta, GA.
        Lucy was William Felix Alexander's second wife. He
        graduated from Yale in 1851 and was a Major C.S.A. His
        brother, a West Pointer, was Edward Porter Alexander
        (5/26/1835-   ), Brig. Gen. C.S.A. Author of MILITARY
        MEMOIRS OF A CONFEDERATE. Lucy met William Felix while
        visiting the home of her kinsman, Governor Gilmer in
        Lexington, GA. Reproduction of portraits of Adam
        Leopold, Sarah and William Felix appear in THE ALEXANDER
        LETTERS.
541131 Jane Elvira ("Ella") Grattan Alexander (1/4/1869-1937),
        m. 11/12/1891, Edgeworth Bird Baxter (7/18/1868-1906),
        son of Richard Bolling and Kate Rucker Baxter.
        Edgeworth was appointed in the 1920's to two chairs
        at Princeton (Jurisprudence and Philosophy) by
        President Wilson.
5411311 Lucy ("Nanny") Alexander Baxter (3/15/1900-10/15/1993),
        m 1927, Hayden ("Breeze") Freeman (11/7/1901-1/3/
        1967), Col. U.S.M.C., son of Dean and Lena Hayden
        Freeman of Winthrope, MA. Died Moorehead City, NC.
        Buried Arlington
54113111 Ann Hayden Freeman (10/30/1927-   ) of Morro Bay, CA
54113112 Dean Giffin Freeman (11/12/1931-2/28/1995), m. 10/17/
        1953, Marilyn ("Mickey") Romieux. Residence:
        Lynchburg.
541131121 Michael Dean Freeman (9/26/1954-   ), m. 1974,
        Jeannie Marie Kirkman. Residence: Williamsburg.
5411311211 Amanda ("Mandy") Marilyn Freeman (10/21/1977-   )
5411311212 Kirk Michael Freeman (10/3/1980-   )
541131122 Stephen Harry Freeman (1/13/1956-   ), m. Cynthia
        Scudder
5411311221 Amy Catherine Freeman (10/30/1988-   )
5411311222 Georgia Helen Freeman (7/16/1990-   )
541131123 Jeanne Hayden Freeman (7/26/1957-   ), m. John Glover
5411311231 Jacob ("Jake") Freeman Glover (7/16/1990-   )
541131124 Joseph Kristin Freeman (4/11/1960-   ), m. Ann Morris
        Milliner
5411311241 Joseph Trevor Freeman (5/9/1987-   )

```
5411311242  Stewart Kristin Freeman (3/12/1990-   )
5411311243  Genevieve ("Genna") Scott Freeman (11/3/1992-   )
54113125    Phillip Giffin Freeman (7/17/1965-   ), m. Pamela
              Ajac
54113113    Lucy Grattan Alexander Freeman (6/26/1933-   ), m.
              (1st) 1954, John ("Jack") Thomas Skelly (6/1/1926-
                ), m. (2nd) 1974, Joseph E. Modrak (who had
              two children before his marriage to Lucy)
541131131   Ann Hayden Skelly (2/7/1955-   ). Born Alexandria.
              M. (1st) 1982, Mike Reed, m. (2nd) 1995, Don Rhodes
5411311311  Benjamin Skelly Reed (8/14/1984-   ). Born Spring-
              hill, MA
541131132   John Thomas Skelly, Jr. (2/2/1956-   ). Born Lake-
              land, FL. M. (1st) 1982, Cecilia Malmquist, m.
              (2nd) 1990, Maria Frederickson
541131133   Elizabeth ("Beth") Frances Bolling Skelly (5/18/1957-
                ). Born Washington, DC. Twin. M. 1982, Dr.
              Douglas James Borgman (7/3/1957-   ), son of Col.
              John and Patricia Ransom Borgman.
5411311331  Andrew Howard Weilgus (6/16/1978-   ). Born
              Washington, DC.
5411311332  Patrik Ransom Bolling Borgman (3/27/1983-   ). Born
              Austin.
5411311333  Douglas James ("Jamee") Bolling Borgman (1/8/1985-
                ). Born Austin.
5411311334  Marguerite ("Maggie") Colleen Skelly-Borgman (12/2/
              1988-   ). Born Austin.
541131134   Patricia Marie Ferguson Skelly (5/18/1957-   ). Born
              Washington, DC. Twin. M. 1981, Stephen T. Grove.
              Residence: Mt. Pelier, VT.
5411311341  Daniel Thor Grove (9/22/1981-   ). Born Portland, OR
5411411342  Eric Skelly Grove (10/7/1983-   ). Born Portland, OR
54113135    Christopher Martin Skelly (3/31/1959-   )
54113136    Lucy Bolling Alexander ("Rita") Skelly (7/5/1961-   )
              m. (1st) 1982, Luc Maranda, m. (2nd) 1993, Charlie
              Brown
5411311361  Jessee Roland Maranda (7/14/1987-   ). Born Ft.
              Lauderdale, FL
5411311362  Louis ("Louie") Jackson Maranda Brown (7/7/1994-   ).
              Born Burlington, VT.
541131137   Louis Joseph Skelly (2/16/1962-6/10/1991). Born and
              died Alexandria, VA.
5411312     Elvira ("Vera") Grattan Baxter (4/25/1903-3/19/1994).
              Born Augusta, GA. M. (1st) 1924, Julius Raiford
              Watkins, m. (2nd) Louis C. Fink
54113121    Baxter Raiford Watkins (11/17/1928-   ). Born
              Augusta, GA. M. Patricia Ann O'Brien. Residence:
              Ormand Beach, FL.
541131211   Catherine Mary Watkins (12/3/1956-   ), m. Paul Camp
541131212   Stephen Baxter Watkins (8/13/1958-   ), m. Helen
              Frank
5411312121  Stephen Baxter Watkins, Jr. (3/30/1993-   )
5411312122  Lauren Patrice Watkins (4/10/1996-   )
```

541131213 Nancy Patricia Watkins (8/20/1961-   ), m. Michael
           Brown
541131214 David Louis Watkins (8/26/1962-   ), m. Victoria
           Duvalde
5411312141 Sophia Danielle Watkins (1/26/1996-   )
541131215 Allen Raiford Watkins (3/21/1965-   )
541132 Peachy Ridgeway Grattan Alexander (lived a few months).
541133 Adam Leopold Alexander. Died at birth.
541134 George Grattan Alexander. Died at birth.

54116   James B. Ferguson Grattan (7/9/1829-lived only a few
        months).
54117   Mary Peachy Grattan (5/8/1831-1838)
54118   Jane Gay Grattan (11/16/1832-1838)
        Note: 54117 and 54118 died of scarlet fever.
54119   Robert R. Grattan (9/21/1835-1850?)
5411x   Lavinia Payne Grattan (8/7/1842-lived sixteen months).
5411a   Jane Elvira Grattan (3/31/1848-1854)
542 Jane Eldridge Ferguson (7/9/1778-12/11/1785). Chesterfield
     County.

562 Susanne Everard Eldridge, m. (2nd)
5621 Courtney T.

56344   Thomas Walker Eldridge (7/16/1868-7/17/1935), m. (1st)
        12/23/1899 Ruth Fore (7/23/1879-11/29/1905), m. (2nd)
        11/22/1906 Maude Maria ("Memeo") Fore (10/23/1873-1961)
        (sister to Ruth Fore).
    Children by first wife:
563441 Thomas Leslie Eldridge (8/23/1900-6/6/1977), m. Bessie
        Walters
5634411 Leslie Willard Eldridge, m. Myrtle Thomas
56344111 Constance Eldridge, m. E. G. Totty. Div. M. (2nd)
          Richard Hughes (died). M. (3rd) Jim Engle. No
          children by 2nd and 3rd husbands.
563441111 Scotty Totty
563441112 Kelly Noel Totty, m. David Revel
5634411121 Sarah Revel (6/9/1995-   )
56344112 Leslie Willard Eldridge, Jr., m. Frances
563441121 Emily Eldridge
5634412 Raymond Eugene Eldridge, m. Doris Seay
56344121 Cathy Eldridge
56344122 Laurie Lee Eldridge
56344123 Ronnie Eldridge
56344124 Randy Eldridge
563442 Margaret Amanda Eldridge (7/7/1902-7/26/1987), m. 3/30/
        1929 Harold Gilbert Gill (7/14/1887-11/17/1967)
5634421 Patricia Gilbert Gill (12/26/1937-1/28/1938)
5634422 Leslie Faye Eldridge Gill, m. (1st) 11/5/1960 George
         Oswald Bullis (d. 7/31/1963), m. (2nd) 2/7/1965 Donald
         Jeffery Harkey. Div. 2/22/1971. M. (3rd) 11/9/1972
         Bernard T. C. Purol. Div. 3/25/1977.
5634423 Cary Lynn Gill (2/24/1946-   )
    Children by second wife:

563443   David Ferdinand Eldridge (6/12/1909 Richmond-   ), m.
         Mattie Henley (11/3/1918 Richmond-   )
5634431 Diana Letitia Eldridge (11/29/1941-   ), m. 5/17/1958,
         Wesley Frederick Coleman (9/8/1938-   )
56344311 Mina Lynn Coleman (1/31/1959-   ), m.   Carpenter
563443111 Chad Coleman Carpenter (6/13/1990-   )
56344312 Wesley Frederick Coleman, Jr. (5/8/1960-   ), m.
         11/20/1989, Gema Elizabeth Campas (5/28/1970-   )
563443121 Wesley Frederick Coleman III (1/30/1993-   )
563444   James Oscar Eldridge (4/30/1913- Richmond 3/4/1993).
         Married three times. No children.

573 Martha ("Patsy") Rives, m. John Wilkinson, son of William
     and Elizabeth Stith Wilkinson. Elizabeth Stith was dau.
     of Drury Stith. (William Wilkinson father was John
     Wilkinson of Surry and his mother was Agnes Bolling
     Wilkinson of Charles City).

5735 Thomas Edward Wilkinson (10/27/1807-9/2/1859), m. Susan J.
     Wells (1821-7/15/1874), dau. of John and Elizabeth Wells
     of Petersburg, VA.
57351 William T. Wilkinson (1840-   ). Unm.
57352 George E. Wilkinson (1840-7/24/1889), a Civil War soldier,
      m. Roberta A. Harwell (1844-8/15/1874), dau. of Redmond
      Y. and Temperance Redding Cain Harwell of Prince George.
573521 Hattie A. Wilkinson (1840-1908), m. Arthur Dunn
573522 Thomas Redmond Wilkinson (11/17/1872-5/31/1917), m. Linda
       Harville Magee (6/20/1876-3/29/1958), dau. of William
       Ellison Magee of Prince George and Ann Lucas Leonard
       Magee of Sussex.
5735221 Winnie Magee Wilkinson (12/19/1901-10/22/1924). Unm.
5735222 Thomas Overton Wilkinson (10/1/1906-10/10/1941), m.
        Celia Rosi of Tarreytown, NY. No children.
5735223 George Carroll Wilkinson (8/9/1908-8/25/1993), m.
        Virginia Lee Cox (2/8/1908-10/22/1968), dau. of
        Eugene Lee Cox of Sussex and Alice Greenaway
        Goodwyn Cox of Dinwiddie.
57352231 George Carroll Wilkinson, Jr. (1/30/1937-   ), m.
         Margaret Anne ("Peggy") Capehart (8/5/1939-   ),
         dau. of Leroy Simpson Capehart of Bertie County, NC
         and Fairice Mary Smith Capehart of Norfolk County.
573522311 Cathryn Anne Wilkinson (9/17/1961-   ), m. Jade
          John Litcher (2/22/1961-   ) of North Carolina.
5735223111 Cameron Jaye Litcher (6/30/1994-   )
5735223112 Shane Wilkinson Litcher (6/30/1996-   )
573522312 Thomas Scott Wilkinson (8/31/1963-   ), m. Beth
          Allison Davis (10/25/1963-   ) of New York.
5735223121 Caroline Paige Wilkinson (3/9/1995-   )
57352232 Gene Cox Wilkinson (1/2/1945-   ). Unm.
5735224 William Redmond Wilkinson (5/24/1910-1/10/1970), m.
        Lucille Dempsey of New York. No children.
5735225 Ann Elizabeth Wilkinson (10/15/1912-   ), m. Edgar
        Claiborne Wilkinson (10/21/1916-1985). No children.

57353   Monroe Wilkinson (1843-   ), a Civil War soldier, m.
        Henrietta S. Daniel, dau. of William and E. Daniel of
        Prince George.
57354   James Wilkinson (1845-   )
57355   Robert William Wilkinson (1847-   ) (twin). M. Nora E.
        Wood, dau. of Albert and Henrietta J. Wood of Sussex.
57356   Susan Frances Wilkinson (1847-   ) (twin). Unm.
57357   Sarah J. Wilkinson (1851-   )
57358   Ann Elizabeth Wilkinson (1853-   ), m. John T. Brown

574566   Mary Arthur Rives (2/15/1889-7/14/1969), m. John George
          Mengel III (9/10/1889-11/27/1965)
5745661   John George Mengel IV (5/24/1912-11/7/1988, m. Ida
          Lucille Lane (1/7/1918-   )
57456611 John George Mengel V (7/28/1940-   ), m. Joan Travis
          Armistead (5/13/1941-   )
574566111 Caroyln Lane Mengel (3/18/1972-   ), m.   Simpson
57456612 Jacqueline Lane Mengel (9/16/1941-   ), m. (1st)
          Harry Culpen (11/26/1936-   ). M. (2nd) Wayne
          Dilks. M. (3rd) William Benjamin Duke, Jr. (6/5/
          1958-   )
574566121 Scott Simpson Culpen (11/20/1963-   ), m. Tammi
          Krupa
574566122 Christopher Rives Culpen (5/31/1966-   )
5745662   Arthur Williamson Mengel (6/29/1913-   ), (1st) m.
          Betty Lou Hedrick (9/23/1924-   ). M. (2nd) Ethel
          Virginia Brittingham (10/18/1915-12/2/1965)
57456621 Arthur Williamson Mengel, Jr. (8/21/1945-   )
57456622 William Brittingham Mengel (10/28/1950-   )
57456623 Robert Burke Rives Mengel (1/13/1953-   ), m. Randi
574566231 Burke Aaron Mengel (3/31/1987-   )
5745663   Mary Elizabeth Mengel (9/6/1915-10/15/1971), m. Harry
          Diggs Oliver, Jr. (6/6/1913-3/3/1986)
57456631 Mary Frances Oliver (b. and d. 4/3/1939)
57456632 Mary Frances Oliver (3/28/1940-   ), m. Larry Lambert
57456633 Harry Diggs Oliver III (8/23/1941-3/3/1986), m.
          Elizabeth
57456634 Elizabeth Ann Oliver (10/23/1943-   ), m. Larry H.
          Goff
574566341 Larry H. Goff II (10/14/1969-   )
574566342 Dana Ann Goff (9/3/1970-   )
57456635 Loretta Oliver (1/3/1945-   ), m. Michael Kenneth
          Butler
574566351 Amy Elizabeth Butler, m. Mark Joseph Kallenbach
574566352 Michael Kenneth Butler, Jr.
574566353 Mathew Brounley Butler
57456636 John Patton Oliver (4/3/1945-   ), m. (1st) Perry
          . M. (2nd) Dena Chesley Branch
574566361 Jacqueline Alexander Oliver (4/17/1992-   )
57456637 Theresa Martin Oliver (8/8/1947-1/7/1949)
57456638 Martin Vianey Oliver (7/26/1950-   ), m. Kay
          Edwards (8/27/1954-   )
574566381 Jonathan Edwards Oliver (12/14/1987-   )
574566382 Elizabeth Sterling Oliver (2/5/1992-   )

5745664 Anne Rives Mengel (6/27/1918-1/24/1992), m. Joseph
         Gerald Mullen, Jr. (7/20/1916-11/20/1990)
57456641 Joseph Gerald Mullen III (6/10/1942-   ), m. (1st)
         Linda   . M. (2nd) Mary Elizabeth Rice (4/27/
         1947-   )
574566411 Joseph Gerald Mullen IV (10/28/1972-   )
574566412 David Lloyd Mullen (7/23/1975-   )
57456642 Robert Rives Mullen (7/17/1946-   ), m. (1st)
         Kathleen Cordia Howard (7/11/1946-   ). M. (2nd)
         Sandra Elizabeth Farris (9/15/1942-   )
   Child by second wife:
574566421 Jennifer Anne Mullen (4/14/1982-   )
57456643 Michael Randolph Mullen (10/1/1951-   ), m. (1st)
         Cindy Lakey. M. (2nd) Cheryl Ann Garrison (3/10/
         1954-   )
   Child by first wife:
574566431 Sarah Mullen (4/ /1991-   )
   Children by second wife:
574566432 Elizabeth Rives Mullen (1/11/1971-   ), m. Charles
         Randall Womble (3/16/1968-   )
5745664321 Brandi Elizabeth Womble (2/15/1991-   )
574566433 Michael Scott Mullen (5/7/1976-   )

5745665 Margaret Hall Mengel (9/29/1921-   ), m. John Gilbert
         Grubb, Jr. (4/28/1925-11/5/1983)
57456651 John Gilbert Grubb III (12/3/1961-   ), m. Elisa Ann
         Bermudez (10/31/1960-   )

61111 William Murray Robinson. Changed his name.

6131 Rebecca Bolling Murray

623111 Jean Ruffin Robertson, m. Captain Adams at Port Lavaca, TX
        (d. 1853 of yellow fever). He was private secretary to
        Sam Houston.

62311114 Lillian Evelyn Dobbins, m. Jackson Chadwick Minge (d.
            4/11/1908).
62311115 Olive Hill Dobbins, m. Charles Hatcher. No issue.
6231112 Willie Georgine Adams, m. Capt. Lemuel Durant Hatch, a
          widower. No issue. Home: Perdido Beach, AL

623114 Elizabeth Royal Robertson, m. Joseph Asbury Groves, M.D.
          Surgeon in the Battle of Atlanta.

623116 Anne Eliza Robertson (d. 11/17/1911), m. Thomas Moseby
          Cunningham (d. 5/15/1877)
6231161 Mary Lee Cunningham (d. 10/6/1908), m. Peter Conrey
          James (3/14/1846-8/28/1888). No issue.
6231162 Eliza Cunningham (d. 1885), m. Eyre Damer (1854-1922)

6231163 Annie Bondurant Cunningham (d. 1919)
6231164 George Adams Cunningham , m. Mary Gilliard Pickens
          (1/23/1866-9/26/1949). Granddaughter of Alabama
          Governor Pickens.

6231166 Carrie Shields Cunningham (ca. 1871 or 1872?), m. 12/1/
          1891, Dallas County, AL, Benjamin Diggs

623116x William Gordon Cunningham (d. 1918)

62312 Ann Cocke, m. Sterling Edmunds
623121 Emmett Edmunds, m. Amanda McNeal
6231211 Louisa Edmunds
6231212 Irby Edmunds

63 Anne Bolling Murray (1746-   ) of Moss, m. Neil Buchanan
      (1733-1777) of Auchentoshan, an estate a mile to the west
      of Old Kilpatrick, Dumbartonshire, Scotland. Two daughters
      were baptised at Old Kilpatrick.
            Moss of the family of Buchanan, the poet and
            historian. Auchentoshan of the family of
            Hamilton, the first of whom was Andrew of
            Cochna, Provost of Glasgow and Governor of
            Dumbarton Castle for Mary Queen of Scots.
631 Ann Bolling Buchanan (2/16/1774-   ). After the death of
      her sister, Mary, she became sole heiress of Auchentoshan.
      M. 10/25/1793 in Glasgow William Cross (originally Course)
      (1763-1813), merchant of Glasgow. Ref: Alexander
      Henderson, AUSTRALIAN FAMILIES (1941) 127.
            Children: all baptised at Old Kilpatrick.

6311 Anna Cross (9/10/1794-   ), bapt. 10/8/1794, m. in Glasgow
      4/18/1814 Robert Yuille (2/30/1777-   ) of the Darleith
      family. Ref: Henderson
          Yuille, son of George Yuille of Farleith and Margaret
      Murdock. A merchant in Glasgow. Admitted 4/14/1808 as
      a Burgess and Guild Bother. Ref: BURGESSES & GUILD
      BRETHEREN OF GLASGOW (1751-1846) 250.
          Children: all baptised at Glasgow.
63111 Ann Bollingbroke Buchanan Yuille (4/25/1815-   )
63112 Margaret Murdock Yuille (7/17/1816-   ), m. 4/2/1833
      Robert Strang
63113 George Yuille (11/4/1817-   )
63114 William Cross Yuille (3/28/1819-   ). Born at Cardross,
      Dumbartonshire. Ref: Henderson. Educated in Glasgow.
      Apprentice in the West India house of James Ewing & Co.
      Emigrated to Australia at the age of seventeen.
      Prominent in Victoria as a pastoralist and was one of
      the principal breeders of rams. A turf expert and
      bloodstock agent. Founded the Australian Stud Book.
      M. in Melbourne, Victoria 7/7/1842 Mary Denny (1824-   )
      who was born in Glasgow, Scotland, dau. of James
      Oliphant Denny and Bertha Adam.
631141 Betsy ("Bessie") Yuille (4/14/1843-12/27/1907). Born at
      Rockbank, the family property north of Melbourne. M.
      at Charlotte Plains at Carisbrook, Victoria (her
      residence) 8/7/1862 Matthew Bryant, "Squatter" (age 33,
      residing at Cairn Curran). Ref: Marriage certificate.
      He died 7/3/1886 at Winter's Flat, Castlemaine,
      Victoria following an accident. She died of breast
      cancer in Melbourne, Victoria.
6311411 William Cross Yuille Bryant (1863-   ). Born Melbourne
      (VIC DMN index). Pastoralist and racehorse owner.
      Died unm. (Henderson)
6311412 Jane Elsie Bryant (1865-1919). Born Cairn Curran (VIC
      BDM index). M. W. Ley (Lee ?) Grantham. Died at
      Rutherglen (Henderson). Had six sons and four
      daughters.
63114121
63114122
63114123
63114124
63114125
63114126
63114127
63114128
63114129
6311412x
6311413 Mary ("May") Elizabeth Bryant (1866-1/16/1939). Born
      at Cairn Curran (VIC BDM index). Educated at Rothwell
      Girls School, St. Kilda. M. Hector Norman Simson
      Hewitt. Died at Malvern, Melbourne. (Henderson).
      Had three sons and one daughter.
63114131
63114132

63114133
63114134
6311414 Annie ("Nanny Puss") Bryant (1867-1945). Born at Cairn
         Curran (VIC BDM index). M. at St. Columb's Church of
         England, Hawthorne, Melbourne, 11/30/1916 (LDG family
         Bible) (as his second wife) Llewellyn Downes Griffith.
         No children.
6311415 Felicia Marion Victoria Bryant (5/25/1869-11/28/1914).
         Born at Cairn Curran (birth certificate). M. 9/3/1890
         at St. Mary's Church of England, Caulfield, Melbourne,
         Llewellyn Downes Griffith (11/4/1859-   ). She is
         buried at Brighton General Cemetery, Melbourne (LDG
         family Bible). He was son of Arthur Hill Griffith
         and Hannah Rose Cottingham and was born at 14 Russell
         Street, Dublin, Ireland, the home of his mother's
         parents James Courtney Cottingham and Hannah Robinson.
             Children, all except the last, were christened at
         St. Mary's, Caulfield, by Rev. H. B. Macartney, Dean
         of Melbourne.
63114151 Maurice Edmund de Burgh Griffith (6/6/1891-1/25/1964).
         Born in the residence at Melbourne Savings Bank,
         Windsor, Praham, where his father was manager. M.
         (1st) 2/24/1919 Marie Yorstoun Kennedy Stuart (1896-
         1925) at Hove, Sussex, England. Had a daughter and
         two sons. M. (2nd) 9/11/1925 Yrene Thorburn (1893-
         1984). Had two daughters and a son. He died at
         Hawthorne, Melbourne, Victoria, of a heart attack.
      Children of Marie:
631141511 Daughter. Died as an infant.
631141512 Son. Killed over France in 1944.
631141513 W. S. Griffith (   ), m.
             Lives north of Sydney, New South Wales at 87 Kalakau
             Avenue, Forrester's Beach.
6311415131 Daughter. Resides in Chippenham, England.
6311415132 Daughter. Resides in Sydney, New South Wales.
6311415133 Daughter. Resides in Brussels, Belguim.
6311415134 Daughter. Resides in Perth, Western Australia.
      Children of Yrene:
631141514 Son. Resides in Brisbane, Queensland.
631141515 Daughter. Resides in Mount Martha, Victoria.
631141516 Daughter. Resides in Sheffield, England.
6311416 Helen Vernon ("Nellie") Bryant (1871-   ). Born at
         Cairn Curran. Died age 6. Buried 3/3/1877 at
         Barringhup Cemetery (No. 18 Cemetery Burial Register).
6311417 Matthew Bryant (1872-   ). Born at Cairn Curran (VIC
         BDM index). Educated at Brighton Grammar School.
         Died about 1910 in Central Australia (Henderson). M.
         Louisa Walsh. Had a son and a daughter.
63114171
63114172
6311418 Edmund Archibald Highett Bryant (7/11/1873-2/16/1906).
         Born at Cairn Curran. Educated at Brighton Grammar
         School. Grazier and Station owner. M. Bettina Morea
         Cole. He died at Malvern, Melbourne. (Henderson)

63114181 Daughter

631142   George Yuille (1844-   ), m. Ann McMillan (1844-   )
6311421   Mary Denny Yuille (1867-   ), m. William Collis
63114211   Noel Vincent Collis (1897-   )
6311422   William Cross Yuille (1869-   )
6311423   Florence Isabel Yuille (1871-   )
6311424   George Arthur Yuille (1873-   ), m. Mary Casey
63114241   Annie Veronica Yuille, m. W. H. A. Tracey
6311425   Frank Archibald Yuille (1875-   ), m. Catherine
           O'Rielly
63114251   George Yuille (1912-   )
63114252   Helen Catherine Yuille
63114253   Dorothy Vernon Yuille
6311426   John Oliphant Yuille (1878-   )
6311427   Annie Elsie Yuille (1879-   ), m. Hugh Frederick
           Christie
63114271   Frederick A. Christie (1905-   ), m. Jean Hay
631142711   Janeene Yuille Christie
63114272   George C. D. Christie
63114273   James N. M. Christie (1912-   ), m. Ruth Prince
631142731   Diana Christie
63114274   Helen M. Christie, m. Geoffrey Thomas
631142741   Geoffrey Thomas, Jr.
631142742   Anne Thomas
631142743   Elizabeth Thomas
631142744   Jennifer Thomas
63114275   Alison L. Christie
63114276   Nancy Christie
63114277   Florence Christie
6311428   Muriel Margaret Yuille (1881-   ), m. Ernest Fairclough
           Nicholson
63114281   Roger Dalzeil Nicholson
63114282   Mary Nicholson
63114283   Gertrude Nicholson
63114284   Margaret Nicholson
63114285   Anne Nicholson
63114286   Janet Dalziel Nicholson
6311429   Helen Yuille (1883-   ), m. Norman Leslie Galloway
           Wilson
631142x   Milicent Beatrice Yuille (1885-   ), m. Arnold Mercer
           Davies
631142a   Anthony Ashley Angus Yuille (1887-   )
631142b   Donald Reginald Yuille (1888-   )
631143   William Yuille (1846-   ), m. (1st) Adela Kilburn. M.
           (2nd) Fanny De St Helier Cox (1847-   )
     Children by first wife:
6311431   Elana Beatrice Mary Yuille (1877-   )
6311432   William Douglas Yuille (1878-   ), m. Constance
           Victoria Bartram Green
631144   James Yuille (1847-   )
631145   Anne Agnes Yuille (1849-   ), m. George Henry O'Hea
6311451   Foliola Lucy Linda O'Hea (1880-   )
6311452   Elizabeth Agnes Catherine O'Hea (1881-   )

```
6311453   Stella Cecilia Marguerita O'Hea (1882-    )
6311454   Sebastian John Adolphus O'Hea (1883-    )
6311455   Charlotte Augusta O'Hea (1885-    )
6311456   George Fitz Henry O'Hea (1887-    )
6311457   Eileen Martha Sicily O'Hea (1888-    )
6311458   Charles Phillip Randolph O'Hea
6311459   Francis Andrew Llewellyn O'Hea (1891-    )
631145x   Reginald Archibald Jerome O'Hea (1896-    )
631146    Archibald Yuille (1851-    ), m. Annie Denny
6311461   Ravenna Anne Yuille (1882-    )
6311462   Archibald Denny Yuille (1883-    ), m. Nellie Sherrard
63114621  Margaret Yuille
63114622  Barbara Yuille
63114623  Heather Yuille (1926-    )
6311463   Nancy May Yuille (1885-    ), m. Reginald Perrins
63114631  Nancy Mona Perrins
63114632  Elizabeth Anne Perrins
63114633  Neil Perrins
63114634  Peggy Perrins
63114635  Margaret May Perrins
6311464   Guy Ulick Yuille (1887-    )
6311465   Allan Neil Yuille (1888-    ), m. Violet Marion Wilson
            Binnie
63114651  Archibald Binnie Yuille (1915-    )
63114652  George Binnie Yuille (1916-    )
63114653  Alan Binnie Yuille (1925-    )
63114654  Violet Binnie Yuille
6311466   Max Yuille (1889-    ), m. Florence Nita Scott
6311467   Albert Lodden Yuille (1891-    ), m. Clara Bindi
            Margetts
63114671  Alexander Lodden Yuille
63114672  William Lodden Yuille (1920-    )
63114673  Bruce Yuille (1922-    )
631147    Mary Yuille (1853-    )
631148    Charles Henry Yuille (1855-    )
631149    John Richard Randolph Yuille (1857-    )
63114x    Albert Loddon Yuille (1861-    ), m. Ethel Maria Clarissa
            Pike
63114x1   Helen Buchanan Yuille (1883-    ), m. George Alfred
            Chadwick
63114x2   Marjorie Cross Yuille (1885-    ), m. Henry Hume
            Turnbull
63114x21  Nicholas Hume Turnbull (1911-    )
63114x22  Henry Hume Turnbull (1923-    )
63114x23  Clarissa Mary Turnbull
63114x24  Jean Turnbull
63114x3   Ethel Elsie Vincent Yuille (1887-    ), m. Philip
            Burgoyne Hudson
63114x31  Philip Burgoyne Hudson, Jr. (1914-    )
63114x32  Mary Burgoyne Hudson, m. Arthur Russel Stewart
63114x321 Elizabeth Stewart
63114x33  Pamela Burgoyne Hudson
63114x4   Geoffrey Buchanan Yuille (1894-    )
63114x5   Jack Buchanan Yuille (1900-    ), m. Mabel Lois Berthon
```

63114x51 Arthur D. Buchanan Yuille (1928-   )
63114x52 Elizabeth Ann Yuille
63114a Helen Mary Yuille (1863-   ), m. John Matthew Vincent
         Smith (1886-   )
63114a1 John Matthew Smith (1886-   ), m. Mabel Palmer
63114a2 Dudley Vincent Smith (1890-   ), m. Jean M. McCracken
63114a3 Dorothy Smith, m. John Govett
63114a4 Alice Felicia Smith, m. George Lewis
63115 Robert Yuille (9/2/1820-   ), m. Ellen Littlejohns (1830-
)
631151 Robert William Yuille (1851-   )
631152 Annie Ellen Yuille (1855-   ), m. George Martin (1846-
)
6311521 Mary Ann Martin
6311522 John Robert Martin (1876-   ), m. Lavinia Therese
          Carpenter (1895-   )
63115221 Dorothy Martin, m. Roy Ludlow
63115222 Kelvin Francis Martin (1920-   ), m. Agnes Elizabeth
           Dowling (1921-   )
631152221 Anthony Paul Martin (1950-   ), m. Beverley Anne
            Boadle (1950-   )
631152222 Paul Damian Martin (1954-   ), m. Margaret June
            Kenwright
6311523 George Martin (1878-   )
6311524 Bessie Jane Martin (1881-   )
6311525 Sydney Clarence Martin (1884-   )
6311526 Albert William Martin (1886-   )
6311527 Lillian Victoria Martin (1888-   )
6311528 Ivy Valetta Martin (1891-   )
631153 Victoria Leonard Yuille (1861-   ), m. Joseph Frederick
         Henshaw
6311531 Ellen Hannah Henshaw (1887-   )
6311532 Frederick Thomas Henshaw (1890-   )
6311533 May Victoria Henshaw (1892-   )
6311534 Eliza Henshaw (1894-   )
6311535 Eva Stella Henshaw (1896-   )
6311536 Joseph William Henshaw (1899-   )
6311537 Margaret Yuille Henshaw (1900-   )
631154 William Robert Yuille (1864-   )
631155 Robert Yuille (1866-   ), m. Kate Malone
6311551 Mary Ellen Yuille (1894-   )
6311552 Eileen Ann Yuille (1895-   )
6311553 Robert Joseph Yuille (1898-   )
6311554 Harry Leonard Yuille (1899-   )
631156 Alexander George Yuille (1869-   ), m. Mary Ellen
         Truscott
6311561 Albert Alexander Yuille (1894-   ), m. Amelia Gladys
          Muriel Curran
63115611 Kelvin Alexander John Yuille (1915-   ), m. Marion
           Hilda Strugnell
631156111 Vaughan Albert Archibald Yuille (1933-   )
631156112 Tannis Margaret Rose Yuille
631156113 Dianne Amelia Yuille
631156114 Dannielle Yuille

631156115 Darys Alexander John Yuille, m. Beverley Anne Worn
631156116 Adrienna Lynn Yuille (1940-   )
631156117 Gaylord Anthony Yuille (1950-   )
63115612   Nelson Albert Slade Yuille (1920-   )
631156121 Slade Brice Nelson Yuille (1956-   )
63115613   Leighton Eldred Truscott Yuille (1923-   ), m. Norma
             Masie June Reed
631156131 Jeffrey Leighton Yuille (1946-   ), m. Margaret Gaye
             Lowrie (1947-   )
6311562   Arthur Leonard Yuille (1895-   ), m. Muriel Ethel
             Bremner
63115621   Margory Agnes Yuille (1919-   )
63115622   Joyce Ellen Yuille (1923-   )
63115623   Alexander Bremner Yuille, m. Rhona Eleanor Miller
631156231 Peter Yuille (1945-   )
633156232 Murray Yuille (1948-   )
631156233 Neville Yuille (1946-   )
6311563   Doris Audley Yuille (1900-   ), m. Francis Carland
631157   Margaret Yuille (1871-   )
63116   Thomas Yuille (4/21/1822-   )
63117   John Cross Buchanan Yuille (10/4/1823-   )
63118   Helen Yuille (5/7/1825-   )
63119   Alexander Yuille (10/15/1826-   )
6311x   Richard Cross Yuille (1/19/1830-   ). Bapt. 2/23/1830.
             Ref: 1G1 and E.S. Pryor.

6312   Marion Cross, bapt. 7/5/1800. M. 10/8/1822 James W. Alston
         of Stockbridge
6313   John Cross, bapt. 3/1/1803, m. Jean Wardrop. Inherited
         Auchentoshan (estate was sold after his death). He
         assumed the surname of Cross-Buchanan and wrote EDITH,
         A TALE OF THE AZORES AND OTHER POEMS. He represented
         the Buchanans of Moss and the Hamiltons of Cocho. Ref:
         Irving, THE BOOK OF EMINENT SCOTSMEN 48.
6314   Neil Cross, bapt. 12/29/1807.
6315   William Cross (1809-1862), bapt. 3/1/1809, m. Anna Chalmers
         Wood (1812-1878), dau. of John Wood (1779-1821) and his
         wife Elizabeth Dennistoun (1787-1837). He was of
         Dennistoun Cross and Company.
6316   Richard Cross, bapt. 2/21/1810. 92nd Highlanders.
         Ref: John Guthrie Smith, HISTORY OF STRATHENDRICK (1896).
6317   Mary Cross, bapt. 2/9/1798. D. unm.
6318   Lillias Cross, bapt. 9/9/1796. D. young (?).
632   Mary Buchanan

641   Anne ("Nancy") Gordon (1776-6/7/1824 "Woodlawn", Halifax
         County), m. 6/13/1795, Col. Henry Embry Coleman (4/27/1768
         "Woodlawn"-12/16/1837 "Woodlawn").
6411   Elizabeth Ann Coleman (11/12/1796-8/19/1821), m. Col.
         Baskerville

6411131 Susannah Riddick Baskerville (1866-1947), m. Rev.
           Alexander Peirce Saunders (1865-1900)

64111311   Charles Baskerville Saunders (1891-1973), m. 1927, Lucy
           Ashby Carmichael (1897-1985), member of the faculty
           of St. Mark's School, Southboro, MA for 36 years.
641113111 Charles Baskerville Saunders, Jr. (1928-   ), m.
           1950, Margaret MacIntire Shafer of Montrose, PA
6411131111 Charles Baskerville Saunders III (1952-   ) of
           Reston, VA, m. 1975, Mary Cornell Rus
64111311111 Mahrya MacIntire Saunders (1985-   )
64111311112 Gillian Cornell Saunders (1990-   )
6411131112 George Carlton Saunders (1954-   ), of New Hope, PA,
           m. 1984, Dr. Cyntia Matossian
64111311121 Nora Saunders (1988-   )
6411131113 Margaret Keyser Saunders (1957-   ) of Chevy Chase,
           MD, m. 1989, Stephen David Spector
64111311131 Julian Spector (1992-   )
64111311132 Cary Spector (1995-   )
6411131114 Lucy Carmichael Saunders (1958-   ) of Norway, ME,
           m. 1989, Glenn Paul Kish
64111311141 Devin Glenn Kish (1989-   )
64111311142 Autumn Hannah Kish (1995-   )
641113112 Susie Baskerville Saunders (1930-   ), m. 1955,
           John Francis McClatchey, of Cleveland
6411131121 John Francis McClatchey, Jr. (1957-   )
6411131122 Mary Spottswood McClatchey (1960-   )
641113113 Ashby Carmichael Saunders (1932-   ) of Solbury, PA,
           m. 1956, Mary Virginia Swain of Newark
6411131131 Charles Spencer Saunders (1958-   ), m. 1995, Amy
           Clinton Heffner
6411131132 Elizabeth Ashby Saunders (1960-   )
6411131133 Susannah Baskerville Saunders (1966-   ), m. 1996,
           David George Roberts
64111312   Alexander Peirce Saunders (1898-1981), for many years
           dean of the Hill School, Pottstown, PA. M. 1927,
           Isabel Potts of Pottstown, PA
641113121 Alexander Peirce Saunders, Jr. (1828-1934)
641113122 William Campbell Saunders (1931-   ) of Florida
641113123 Emlie Saylor Potts Saunders (1936-   ), m.
           Mazepa. Pottstown, PA
64111313   Hugh Saunders (1893-1896)
6411134   Alice M. Baskerville (1872-1961), m. 1896, George
           Robson (1868-1900)
64111341   George Robson, Jr., M.D. (1899-1935), m. 1926, Naomi
           Fithian of New Jersey.
641113411 Marianna Robson, m. Edward Johnson. Haddonfield, NJ
641113412 George M. Robson III, m.   . Glendale, CA
64111342   Charles Baskervill Robson (1900-1993) of Chapel Hill,
           NC, m. 1936, Harriett Hardison (1899-   )
641113421 Charles Baskervill Robson II (1937-   ) of Raleigh,
           NC, m. Lucie Lea Wurtz
6411134211 Charles Baskervill Robson III (1972-   )
6411134212 Patrick Lea Robson (1975-   )

64111352   Frances Baskerville, m. Robert C. Platt, Jr. of
           Wilmington, NC

6411136 Lula Baskerville (d. 1920)

6411137 Ellen Baskerville, m. Rev. Orville Yates. Missionaries
      to China in 1930's.
64111371 Dau.
64111372 Dau.
64111373 Dau.

6412 Mary Margaret Coleman (9/12/1798-11/22/1869), m. 5/15/1821,
      Richard Logan (1/10/1792 "Oakville", Halifax County-
      5/12/1869)
64121 Julia Logan (8/23/1836-8/18/1894), m. 1/27/1858
      "Oakville", Col. Henry Eaton Coleman (1/5/1837
      "Woodlawn"-6/25/1890) (both bur. "The Oaks" Cemetery,
      Halifax County).
641211 Charles Baskerville Coleman (11/10/1859 Cedar Grove,
      Granville County, NC-8/23/1906 VA)
641212 Richard Logan Coleman (12/12/1861 in VA-5/1/1925
      "Woodside", Pittsylvania County near Java), m. (1st)
      4/3/1888, Sarah Anne Powell (5/5/1862 VA-11/17/1904
      "Woodside") (both bur. "The Oaks" Cemetery, Halifax
      County), m. (2nd) 7/18/1906 Chatham, Jane Caroline
      Hurt (1/11/1886 in Chatham-12/26/1960 Danville)
   Children by first wife:
6412121 Julia Logan Coleman (1/31/1889-1/26/1964 Luray, VA),
      m. Ross H. Benson (5/8/1884-7/17/1967 Luray)
6412122 Rebecca Leigh Coleman (8/12/1891 "Woodside"-12/1/1973
      Atlanta), m. 7/9/1919 Norfolk, William Walker Hurt
      (9/17/1871 Pittsylvania County-3/14/1944 Lynchburg)
      (both bur. Chatham, VA Cemetery)
64121221 Rebecca Leigh Hurt (9/13/1920 Lynchburg-   ), m.
      6/12/1943 Lynchburg, Michael Albert Hans Rosenberg
      (6/6/1912 Giessen, Germany-11/13/1979 in Wilmington,
      DE)
641212211 Elizabeth Powell Rosenberg (1/30/1945-   )
641212212 Catherine Leigh Rosenberg (9/4/1952-   )
64121222 Ellen Carter Hurt (3/6/1927 Lynchburg-   ), m. 8/28/
      1949 University of Virginia Chapel, Charlottesville,
      Harry Douglas Allen, Jr. (2/12/1928 Atlanta-   )
641212221 Rebecca Leigh Allen (9/21/1950 Richmond-   ), m.
      6/8/1969 Atlanta, Richard Lawson Leake, Jr. (1/15/
      Atlanta-   )
6412122211 Melanie Rebecca Leake (1/7/1975 Chattanooga-   )
6412122212 Alison Marie Leake (2/5/1977 Summerville, SC-   )
6412122213 Jonathan Richard Leake (7/2/1979 Summerville-   )
6412122214 Stephanie Ellen Leake (2/18/1982 Summerville-   )
6412122215 Benjamin Douglas Leake (1/18/1986 Summerville-   )
641212222 Harry Douglas Allen III (12/1/1952 Charlottesville-
)
641212223 Caroline Marie Allen (5/3/1954 Charlottesville-   ),
      m. 5/23/1981 Chapel Hill, NC, Thomas Scott
      Cunningham (4/20/1958 Chateauroux, France-   )
6412122231 Claire Ellen Cunningham (12/28/1985-   )

641212224 Virginia Carter Allen (6/3/1956 E. Islip, Long Island,
           NY-   ), m. (1st) 7/1/1975 Camden, SC, Lee VanOrden
           (ca. 1958 NJ-   ), m. (2nd) 8/8/1981 Atlanta, Tommy
           Hounschell (4/2/1958 Knoxville-   )
     Children by first husband:
6412122241 Jeffrey Lee VanOrden (5/3/1976-   )
6412122242 Jessica April VanOrden (5/26/1979-   )
     Child by second husband:
6412122243 Christina Marie Hounschell (7/6/1982-   )
641212225 William Walker Allen (11/5/1958 Atlanta-   ), m.
           5/11/1991, Gretchen Talmage (6/13/1955 New
           Orleans-   )
6412122251 Abigail Ducote' Allen (12/2/1991 Acworth, GA-   )
6412122252 Jona Lanier Allen (4/9/1995 Acworth, GA-   )
641212226 Nancy Lynn Allen (9/7/1960 Atlanta-   ), m. 4/5/1986
           Sandy Springs, GA, Robert Benjamin Shuford (3/2/1951
           Arden, NC-   )
6412122261 Sara Rebecca Shuford (6/22/1989 Atlanta-   )
6412122262 Amanda Gail Shuford (10/15/1991-   )
6412123   Susie Ruffin Coleman (3/16/1893 "Woodside", Java, VA-
           d. Wyncote, PA), m. 6/27/1916 , Thomas Randolph
           Harrison (1/4/1891 VA-ca. 1990 Wyncote)
64121231   Thomas Randolph Harrison, Jr. (4/19/1921-   )
64121232   Sarah Powell Harrison (12/7/1925-   ), m. 8/15/1953,
           William H. Binns, Jr.
641212321 Bruce William Binns (8/15/1954-   )
641212322 John Powell Binns (8/26/1956-   )
641212323 Paul Harrison Binns (6/10/1959-5/30/1965) (b. & d.
           Wyncote)
641212324 David Paul Binns (8/14/1966-   )
64121233   Richard Logan Harrison (1/24/1927-4/12/1995 CA)
           (bur. New Kent Cemetery, VA), m. 2/27/1960, Deborah
           Jopson
641212331 Virginia Logan Harrison (9/19/1964-   )
641212332 Caroline Pearson Harrison (5/15/1967-   )
6412124   Richard Logan Coleman, Jr. (12/12/1896 "Woodside"-ca.
           1970 Hartford, CT), m. (1st) Ellen Douglas Martin,
           m. (2nd) Katherine Moran
6412125   Sarah Powell Coleman (4/25/1898 "Woodside"-8/12/1961)
6412126   John Powell Coleman (7/1/1900 "Woodside"-1/20/1954 VA)
6412127   Annie Eaton Coleman (11/1/1904 Pittsylvania County-
           ), m. 9/10/1932, William Ralston
64121271 William Ralston, Jr. (3/11/1938-   )

     Richard Logan Coleman's children by second wife (Jane
     Caroline Hurt:
6412128 Henry Eaton Coleman (5/5/1907 "Woodside"-12/23/1982
           Greenville, NC), m. 6/30/1936, Mildred Courtney
           Chalkley
64121281 Mildred Chalkley Coleman (12/20/1940-   ), m.
           Christopher Grooby (ca. 1965-   )
64121282 Melinda Courtney Coleman (7/8/1943-   )
641212821 Jennifer Coleman (ca. 1971-   )
641212822 Amanda Coleman (ca. 1975-   )

6412129   William Logan Coleman (7/18/1910-8/20/1968 Winnsboro,
           SC), m. (1st) 5/6/1933, Margaret Mays (5/8/1906-4/27/
           1935 Charlottesville), m. (2nd) 8/20/1939, Martha
           Elizabeth Smith
   Child by first wife:
64121291   Margaret Logan Coleman (3/30/1935-   ), m. Ralph
           Douglas Giles
641212911 Sharon Lee Giles (3/29/1957-   )
641212912 Lisbeth Giles (7/30/1958-   ), m. David Gaddy
641212913 Ralph Douglas Giles, Jr. (4/9/1960-7/ /1993
           Columbia, SC)
   Children by second wife:
64121292   William Logan Coleman, Jr. (6/23/1940-   ), m. Carolyn
           E. Patrick
641212921 Kathryn Coleman (1965-   )
641212922 Carolyn Coleman (1967-   )
64121293   Claude Smith Coleman (3/13/1945-   )
641212x   James Carter Coleman (10/20/1912 "Woodside"-5/26/1994
           Java, VA), m. 6/14/1942, Susan Hay Wilson (1/2/1917
           Roanoke-   )
641212x1   Susan Caroline Coleman (7/14/1943-   ), m. George
           Anthony Salah

6413   John Coleman (5/23/1800-   ), m. (1st) Miss Love, m. (2nd)
       7/28/1825, Elizabeth Sims Clark

6415   Henrietta Marie Coleman (12/26/1803-1/12/1844), m. 10/24/
       1833, Rev. John T. Clark

6416   Henry Embry Coleman, Jr. (1/16/1806-   ), m. (1st) Bester
       , m. (2nd) 4/11/1832, Ann Turner.
       Brawley-Perry states H. E. m. (2nd) Mary Eaton

6417   Dr. Ethelbert Algermon Coleman (2/12/1812-d. "Creekside",
       Halifax County), m. (1st) Martha Frances Ragsdale (b.
       "Riverside", Halifax County), m. (2nd) 10/23/1833, Mary
       Elizabeth Sims (-10/8/1936)

6418   Sarah Embry Coleman (3/5/1810-   ), m. 11/28/1826, David
       Chalmers

6419   Charles Baskerville Coleman (6/13/1814 "Woodlawn", Halifax
       County-5/7/1849 "Woodlawn"), m. (1st) 3/3/1836, Sarah
       Anne Eaton (b. Granville County, N.C.-1/5/1837), m. (2nd)
       4/29/1846, Alice Ann Sydnor (1824-   )

641x   Jane Catherine Coleman (12/1/1820-   ), m. 1840, Charles
       E. Patrick Hamilton

641a   William Murry Coleman (1/2/1808-7/18/1821)
641b   Virginia Francis Coleman (12/22/1816-7/7/1817)

6512   Sophia Knox, m. John Buford, son of Henry (Jr.) and Frances
       Corbin Buford

6516   Henry Green (1767-   ), m. Jean Davidson, dau. of Gen.
          William Lee and Mary Brevard Davidson

652   Mary Ann Davies, m. Fortesque Whittle, born in County
          Antrim, Ireland

6523   James Murray Whittle

6528   Francis McNeece Whittle (b. 7/7/1823 Mecklenburg County)
          (twin), m. 5/15/1848, Emily Cary
6529   Powhatan Bolling Whittle (b. 7/7/1823 Mecklenburg County)
          (twin)

Index

NOTE: The name of the spouse of a Pocahontas descendant is indexed even though that spouse is not a descendant of Pocahontas, but the name of a parent of such a spouse is not indexed unless, of course, that parent is a descendant of Pocahontas.

-A-

Alexander, Frederick   111x643
Alexander, Frederick, Jr.   111x6431
Alexander, George Grattan   541134
Alexander, Hugh Howard   511111471
Alexander, Iska Lynn ("Aunt Mickey")
                          1783513
Alexander, Jane Elvira ("Ella") Grattan
                          541131
Alexander, Janet Lee   111x6431
Alexander, Jason Scott   5111114732
Alexander, Jeannie Jordan   5111114722
Alexander, Joe Wheeler   1783518
Alexander, John Gordon   1783515
Alexander, John Tillman   178351
Alexander, JoLynn   5111114721
Alexander, Keith Ernest   5111114712
Alexander, Kenneth Warren   511111472
Alexander, Kevin Michael   5111114711
Alexander, Leona   1783514
Alexander, Letha Aline   1783517
Alexander, Linda   11138122
Alexander, Lucy Gilmer Grattan   54113
Alexander, Markham Robertson   111x6433
Alexander, Mary Faukerson White   111x643
Alexander, Michael Ernest   5111114773
Alexander, Michael Scott   5111114733
Alexander, Nell Katherine Warren   51111147
Alexander, Otto Tillman   1783514
Alexander, Patricia Ware McGriff Halcomb
                          511111472
Alexander, Paul Wilson   178351x
Alexander, Peachy Ridgeway Grattan   541132
Alexander, Ruth Electra   1783511
Alexander, Sally Maxine Swartz Burden
                          511111473
Alexander, Samuel David   5111114722
Alexander, Sharon Amalie   5111114723
Alexander, Staci Michele   5111114731
Alexander, Taylor Lee   51111147121
Alexander, Virginia Meeks   5111114721
Alexander, William Felix   54113
Algrant, Deborah ("Debbie")   41426213
Alix, Alfred   15354123
Alix, Benjamin   153541232
Alix, Dabney Alice   153541233
Alix, Erin   153541231
Alix, Martha Venable Harfst   15354123
Allen, Mr.   1783383
Allen, Abigail Ducote'   6412122251
Allen, Alma Gertrude Creely   178372
Allen, Bernice   1783722
Allen, Brenda   17837211
Allen, Caroline Marie   641212223
Allen, Deborah Sue   51111122211
Allen, Ellen Carter Hurt   64121222
Allen, Gaston   178372
Allen, Grace Malone   1783722
Allen, Gretchen Talmage   641212225
Allen, Harry Douglas III   641212222
Allen, Harry Douglas, Jr.   64121222
Allen, James Nolen   17833831
Allen, Jane Dandridge   1781
Allen, Jimmie Lee   1783721
Allen, Jona Lanier   6412122252
Allen, Kimberly Leigh   514241112
Allen, Lee Olen   17833832
Allen, Lelia Jordan   1783383

Allen, Mamie   172172
Allen, Margaret Rynie   17833833
Allen, Nancy Lynn   641212226
Allen, Patricia   17511312
Allen, Rebecca Leigh   641212221
Allen, Reuben   1781
Allen, Susan Lanell   17833834
Allen, Virginia Carter   641212224
Allen, William Walker   641212225
Alston, James W.   6312
Alston, Marion Cross   6312
Alvery, Emma Glass   1117933
Alvery, Lelia Bernard Scott   111793
Alvery, Martin Scott   1117933
Alvery, Richard Henry   111793
Alvery, Richard Henry, Jr.   1117932
Alvis, Eleanor Myrtle Dandridge   1722425
Alvis, Emory   1722425
Amos, Benjamin Franklin   1722x
Amos, Eunice Dandridge   1722x
Anderson, Anna Marie Call   222334161
Anderson, Bradley Kent   111381212
Anderson, Cynthia Lynn   111381211
Anderson, Gordon   13311254
Anderson, Grace Gilliam   133112541
Anderson, Helen Patricia Robertson
                          11138121
Anderson, Jessie Love Adams   13311254
Anderson, Kerry William   222334161
Anderson, LaTriccia   172234121
Anderson, Richard   11138121
Andrews, Christina   111418122
Anthony, Sarah Ruth   1721221
Aquino, Elton Michael   2223341222
Aquino, Leslie M.   22233422
Aquino, Lisa Kay Lawwill   22233422
Aquino, Ryan Thomas   2223341221
Archer, Anna Bolling   12152
Archer, Caroline Wooldridge   33242
Archer, Edward   1215
Archer, Edward Cunningham   33242
Archer, Eleanor ("Ellen") W.   1213
Archer, Elizabeth Westerstone Price   1211
Archer, Lucy Ann   1215
Archer, Lucy Ann Archer   1215
Archer, Martha Bolling   121
Archer, Martha C.   1212
Archer, Martha Jones Walthall   1211
Archer, Mary   1214
Archer, Mary Bolling   332425
Archer, Peter Field   121
Archer, Pocahontas   121x
Archer, Powhatan Bolling   1211
Ardino, Joanne   111326531
Ariel, Ari   511111765
Ariel, Joshua Ari   5111117651
Ariel, Laurel Elaine Williamson   511111765
Armistead, Joan Travis   57456611
Armstrong, Allie Azalee Creely   178378
Armstrong, Bonner Motley   1783811
Armstrong, Carl   1783811
Armstrong, Elzie Grady   178378
Armstrong, Lorraine   1783781
Armstrong, Mary Elizabeth   241513432
Armstrong, Mary Lou   1783782
Armstrong, Sarah Frances   17223

Arnold, Mary 511119
Arnold, Patricia 5111114311
Arrington, Ada 172233
Askew, John Douglas 1722355
Askew, Virginia Pearl Culpepper Montgomery
                                        1722355
Atkins, Harold Edward 172122121
Atkins, Martha Shannon Sofield Overton
                                        172122121
Atkinson, Andrew Jackson 1722411
Atkinson, Betty Jane Toler 1722411
Atkinson, Eliza 3665
Atkisson, Elizabeth Jane 17224
Attaway, Norma Kay 5111111111
Augh, Erna Agusta 511119c
Austin, Carol 222131414
Ayers, Joshua Curtis 22213141111
Ayers, Michael 2221314111
Ayers, Quanita Lynn Smith 2221314111

-B-

Babbit, Becky 5111112235
Bacon, Bessie Louise 1721741
Bagby, Parke Chamberlayne 2193x
Bailey, Jossie Ruth 511111223
Baillio, Linda Sue (Chandler) 133144662
Baillio, Robert Langdon 13314466
Baillio, Sallie Love Terry Chandler
                                        13314466
Baine (Raine?), _____ Gay 41635
Baine (Raine?), Thomas B. 41635
Baird, Averie Ann 511111111121
Baird, Kerry 51111111112
Baird, Sharon Michelle Boydston
                                        51111111112
Baker, Anna Laurie 5111117112
Baker, Donna Jean Moncrief 5111117113
Baker, Dwight Daniel ("Danny") 5111117114
Baker, Jacob Dwight 51111171142
Baker, Jason Daniel 51111171141
Baker, Mary Catherine ("Cathey") 5111117111
Baker, Pamela Ann Sanders 5111117114
Baker, Phillip Dwight 511111711
Baker, Phillip Samuel ("Bo") 51111171131
Baker, Phillip Samuel 5111117113
Baker, Rosemary Morris 511111711
Balch, Calvin Edward 5111112433
Balch, Carey Edward 51111124331
Balch, Carolyn Diane Aderholt 5111112433
Balch, Cecil Edward 511111243
Balch, Mary Alice White 5111112433
Balch, Mary Frances Strange Locke 511111243
Baldwin, Beate Hintennach 15354823
Baldwin, Elizabeth Blair 15354821
Baldwin, Felicia Garcia 15354824
Baldwin, George Weldon 15354822
Baldwin, Jennifer Annin 153548221
Baldwin, Martha Venable ("Teeka") Long
                                        1535482
Baldwin, Mary Roberts 15354822
Baldwin, Ollie Mae 178373
Baldwin, Pete 1535482
Baldwin, Peter Roberts 153548222
Baldwin, Samuel Long 15354823
Baldwin, Taylor Benton 153548241
Baldwin, Thomas Benton 15354824

Balog, Patricia Ann 511111283
Bandarnt, Ginger Hatchett 511116632
Bandarnt, Mr. 511116632
Banhook, Octavia E. 1784
Banister, Corrilla Nations 131153
Banister, John Monro, Jr. 13115
Banister, Mary Caroline Noltenius 131152
Banister, Mary Louisa 1311531
Banister, Robert Bolling 131153
Banister, William Broadnax 131152
Barber, Brad Alan 51111132113
Barber, Chad Lynn 51111132112
Barber, Donald Ray 5111113211
Barber, Donna Yvette Williamson McElvain
                                        5111113211
Barbough, Mr. 1783517
Barbdugh, Letha Aline Alexander 1783517
Barksdale (infant) 111425
Barksdale, Alice Stith 1114241
Barksdale, Anne Robertson 1114242
Barksdale, Gay Robertson 1114245
Barksdale, Winifred Elizabeth Lewis 1114244
Barlow, Devin Michael 33242521321
Barlow, Jonathan Gary 33242521322
Barlow, Keith Monroe 3324252132
Barlow, Mary Darrington Sexton 241c114223
Barlow, Melissa Carolyn Wood 3324252132
Barlow, William Lyle 241c114223
Barlow, William Nelson 241c1142231
Barnett, Margie 51111652
Barney, Carol Marie Rizzo 5111112712
Barney, Justin Kenneth 51111127121
Barney, Kenneth D. 5111112712
Barney, Nathan Philip 51111127122
Barnhardt, Byrd (A?) 222314
Barnhardt, Cara Lee 2223112
Barnhardt, Cary Lee 222311
Barnhardt, Charles 222316
Barnhardt, Emma (Emmeline?) 222315
Barnhardt, Mary Olive 222313
Barnhardt, Mary Susan Randolph 22231
Barnhardt, Nannie Woodson 222311
Barnhardt, Robert 22231
Barnhardt, Robert E. 2223111
Barnhardt, William Randolph 222312
Barr, Amy 13311215112
Barr, Brad 133112122
Barr, Christopher West 13311215111
Barr, Grace Ellen Booker 133112122
Barr, Grace Mildred 172123
Barr, Linnie Wilson 1331121511
Barr, Susan Glenn Womack 1331121511
Barrett, Florence Worden 111x8842
Barrett, Mr. 111x8842
Barton, A. L. 1783365
Barton, Andrew Jackson ("Mac") 178333
Barton, Bulah Moore 178332
Barton, Carrie Heart 178333
Barton, Elizabeth Milner 178331
Barton, Hance H. 178332
Barton, Howard 1783312
Barton, Inez Hightower 178336
Barton, James ("Jim") Robert 178331

Barton, John Dandridge 178336
Barton, John Dandridge, Jr. 1783361
Barton, Lelia 178338
Barton, Margaret ("Mag") J. B. Crielly
                                    17833
Barton, Mary Margaret 1783362
Barton, Mary N. ("Sis") 178334
Barton, Mildred 1783311
Barton, Mildred 1783321
Barton, Sarah ("Sally") Azile 178335
Barton, Thomas E. 1783363
Barton, Troy 178337
Barton, Willey Shirley 178332
Barton, William L. 17833
Baskerville, Alice M. 6411134
Baskerville, Col. 6411
Baskerville, Elizabeth Ann Coleman 6411
Baskerville, Ellen 6411137
Baskerville, Frances 64111352
Baskerville, Lula 6411136
Baskerville, Susannah Riddick 6411131
Bates, Mr. 1783512
Bates, Betty Low 17835122
Bates, Carolyn Sue 17212121
Bates, Ethel Donnon Alexander 1783512
Bates, Jo Ann 17835121
Bates, Patricia Ann 51424323
Bates, Zelma Elizabeth 51111142
Baukages, Elizabeth 15354121
Baxter, Edgeworth Bird 541131
Baxter, Elvira ("Vera") Grattan Baxter
                                    5411312
Baxter, Jane Elvira ("Ella") Grattan
                                Alexander 541131
Baxter, Lucy ("Nannie") Alexander 5411311
Baxter, Mary Alice 511111324
Baxter, Ruby Ann 511111323
Baya, Harry Porche 111x6442
Baya, Paul Emery 111x64422
Baylor, Anne Robertson Barksdale 1114242
Baylor, Bernard Hoskins 1114242
Baylor, Elizabeth Cushing Herring 11142421
Baylor, Margaret ("Margo") Hazen 111323214
Baylor, William Barksdale 11142421
Bearman, Audra 111344375
Beasley, Brandi Michelle 5111117311
Beasley, Joshua Dale 5111117312
Beasley, Lucille Catherine 17224132
Beasley, Randy Dale 511111731
Beasley, Tammy Nell Williamson 511111731
Beattie, Carolyn Nickels 2422211212
Beattie, Jean G. Nickels 242221121
Beattie, John W. 242221121
Beattie, Susan Nickels 2422211211
Beechner, Jackie Lynne Black 5111112732
Beechner, Ricky Paul 5111112732
Bell, Barbara Jean Cehan 17212241
Bell, Christine Lee 172122413
Bell, Elizabeth Lee 172122412
Bell, Frances Etoile Gault 17834211
Bell, Gerald Ray 178342112
Bell, Hugh Kenneth 17834211
Bell, James Kenneth 178342111
Bell, James William 172122411

Bell, John Thomas 178342113
Bell, Mary Jacqueline 178342114
Bell, William G. 17212241
Beller, Susan 133144612
Bennett, Dena 2221314124
Bennett, Homa Creilly 178343
Bennett, Janet Elaine 511111842
Bennett, Joe 178343
Benson, Julia Logan Coleman 6412121
Benson, Ross H. 6412121
Bermudez, Elisa Ann 57456651
Bernard, Almeda Young 36653
Bernard, Aseneth Johnson 36651
Bernard, Caroline Pocahontas 11179
Bernard, Eliza Atkinson 3665
Bernard, Frances Ruth 1113441331
Bernard, Gay Robertson 11171
Bernard, Mary McConnel 3665
Bernard, Meredith Dorsey 1113441332
Bernard, Nancy 36654
Bernard, Sarah 36652
Bernard, Sarah Abigail 366531
Bernard, Thomas Jefferson 3665
Bernard, Thomas Jefferson, Jr. 36653
Bernard, William 369
Bernard, William P. 36651
Berry, Eleanor ("Ellen") W. Archer 1213
Berry, Martha C. Archer Bolling 1212
Berry, Robert 1212
Berry, Robert 1213
Berry, Robin Rebecca 111x41211
Berschback, Charles 21924613
Berschback, Charlotte Marie 219246131
Berschback, Madeline Ann 219246132
Berschback, Suzanne ("Suzy") Marie King
                                    21924613
Berthon, Mabel Lois 63114x5
Berwanger, Mary Helen Williamson 511111753
Berwanger, Nicole Marie 5111117532
Berwanger, Ralph 511111753
Berwanger, Rebecca Ann 5111117531
Best, Alan 5111112721
Best, Barbara 111x21323
Best, Elizabeth 111x213122
Best, Gaye Kathleen Jordan 5111112721
Best, Helen Harmon 1751163
Best, John 111x213121
Bickford, Linda Denise 11138122
Biebighauser, Elizabeth Hunter Hurst
                                    213524213
Biebighauser, John Hunter 2135242131
Biebighauser, Julia Perrin 2135242132
Biebighauser, Victor Kris 213524213
Bigger, Ruby 24222133
Biggs, Kamelia Pfeiffer 211812513
Biggs, Kathrine Howard 21181251
Biggs, Kathryn Michelle 2118125112
Biggs, Mercedita Delgado 211812511
Biggs, Miriam Kathrine 211812514
Biggs, Robert Michael 2118125111
Biggs, Robert Munford, Jr. 21181251
Biggs, Robert Munford III 211812511
Biggs, Thomas Howard 211812512

rawley, Eloise Gay 4142612
rawley, Helen ("Dee") Wallace Haskins
                              4142613
rawley, Jane Elizabeth Palmer 41426115
rawley, Laura Gay 41426112
rawley, Lori Margaret Lomasito 41426131
rawley, Nancy Lynne Graham 41426114
rawley, Rebecca ("Becky") Gay 41426133
rawley, Ryan William 414261321
rawley, Wendy Mae Dougherty 41426132
rawley, William ("Bill") Gaston 4142611
rawley, William Bolling 41426132
rawley, William Foote 414261
rawley, William Gaston, Jr. 41426113
ray, Gwendolyn Willetta 511111321
razeal, Annie 133147
reckenbridge, Keith Douglas 11133212211
regory, Chelsea Elizabeth 414283212
remner, Muriel Ethel 6311562
renkenridge, Craig Mitchell Douglas
                              11133212212
rewster, Christopher Ralph 51424431
rewster, Jane Eldridge 51424431
rewster, Kathryn Barrett 514244312
rewster, William Eldridge 514244311
ridges, Mary Susan 511119
rightwell, Charles Edwood 1611361
rightwell, Joseph Walker 161136
rightwell, Mary Lillian 1611362
rightwell, Virginia Cabell Davidson
                              161136
rinkman, Irene 511111433
ristol, Kristy Ann 51111122324
rittingham, Ethel Virginia 5745662
roaddus, David Tilghman 111326521
roaddus, David Tilghman, Jr. 1113265212
roaddus, Margaret Collier Cuthbert
                              111326521
roaddus, Suzanne Everard 1113265211
roadwater, Anita Louise 351167112
rock, Joyce 17834222
rock, Mary Bunn Gay 414234
rock, Middleton 414234
rooke, Edith Shepherd 11134435
rooking, Evelyn 1722433
rooks, Bernice Lee Toler 1722412
rooks, Bryant Wallace 111x8882
rooks, George Washington 1722412
rooks, Mary Stuart Worden 111x8882
rooks, Nancy Caroline 172242
rookshire, Jennie Lynn 17835
rown, Andrea 2221314122
rown, Angie Ponzo 1113324151
rown, Ann Elizabeth Wilkinson 57358
rown, Bobby 17837362
rown, Briscoe Baldwin III   1113324151
rown, Buford 1783736
rown, Charlie 541131136
rown, Donna Kay 5111112632
rown, Elizabeth Gay 41426333
rown, Eunice Creely 1783736
rown, John T. 57358
rown, Kathleen 111x646
rown, LeRoy Edwards III 16113621

Brown, Louis ("Louie") Jackson Maranda
                              5411311362
Brown, Lucy Bolling Alexander ("Rita")
                   Skelly Maranda 541132236
Brown, Maria Randolph 161136212
Brown, Maury Briscoe 11133241511
Brown, Michael 541131213
Brown, Misty Leigh 5111117822
Brown, Nancy Patricia Watkins 541131213
Brown, Pat Altwegg 1535471
Brown, Phyllis Anne Coghill 16113621
Brown, Quanita Lynn Smith Ayers 2221314111
Brown, Rick 2221314111
Brown, Robert Thomas 5111117821
Brown, Ruth 17834213
Brown, Susan Lynn Melton 5111117821
Brown, Susanne Page 161136211
Brown, Vernon Dale 351167111
Brown, Wayne 17837361
Browne, Anne Fullerton 41426332
Browne, Elizabeth ("Libby") Bowling
                              4142633
Browne, Hailey Elizabeth 414263321
Browne, James Wade 41426332
Browne, James Wade, Jr. 414263323
Browne, Kathryn Herlong 41426331
Browne, Margaret Fullerton 414263322
Browne, Robert Andes 4142633
Browne, Robert Andes, Jr. 41426331
Browning, Ann Brymer 5111112251
Browning, Annie Irene Willis 511111225
Browning, Becky Babbit 5111112235
Browning, Benton Darby 511111225
Browning, Beverly Joan 5111112233
Browning, Breanna Lee 511111225221
Browning, Brooke Ashley 51111122542
Browning, Carla Gay 5111112235
Browning, Christopher Dewayne 511111225111
Browning, David Mark 5111112235
Browning, Deborah Kay Whateley 5111112234
Browning, Donald Clinton 5111112254
Browning, Donna Scoggins 51111122511
Browning, Elizabeth Margaret 5111
Browning, Garrett Benton 511111225211
Browning, Gayla Kay 51111122512
Browning, Gracie Clara Carroll 51111122
Browning, Harold Dewayne 51111122511

Browning, Harold Ray 5111112251
Browning, Horace Clinton 511111224
Browning, James Juanita 511111226
Browning, Jean Campbell 5111112252
Browning, Jenny Williams 51111122522
Browning, John Clinton 51111122
Browning, John Ryan 51111122523
Browning, Jonathan Adam 51111122341
Browning, Jossie Ruth Bailey 511111223
Browning, Joy Delores 5111112231
Browning, Judy Lavon 5111112232
Browning, Lula May Catherine 511111222
Browning, Michael Allen 51111122521
Browning, Nathan Lewis 51111122541
Browning, Patsy Davis 5111112252
Browning, Robert Anthony 511111225112
Browning, Robert Arthur 511111223

Browning, Robert Edward 5111112234
Browning, Rodney Lamar 5111112252
Browning, Ruthie Etta 511111228
Browning, Ryan Cory 51111122351
Browning, Sally McGee 5111112254
Browning, Shirley Marie 5111112253
Browning, Teresa Nails 51111122521
Browning, Thelma Russell ("Billie")
    511111227
Browning, Timothy Lamar 51111122522
Browning, Virgia Loretta 511111221
Brumbelow, Kathleen ("Kathy") Laura
    5111112742
Brunson, Carolyn Ann Williamson 511111341
Brunson, David Lee 511111341
Brunson, David Michael 5111113411
Brunson, Michelle Diane 5111113412
Bryant, Andi Elizabeth 1331445521
Bryant, Annie ("Nanny Puss") 6311414
Bryant, Betsy ("Bessie") Yuille 631141
Bryant, Danny Ray 133144552
Bryant, Era Lee Williamson Sheffield
    Coltrane 51111172
Bryant, Felicia Marion Victoria 6311415
Bryant, Helen Vernon ("Nellie") 6311416
Bryant, Ira Houston 51111172
Bryant, Jane Elsie 6311412
Bryant, Louisa Walsh 6311417
Bryant, Mary ("May") Elizabeth 6311413
Bryant, Mary Frances Harvey 133144552
Bryant, Matthew 631141
Bryant, Matthew 6311417
Bryant, William Cross Yuille 6311411
Bryant-Collins, Marie Amanda 511111262
Brymer, Ann 5111112251
Bryson, Sherry 511116522
Bryum, Bradley Allen 51111222151

Buchanan, Ann Bolling 631
Buchanan, Anne Bolling Murray 63
Buchanan, Mary 632
Buchanan, Neil 63
Buchanon, Kathleen 111x4432
Buckner, Ann 5111162
Buford, John 6512
Buford, Sophia Knox 6512
Bugg, Gary 111794111
Bugg, Virginia Robbins 111794111
Bullard, Kelly 514244212
Bullis, George Oswald 5634422
Bullis, Leslie Faye Eldridge Gill 5634422
Bunn, Mary 4142
Burden, Sally Maxine Swartz 511111473
Burgin, Armelia Nelson 5111111133
Burgin, Bobby Gene 5111111133
Burgin, Corey David 51111111122
Burgin, Henry Christopher ("Bill")
    511111113
Burgin, Irene Marie Williamson 511111111
Burgin, Jo Ann 5111111132
Burgin, Joe Bob 5111111112
Burgin, Joel Bradley 5111111121
Burgin, Julie Robb 5111111121
Burgin, Kimberly 5111111331

Burgin, Linda Joyce 5111111131
Burgin, Linda Norden 5111111112
Burgin, Lulu Winona Williamson 511111113
Burgin, Norma Kay Attaway 5111111111
Burgin, Rose C. 511111111
Burgin, Rose C., Jr. 5111111111
Burgin, Sheilla Dawn 51111111113
Burgin, Susan Kay 51111111111
Burgin, Teffany Cheri Vanginault 5111111118
Burks, Laura Oglesby 1751161
Burns, Dianna Gayle Williamson 511111763
Burns, John Olen 511111763
Burns, John Stuart 111344135
Burns, Julie Kay Garrison 5111117631
Burns, Kevin Darrell 5111117631
Burns, Robin Denise 5111117632
Burns, Russell Chet 5111117633
Burns, Sarah Kyle Woltz 111344135
Burton, Mary Lavinia 13
Bush, Lacey Jo 51111181432
Bush, Latisha Dawn 51111181431
Bush, Steven Gray 511118143
Bush, Tina Denise Darby 511118143
Butler, Amy Elizabeth 574566351
Butler, Charles Lewis 1722434
Butler, Loretta Oliver 57456635
Butler, Mathew Brounley 574566353
Butler, Maude May Singleton 17222434
Butler, Michael Kenneth 57456635
Butler, Michael Kenneth, Jr. 574566352
Buttenheim, Elizabeth Gay 111362113
Butter, Andrew Thomas 1113443733
Butter, Audra Bearman 111344375
Butter, Benjamin Joseph 1113443731
Butter, Charles Donald, Jr. 111344373
Butter, Daniel 111344375
Butter, Gretchen 111344374
Butter, Joshua Michael 1113443732
Butter, Susan Marie Dosser 111344373
Butterheim, Anne Robertson 111362112
Butts, James P. 222134
Butts, Sandra Kay 5111112263
Butts, Virginia Randolph 222134
Byrd, James 1722367
Byrd, James Ronald 17223671
Byrd, Martha Ann Wade 17834272
Byrd, Mary Frances ("Toodlum") Dandridge
    1722367
Byrd, Mary Willing 2223
Byrd, Teresa Anne 17223672
Byrd, William 17834272
Byrd, William Wade 178342721
Byrum, Matthew Scott 51111222152
Byrum, Michael Allen 51111122215
Byrum, Sheri Diane Sattich-Nugent
    51111122215

-C-

Cabel, Lelia Marshall 111x812
Cabell, Charles Joseph 132a
Caffey, Angela Charlane 5111117811
Caffey, Charlotte Ann Melton 511111781
Caffey, Cliff 511111781

Caffey, Kimberly Ann 5111117812
Caldwell, Blake Lane 51111921212
Caldwell, Brandon Jeff 51111921211
Caldwell, Jeffery Frank 5111192121
Caldwell, Kayla Elaine 51111921213
Caldwell, Lana Elaine Murray 5111192121
Calkin, Carol 1535481
Call, Alex Randolph 222334163
Call, Anna Marie 222334161
Call, Chester Leroy 22233416
Call, Donna Mae Lawwill 22233416
Call, Eric Osmond 222334162
Call, Michelle Renee Macarelli 222334162
Callahan, Kelvin Jay 5111112633
Callahan, Keri Jaye 51111126332
Callahan, Kimberly Renae 51111126331
Callahan, Tracey Larue Morris 5111112633
Callaway, Alice May 35116712
Callaway, Amelia Isabell Vaughan 351167
Callaway, Frances Geraldine 35116711
Callaway, John Ballard 351167
Callaway, Lottie Bell Moore 3511671
Callaway, Thomas Lee 3511671
Calloway, Beth 51111124122
Calvin, Grace Brooks Hilderbrandt
                          1116132313
Calvin, Matthew 1116132313
Camp, Catherine Mary Watkins 541131211
Camp, Paul 541131211
Campas, Gema Elizabeth 56344312
Campbell, Anne Robertson Bolling 1312
Campbell, Donna Mae 1113324141
Campbell, Gladys 5142432
Campbell, Grace William 1113461122
Campbell, Jean 5111112252
Campbell, Rev. John N. 1312
Campbell, Kenneth Wayne 211812514
Campbell, Lucas Perry 2118125142
Campbell, Matthew Wayne 2118125141
Campbell, Miriam Kathrine Biggs 211812514
Canada, Anita Graham 332425214
Canada, Beverly Ann 332425216
Canada, Brownne Caroline Graham 33242521
Canada, Catherine Carlisle 332425213
Canada, Edward Carlyle 33242521
Canada, Edward Carlyle, Jr. 332425215
Canada, Frances Stanard 332425212
Canada, Joan Carolyn 332425211
Cannon, Elizabeth Young 17511212
Cantrell, Stephenie 511116523
Canup, Chryel 51111122611
Capehart, Margaret Anne ("Peggy") 57352231
Card, Rhonda Gale 17834282
Carland, Doris Audley Yuille 6311563
Carland, Francis 6311563
Carman, Ethel 219246
Carmichael, Lucy Ashby 64111311
Carooll, Jesse Elizabeth 1116227222
Carpenter, Chad Coleman 563443111
Carpenter, Glenna Ree 511111751
Carpenter, Lavinia Therese 6311522
Carpenter, Mina Lynn Coleman 56344311
Carpenter, Mr. 56344311
Carr, Lynn Fairfax 111344123
Carr, Lynn Fairfax 111344331

Carrier, Margaret 211826
Carroll, Adam Burton 51111127433
Carroll, Albert Eugene 5111112312
Carroll, Alene Marie 511111271
Carroll, Alfred Burton 511111262
Carroll, Alfred Losson 51111126
Carroll, Andrew 51111123111
Carroll, Angela Elizabeth 51111123121
Carroll, Ann Marie Valeri Laverdure
                          5111112311
Carroll, Audra Rose 51111126132
Carroll, Avery Nicole 51111127433
Carroll, Barbara Fay 5111112612
Carroll, Barry Lynn 5111112652
Carroll, Beverly Price 5111112613
Carroll, Candice Baylee 51111126613
Carroll, Cassidy Nicole 51111126611
Carroll, Charles 51111121
Carroll, Chella LeeNeece 5111112614
Carroll, Clarion Lee 511111261
Carroll, Deborah Ann Martin 5111112312
Carroll, Donna Mae Schrimsher 511111266
Carroll, Doris Mae 511111273
Carroll, Dorothy Mae Reagan 511111231
Carroll, Earl Williamson 51111125
Carroll, Ellen Sullivan 511111262
Carroll, Evalyn Inez 511111234
Carroll, Frankie Louise 511111232
Carroll, Frankie Rebecca Hower 51111123
Carroll, Frederick Allen 511111275
Carroll, Garrold Alfred 5111112623
Carroll, George Calvin 5111112
Carroll, George Robert ("Bobby") 511111265
Carroll, Gladys Marie Bowers 51111127
Carroll, Glenn Allen 5111112624
Carroll, Gordon Dean 511111266
Carroll, Gracie Clara 51111122
Carroll, Harmon Calvin 511111231
Carroll, Hector Ernest 51111127
Carroll, Heidi Lynn 51111127421
Carroll, Helen English Feldman 51111123
Carroll, James Eric 51111127422
Carroll, James Richard 511111274
Carroll, James Timothy 5111112742
Carroll, Janet Ruth 511111284
Carroll, Janie Lynn 5111112741
Carroll, Jay Phillip 5111112832
Carroll, Jeanette Hinkle 51111126
Carroll, Jeanettie Elnora 511111263
Carroll, Jeffrey Scott 5111112741
Carroll, Jennifer Elaine 51111123131
Carroll, Jeremy Michael 51111231311
Carroll, Jessie Rudolph 51111128
Carroll, Jordan Whitley 51111126133
Carroll, Karen Teresa 5111112625
Carroll, Kathleen ("Kathy") Laura Brumbelow
                          5111112742
Carroll, Kathryn Wanda Penney 5111112744
Carroll, Laquita Joyce Dedmon 511111265
Carroll, Laura Elizabeth 51111126521
Carroll, Laura Watson 511111261
Carroll, Lettie Jeanette 511111233
Carroll, Lula Losson ("Lossie") Williamson
                          5111112

Christie, Janeene Yuille 631142711
Christie, Jean Hay 63114271
Christie, Nancy 63114276
Christie, Ruth Prince 63114273
Clark, Elizabeth Sims 6413
Clark, Gaylord Lee 241c1142
Clark, Gaylord Lee III 241c114241
Clark, Gaylord Lee, Jr. 241c11424
Clark, Henrietta Marie Coleman 6415
Clark, Jane Atkinson 241c114243
Clark, John T. 6415
Clark, Juliana Gaylord 241c11421
Clark, Julie 111x4434
Clark, Lee Ann Saus 241c112421
Clark, Letitia Lee 241c11422
Clark, Madelyn Ruth 241c1142411
Clark, Margery Levering 241c114242
Clark, Margery Wolfe 241c11424
Clark, Margery Wolfe Clark 241c11424
Clark, Mathilde Keyser 241c11423
Clark, Nina Elizabeth 241c1142412
Clark, Peter Jefferson 241c114244
Clark, Sally Cary 241c11425
Clarke, Amy Stewart 24222132122
Clawson, Natalie Nell 111332412
Cline, Hazel 1783351
Cline, Sam 178335
Cline, Sarah ("Sally") Azile Barton 178335
Cline, True Lynn 1783352
Cloud, Billie Hatchett 51111672
Cloud, William 51111672
Cobbs, James Madison 1341
Cobbs, Mary Bolling 1341
Cochran, Bessie 51111176
Cochran, Charlotte 1113443
Cochrane, Beverly Carroll Morris 5111112631
Cochrane, Erica Nicole 51111126311
Cochrane, Gerald Wayne 5111112631
Cochrane, Gerald Wayne, Jr. 51111126313
Cochrane, Tara Denise 51111126312
Cocke, Ann 62312
Cogbill, Augustus E. 1214
Cogbill, Mary Archer Covington 1214
Coggin, Elsie Lee Jones 1331452
Coggin, M. C. 1331452
Coggins, Mary 5111163
Coghill, Harvie deJarnette 1611362
Coghill, Mary Lillian Brightwell 1611362
Coghill, Mary Louise deJarnette 16113622
Coghill, Phyllis Anne 16113621
Cole, Carrie 1331122
Coleman, _____ Love 6413
Coleman, Alice Ann Sydnor 6419
Coleman, Amanda 641212822
Coleman, Ann Turner 6416
Coleman, Anne ("Nancy") Gordon 641
Coleman, Annie Eaton 6412127
Coleman, Bester 6416
Coleman, Carolyn 641212922
Coleman, Carolyn E. Patrick 64121292
Coleman, Charles Baskerville 641211
Coleman, Charles Baskerville 6419

Coleman, Claude Smith 64121293
Coleman, Diana Letitia Eldridge 5634431
Coleman, Elizabeth Ann 6411
Coleman, Elizabeth Dyson 4142622
Coleman, Elizabeth Sims Clark 6413
Coleman, Ellen Douglas Martin 6412124
Coleman, Ethelbert Algermon 6417
Coleman, Gary Wayne 511111284
Coleman, Gema Elizabeth Campas 56344312
Coleman, Henrietta Marie 6415
Coleman, Henry Eaton 64121
Coleman, Henry Eaton 6412128
Coleman, Henry Embry 641
Coleman, Henry Embry, Jr. 6416
Coleman, James Carter 641212x
Coleman, Jane Caroline Hurt 641212
Coleman, Jane Catherine 641x
Coleman, Janet Ruth Carroll 511111284
Coleman, Jennifer 641212821
Coleman, John 6413
Coleman, John Powell 6412126
Coleman, Julia Logan 64121
Coleman, Julia Logan 6412121
Coleman, Katherine Moran 6412124
Coleman, Kathryn 641212921
Coleman, Margaret Logan 64121291
Coleman, Margaret Mays 6412129
Coleman, Martha Elizabeth Smith 6412129
Coleman, Martha Frances Ragsdale 6417
Coleman, Mary Eaton 6416
Coleman, Mary Elizabeth Sims 6417
Coleman, Mary Margaret 6412
Coleman, Melinda Courtney 64121282
Coleman, Mildred Courtney Chalkley 6412128
Coleman, Mildren Chalkley 64121281
Coleman, Mina Lynn 56344311
Coleman, Rebecca Leigh 6412122
Coleman, Richard Logan 641212
Coleman, Richard Logan, Jr. 6412124
Coleman, Sarah Anne Eaton 6419
Coleman, Sarah Anne Powell 641212
Coleman, Sarah Embry 6418
Coleman, Sarah Powell 6412125
Coleman, Susan Caroline 641212x1
Coleman, Susan Hay Wilson 641212x
Coleman, Susie Ruffin 6412123
Coleman, Virginia Francis 641b
Coleman, Wesley Frederick 5634431
Coleman, Wesley Frederick III 563443121
Coleman, Wesley Frederick, Jr. 56344312
Coleman, William Logan 6412129
Coleman, William Logan, Jr. 64121292
Coleman, William Murry 641a
Collier, Eric Wayne 51111225121
Collier, Gayla Kay Browning 51111122512
Collier, Randy 51111122512
Collins, Jane Williams 21182623
Collins, Pauletta Jean 511111343
Collis, Mary Denny Yuille 6311421
Collis, Noel Vincent 63114211
Collis, William 6311421
Coltrane, Era Lee Williamson Sheffield
51111172

Coltrane, Robert Round 511111723
Coltrane, William Lee 511111722
Coltrane, William Ovid 51111172
Colyer, Margaret Elizabeth 414262122
Colyer, Margaret Gay Simmons 41426212
Colyer, Wilkie Schell 41426212
Colyer, Wilkie Schell, Jr. 414262121
Combee, Cheryl Lynn 5111112343
Combee, Christie Lynn 51111123411
Combee, Curtis Eugene 5111112341
Combee, Debrough Lynn Shellnut 5111112341
Combee, Evalyn Inez Carroll 511111234
Combee, Holly Carroll 5111112342
Combee, Mandy Leann 51111123412
Combee, Patricia Diane Mobley 5111112341
Combee, Rhonda Elaine Hinson 5111112341
Combee, Sheena Nicole 51111123413
Combee, William Eugene 511111234
Comer, Wilma 1783772

Compton, connie 511111772
Conant, Georgia Ann 17834

Congalton, Sarah Elizabeth Wheeler Gordon
                    McCulloch 111613223
Congalton, Thomas Edward 111613223
Connor, Mable 5111119
Conrad, Anne Wray Dandridge 17212324
Conrad, Carter Hunter 17212324
Conrad, Carter Hunter, Jr. 172123241
Conrad, Haden Dandridge 172123242
Cook, Alexandra Genevieve 11134411111
Cook, James Bowling 1113441111
Cook, James Bowling III 11134411113
Cook, John Hayden Piercy 11134411114
Cook, Julia Ann 11134411112
Cook, Maribeth Eldridge 514244221
Cook, Melanie Ann Piercy 1113441111
Cook, Mr. 514244221
Cook, Taylor 5142442211
Cooley, Andrew J. 35112
Cooley, Lucy Ann Evans 35112
Cooley, Mary A.A. 351121
Cooper, Kathy 111344124
Cooper, Nannie Ruth 13314462
Copenhaver, Elizabeth Whitman 111x4142
Coppedge, Billy Wayne 511111315
Coppedge, Linda Sue Pusley Story 511111315
Corbin, Gawin Lane 2118
Corbin, Mary A. Hines 2118
Corbin, Virginia Ann Russell 21182
Cossett, Elizabeth A. 172234131
Cossett, James D. 172234132
Cossett, James H. 17223413
Cossett, Patricia J. 172234133
Cossett, Rosa Ann McLaurin 17223413
Costello, David Joseph 51111127231
Costello, John 5111112723
Costello, Victoria ("Vikki") Leigh Jordan
                                 5111112723
Covington, Edward 1214
Covington, Martha 12141
Covington, Mary Archer 1214
Covington, Mary Jefferson Bolling 125
Covington, William 125

Cox, Dorsie 5142422
Cox, Fanny De St Helier 631143
Cox, Virginia Lee 5735223
Crane, Patrice Ann 511111843
Craven, Elizabeth Page 11142122
Crawford, Donald J. 17223411
Crawford, Duncan M. 172234111
Crawford, Mary Martha McLaurin 17223411
Crawford, Mary Southall Shelburne 1534133

Crawford, Robin S. 172234112
Crawford, Teressa Nickleson 172234111
Crawford, William Reddick 1534133
Creekmore, Ann 13314612
Creely, Albert 1783733
Creely, Allen Jones 1783735
Creely, Allie Azalee 178378
Creely, Alma Gertrude 178372
Creely, Andrew Jackson 178373
Creely, Bessie Earl Watson 178375
Creely, Bessie Pool 178374
Creely, Betty Ray 17837322
Creely, Birdie Mae Smith 17837x
Creely, Chris 178337723
Creely, Earl 178337332
Creely, Eunice 178376
Creely, Eunice 1783736
Creely, Georgeanna Ford 17837
Creely, Georgia Ann 17883321
Creely, Gerald 17837331
Creely, Harvey Medford 178374
Creely, Henryetta Hodges 1783733
Creely, Jack 1783772
Creely, Jackie Marie 17837721
Creely, James ("Jimmy") Louis 17837
Creely, Jennie Lee 178371
Creely, Jimmy Lee 1783734
Creely, Katie 1782731
Creely, Lee 17837711
Creely, Leon 1783771
Creely, Louise Curry 1783771
Creely, Mavis 1783741
Creely, Minnie Bell Lee 178377
Creely, Natalie 17837722
Creely, Norman Jones 178377
Creely, Ollie Mae Baldwin 178373
Creely, Raymond 1783743
Creely, Robert H. 1783
Creely, Ronnie 17837712
Creely, Sam Barnes 17837x
[Creely], "Sugar Lumps" 178378
Creely, Tommy 17837323
Creely, Wilma Comer 1783772
Creilly, Alma 178344
Creilly, Andrew Jackson 17832
Creilly, Bonnie Laverne 1783426
Creilly, Byron David 178342822
Creilly, Carl 1783424
Creilly, Carl Thomas 178342312
Creilly, Carlene 17834241
Creilly, Chadwick T. 1783422811
Creilly, Charles Preston 17834232
Creilly, Charlotte Neal 178342322
Creilly, Dessie 178345

Dandridge, James Guy 172233
Dandridge, James Haley 1721a132
Dandridge, James Hurt 17212322
Dandridge, James Spotswood 1721a
Dandridge, James Spotswood 1721a13
Dandridge, James Spotswood 1721b5
Dandridge, James Spotswood 1721cx
Dandridge, James Spotswood, Jr. 1721a3
Dandridge, James T. 17221
Dandridge, Jane Butler 175
Dandridge, Jane Mikelski 17212322
Dandridge, Jane 1781
Dandridge, Janet Lee 1721236
Dandridge, Jennie 172233
Dandridge, Jenny Waller Jeffress 17212321
Dandridge, Jimmie Ophelia 1721a2
Dandridge, JoAnn Hawkins 1721b22
Dandridge, Joanna Stith 172
Dandridge, John 17214
Dandridge, John 1722316
Dandridge, John Bolling 171
Dandridge, John Dallas 17224
Dandridge, John Marshall 17b
Dandridge, John Robert 172122
Dandridge, John Robert 1722
Dandridge, John Terrell 1784
Dandridge, Joyce 17223144
Dandridge, Julia Peyton 172123222
Dandridge, Laura E. Dudley 1711
Dandridge, Lelia Celestial 172243
Dandridge, Lennie 1722316
Dandridge, Leonard 17223141
Dandridge, Leonard Joseph 172231
Dandridge, Lightie Louise 1721b3
Dandridge, Lightie Rivers 1721b23
Dandridge, Louisa Virginia Perkins 1722
Dandridge, Louise M. 17218
Dandridge, Lucille Denison 1722364
Dandridge, Lucille Rangeley 1721222
Dandridge, Lucy Anderson 17229
Dandridge, Lucy Cathey 1721d
Dandridge, Lucy Virginia 1721213
Dandridge, Mable Ruth ("Bootsie") 1722366
Dandridge, Margaret 1722343
Dandridge, Margaret Ann Johnson 1785
Dandridge, Margaret Rebecca 1722362
Dandridge, Maria ("Mattie") Dodd 17213
Dandridge, Marian Arlington 1722423
Dandridge, Marjorie Latham 1721a11
Dandridge, Martha ("Pattie") Washington 1721c8
Dandridge, Martha A. (Anne?) 17a
Dandridge, Martha Ann ("Dolly") Leggett 172234
Dandridge, Martha Ann 1721a212
Dandridge, Martha Elizabeth 172241
Dandridge, Martha H. Fontaine 173
Dandridge, Martha Lightfoot 1734
Dandridge, Martha Roberta ("Burda") 172235
Dandridge, Martha Washington 17219
Dandridge, Martha Washington Pulliam 1722
Dandridge, Marvin Mathew 17223142
Dandridge, Mary Alice 1721225

Dandridge, Mary Ann Shelton 1721212
Dandridge, Mary Belle Preece 1721231
Dandridge, Mary Eliza Cathey 1721a
Dandridge, Mary Frances ("Toodlum") 1722367
Dandridge, Mary Jane 1729
Dandridge, Mary Jane Hamner 1721
Dandridge, Mary North 1722369
Dandridge, Mary Pocahontas 17217
Dandridge, Mary Susan 1721211
Dandridge, Mary Underwood 171
Dandridge, Mattie 1721c7
Dandridge, Meredith Bates 172121212
Dandridge, Mildred Ann 1783
Dandridge, Mildred Hamner 1721b1
Dandridge, Nancy 1721a111
Dandridge, Nancy Caroline Brooks 172242
Dandridge, Nancy Dawn Ward 17212323
Dandridge, Nancy Harris Pulliam 172
Dandridge, Nannie 17372
Dandridge, Nannie Anderson 17216
Dandridge, Nannie Cathey 1721b
Dandridge, Nathaniel V. (or W.) 172131
Dandridge, Nathaniel W(est?) 1728
Dandridge, Nathaniel West 173
Dandridge, Nellie Dewberry 1722314
Dandridge, Octavia E. Banhook 1784
Dandridge, Ollie May Dupuy 1721a1
Dandridge, Patricia Ward 1722368
Dandridge, Paul Rangeley 172122141
Dandridge, Ralph Marlin 1721a122
Dandridge, Rena 1722313
Dandridge, Robert 17226
Dandridge, Robert Bolling 17212
Dandridge, Robert Carey 1722332
Dandridge, Robert Clay 172122111
Dandridge, Robert Edward 1721a121
Dandridge, Robert Edward II 172121211
Dandridge, Robert Honeyman, Jr. 1785
Dandridge, Robert Honeyman 178
Dandridge, Robert Jackson 1721221
Dandridge, Robert Jackson, Jr. 17212211
Dandridge, Robert T. 1727
Dandridge, Rosa Lee 17228
Dandridge, Sallie Ruth Ross 1721226
Dandridge, Sally 111x21112
Dandridge, Samuel Hamner 1721b
Dandridge, Samuel Joseph 1722364
Dandridge, Sarah Frances Armstrong 17223
Dandridge, Sarah Henrietta 1722365
Dandridge, Sarah Jamison 172122112
Dandridge, Sarah Pulliam 1727
Dandridge, Sarah Ruth Anthony 1721221
Dandridge, Sarah T. 1726
Dandridge, Sarah Virginia 17215
Dandridge, Sarah Virginia Nichols 1721
Dandridge, Spotswood B(olling?) 172x
Dandridge, Stephen Price 172234
Dandridge, Susan C. Stith 1732
Dandridge, Susan Catherine Ragland 17224
Dandridge, Susan Ruth 172122123
Dandridge, Susan Webster Rangeley 17212
Dandridge, Theresa Anne Duffey 17212211

Duke, Jacqueline Lane Mengel Culpen Dilks
57456612
Duke, Jane Sharon Hill Jameson 511111771
Duke, Tom 511111771
Duke, William Benjamin, Jr. 57456612
Dulin, Margaret Anne 15341322
Duncan, Anna Elizabeth 22213141313
Duncan, Maria Elizabeth Williams Smith
2221314131
Duncan, Robert Francis III 22213141312
Duncan, Robert Francis, Jr. 2221314131
Duncan, William Kyle 22213141311
Dunlap, John Lacy 175113
Dunlap, Sallie Strother Logan 175113
Dunlap, Sara Logan 1751131
Dunn, Arthur 573521
Dunn, Hattie A. Wilkinson 573521
Dunnian, Mr. 51111645
Dunnian, Roberta Medlock 51111645
Dupuy, Ollie May 1721a1
Durham, Dillard 1722365
Durham, Sarah Henrietta Dandridge 1722365
Durley, Lightie Rivers Dandridge 1721b23
Durley, William Maurice 1721b23
Duthin, Anne Robertson Buttenheim 111362112
Duthin, Dat 111362112
Duthin, Elizabeth 1113621121
Duvalde, Victoria 541131214
Dye, Linda Gail 5111114411
Dyer, Sue 111x8321

-E-

Early, Virginia 24248133
Eastwood, Anna Pearl Dandridge 1721235
Eastwood, Beverly Barr 17212353
Eastwood, Daniels Marie Ehman 17212351
Eastwood, Dean Raymond 17212352
Eastwood, Gary Dandridge 17212351
Eastwood, Harold T. 1721235
Eastwood, Linda 17212352
Eaton, Chryel Canup 51111122611
Eaton, Dorothy Mae Casteel 5111112262
Eaton, Eric Leslie 51111122613
Eaton, Ginger Shields 51111122613
Eaton, Gregory Lee 51111122611
Eaton, Janice Laverne Casteel 5111112261
Eaton, Jerrica Licole 51111122613
Eaton, Kenneth Dewayne 5111112262
Eaton, Lisa Ann Pitts 51111122611
Eaton, Mary 6416
Eaton, Michele Lynn 51111122612
Eaton, Paula Ramsey 51111122622
Eaton, Sarah Anne 6419
Eaton, Teresa Delaine 51111122621
Eaton, Tiffany Shea 511111226221
Eaton, Timothy Dewayne 51111122622
Eaton, Troy Daniel 51111122623
Eaton, Tylar Shane 511111226222
Eaton, William Lee 5111112261
Eben, Debra Ann 1116132241
Eben, Frances 1116132243
Eben, kelly Lynn 1116132242
Eben, Margaret Ransom Gordon 111613224

Eben, Paul Stewart 1116132243
Eben, Robert Paul 111613224
Ebert, Jennifer Sara 175113111
Ebert, Lee Allen 17511311
Ebert, Maryam Joan 175113112
Ebert, Sallie Lukens 17511311
Ebert, Sara Juliette 175113113
Eck, Stephanie 511111223111
Eck, Steve 51111122311
Eck, Tammy Marie Myrick 51111122311
Edelen, Stephen Fenwick 111713336
Edge, James 5111114421
Edge, Kimberly Germaine 51111144211
Edge, Linda Diane Garst 5111114421
Edmunds, Amanda McNeal 623121
Edmunds, Ann Cocke 62312
Edmunds, Emmett 623121
Edmunds, Irby 6231212
Edmunds, Louisa 6231211
Edmunds, Sterling 62312
Edwards, Brenda 17834271
Edwards, Kay 57456638
Eglehart, Mary Alison 111794221
Ehman, Daniels Marie 17212351
Eldridge, Annie Irene 514243
Eldridge, Beatrice Spivey 5142426
Eldridge, Bessie Walters 563441
Eldridge, Billie Neal 51424421
Eldridge, Bogardus 51411
Eldridge, Cathy 56344121
Eldridge, Charles Ryan 5142422113
Eldridge, Charlette ("Schatzie") Hale
51424422
Eldridge, Constance 563444111
Eldridge, Daniel Ferdinand 563443
Eldridge, Deotta Pool 51424422
Eldridge, Dexter Charles 51424221
Eldridge, Diana Letitia 5634431
Eldridge, Doris Seay 5634412
Eldridge, Dorsie Cox 5142422
Eldridge, Edwin David 5142442
Eldridge, Edwin David, Jr. 51424422
Eldridge, Elizabeth Margaret Browning 5111
Eldridge, Emily 563441121
Eldridge, Emily Ann 5142422112
Eldridge, Eva Merle 5142421
Eldridge, Fannie May 514241
Eldridge, Frances 56344112
Eldridge, Frances M. A. C. Powell 5142
Eldridge, George Wilburn 514242
Eldridge, George Wilburn 5142425
Eldridge, Georgia Afton Hurt Kinzy 5142443
Eldridge, Helen 5142424
Eldridge, Helen Merle Moore 514242
Eldridge, Henry O'Neal 5142426
Eldridge, Irene Agatha 5142423
Eldridge, James 51113
Eldridge, James Oscar 563444
Eldridge, Jane 51424431
Eldridge, Janice Carolyn Wickersham 514244
Eldridge, John 51114

Fleming, Charles Campbell 4165
Fleming, Charles Campbell, Jr. 41651
Fleming, Hugh, Jr. 24222141
Fleming, John 32
Fleming, Minnie Wellford Gay 4165
Fleming, Susanna ("Sukey") 323
Fleming, Thomas 31
Fleming, William 33
Fletcher, Nora Gertrude Singleton 1722435
Fletcher, Woodrow Wilson 1722435
Flores, Maya 1116222461
Flournoy, Alice Eliza 15354
Flournoy, Alice Fitzgerald 1535461
Flournoy, Mildred Carrington 1535462
Flournoy, Sallie Tazewell Fitzgerald 153546
Flournoy, Sally Tazewell 1535463
Flournoy, Thomas 153546
Fontaine, Martha H. 173
Ford, Culvin 13315
Ford, Georgeanna 17837
Ford, Olivia Wilcox Jones 13315
Fore, Maude Maria ("Memeo") 56344
Fore, Ruth 56344
Fortner, Hannie 1783511
Fortner, Ruth Electra Alexander 1783511
Foster, Fannie 1331123
Foster, Helene 13312213
Foster, John Newton III 24222133114
Foster, John Newton, Jr. 2422213311
Foster, Louise Wise Lewis Gray 2422213311
Fox, Beverly Barr Eastwood 17212353
Fox, Clay A. 17212353
Fox, Jenne Nicole 172123532
Fox, Laura Elizabeth 511111791
Fox, Ryan Allen 172123531
Frady, Allison Gay 414262211
Frady, Richard Allen 41426221
Frady, Sallye Coleman Gay 41426221
Frank, Helen 541131212
Franklin, Churchill Halstead 111x213131
Franklin, Elizabeth 111x213112
Franklin, Jennifer 111x213111
Franklin, John Weed III 111x213113
Franklin, Katherine 111x213132
Franklin, Lindsey 111x213133
Franklin, Paula 5111165111
Frederick, Bethann Kuver 111344443
Frederick, John Edward, Jr. 17511521
Frederick, Katharine Taylor 175115211
Frederick, Kimberley 1113444431
Frederick, Mr. 111344443
Frederick, Ricky 1113444432
Frederick, Susanne Lee Logan 17511521
Frederickson, Maria 541131132
Freeman, Amanda ("Mandy") Marilyn
   5411311211
Freeman, Amy Catherine 5411311221
Freeman, Ann Hayden 54113111
Freeman, Ann Morris Milliner 541131124
Freeman, Anne Dandridge 1721b21
Freeman, Carol Diane 1721b211
Freeman, Cynthia Scudder 541131122
Freeman, Dean Griffin 54113112

Freeman, Genevieve ("Genna") Scott
   5411311243
Freeman, George Hugh 1721b21
Freeman, Georgia Helen 5411311222
Freeman, Hayden ("Breeze") 5411311
Freeman, Jeanne Hayden 541131123
Freeman, Jeannie Marie Kirkman 541131121
Freeman, Joseph Kristin 541131124
Freeman, Joseph Trevor 5411311241
Freeman, Kirk Michael 5411311212

Freeman, Lucy ("Nannie") Alexander Baxter
   5411311
Freeman, Lucy Grattan Alexander 54113113
Freeman, Marilyn ("Mickey") Romieux 54113112
Freeman, Michael Dean 541131121
Freeman, Pamela Ajac 541131125
Freeman, Patricia 1721b212
Freeman, Phillip Giffin 541131125
Freeman, Stephen Harry 541131122
Freeman, Stewart Kristin 5411311242
French, Michelle 51111126411
Frey, Cashew Cefalu 178342413
Frey, Wm. Jude 178342413
Friend, Bessie Meade 11132611
Friend, Hibernia McIlwaine 11132636
Frye, David Randolph Pusley 1113113111
Fruge, Andrew Dandridge 178378212
Fruge, John Larry 17837821
Fruge, Nancy Angela Parker 17837821
Fruge, Parrish Hunter 178378211
Fry, George T. 351121
Fry, George T., Jr. 3511211
Fry, Jennie Owen 3511211
Fry, Julia 35112111
Fry, Mary A. A. Cooley 351121
Fulgum, Elizabeth Harris 17212214
Fulks, Ashley Breanne 51111111512
Fulks, Kendra Lynn 51111111511
Fulks, Kent Bryan 5111111151
Fulks, Megan Elizabeth 51111111513
Fulks, Vicki Lynn Williamson 5111111151
Fullerton, Anne 41426332

-G-

Gaddy, David 641212912
Gaddy, Lisbeth Giles 641212912
Gagnon, Gay Lynn Piercy 111344112
Gagnon, Jennifer Lynn 1113441122
Gagnon, Louis Fernand 111344112
Gagnon, Louis Fernand, Jr. 1113441121
Gagnon, Walter Holmes Robertson 1113441123
Gaines, Harriet Elizabeth Fenner 36653111
Gaines, Robert W. 36653111
Galahan, Hazel Elizabeth 1113324141
Galt (son) 1241271
Gambill, Michael Berry 351167122
Gambill, Sherri Diane Moore Richardson
   351167122
Gambill, Tracy Michelle 3511671223
Gammon, Daisy Estelle 1722415
Gammon, Lady Rozelle 1722431
Ganner, Christi Ann 24222132111
Garcia, Felicia 15354824

Gifford, C. 178342412
Gifford, Cade Camillo Cefalu 178342412
Gifvert, Lydia 15354114
Gilbert, Jeanette 24222112
Gilbert, Sandra Jo 5111112421
Gilchrist, Aaron Cameron 13312119223211
Gilchrist, Catherine Elizabeth
                      13312119223212
Gilchrist, Pauline Elizabeth Jackson
                      133121922321
Gilchrist, Randy 1331211922321
Giles, Lisbeth 641212912
Giles, Margaret Logan Coleman 64121291
Giles, Ralph Douglas 64121291
Giles, Ralph Douglas, Jr. 641212913
Giles, Sharon Lee 641212911
Gill, Cary Lynn 5634423
Gill, Harold Gilbert 563442
Gill, Leslie Faye Eldridge 5634422
Gill, Margaret Amanda Eldridge 563442
Gill, Patricia Gilbert 5634421
Gillander, Jean Kollen 21182621
Gilliam, Elgie 13311215
Gilliam, Olive West 1331441
Gilsdorf, Barbara 1113324121
Glass, Emma 1117933
Glaw, Cheryl Ann 511111761
Gloninger, Miss 13115311
Glover, Jacob ("Jake") Freeman 5411311231
Glover, Jeanne Hayden Freeman 541131123
Glover, John 541131123
Goddard, Angela Charlane Caffey 5111117811
Goddard, David Scott 5111117811
Goddard, Tyler Scott 51111178111
Godwin, Lisa 511111775
Goff, Dana Ann 574566342
Goff, Elizabeth Ann Oliver 57456634
Goff, Larry H. 57456634
Goff, Larry H. II 574566341
Gomes, Madelyn 1722359
Goode, Grace Lee Singleton 1722432
Goode, Waverly Samuel 1722432
Goodman, Carroll 111345122
Goodson, Angus Cameron II 17511314
Goodson, Kathryn Lemon 175113141
Goodson, Mary Wilson Lukens 17511314
Goodwin, Ann Jenning 133144412
Goodwin, Brian Addison 1331444112
Goodwin, Claire 1331444111
Goodwin, Cleon Walton 13314441
Goodwin, Cleon Walton, Jr. 133144411
Goodwin, Harry Abbitt 133144412
Goodwin, Harry Abbitt, Jr. 1331444121
Goodwin, Margaret Dixon Abbitt 13314441
Goodwin, Susan Rye 133144411
Gordon, Anne ("Nancy") 641
Gordon, Beverley Poe 111613222
Gordon, Brian Stewart 1116132223
Gordon, Carol Diane 24222133111
Gordon, Charles Herbert 1722436
Gordon, Cornelia Holt Castleton 111613221
Gordon, Elizabeth Graham 1116132322
Gordon, Frances Virginia Willis 11161322

Gordon, Henry Skipwith III 11161321
Gordon, Henry Skipwith V 111613221
Gordon, Henry Skipwith VI 1116132211
Gordon, Herny Skipwith IV 11161322
Gordon, James Fitzhugh 111613222
Gordon, Janie Shelton Singleton 1722436
Gordon, Joe 51111181
Gordon, Joe Gene 511111811
Gordon, Johanna Hesthag Seggern 111613221
Gordon, Karen Lynn 1116132221
Gordon, Katherine Stewart 1116132321
Gordon, Kathryn 1331461
Gordon, Lydia Ann 1116132212
Gordon, Margaret Ransom 111613224
Gordon, Margaret Stewart 111613231
Gordon, Mary Gardiner Blake 11161323
Gordon, Michael James 1116132222
Gordon, Millicent Tilghman Pascault 11613221
Gordon, Nancy Weiss 111613225
Gordon, Sarah Elizabeth Wheeler 111613223
Gordon, Stewart Eccleston ("Chip") III
                      1116132324
Gordon, Stewart Eccleston 11161323
Gordon, Stewart Eccleston, Jr. 111613232
Gordon, Walter Conrad 1116132213

Gordon, William Stewart 11161323
Gordon, Willie Beatrice Williamson 51111181
Govan, Ayanna Reade 111x412111
Govan, Mr. 111x41211
Govan, Robin Rebecca Berry 111x41211
Govett, Dorothy Smith 63114a3
Govett, John 63114a3
Graham, Brownne Caroline 33242521
Graham, Diana Gail 175112
Graham, Frances Stanard Emanuel 3324252
Graham, James Milton 3324252
Graham, Nancy Lynne 41426114
Grandstaff, Kenneth Armistead II 111x4412
Grank, Mr. 111x8132
Grant, Lois Marie 111x81322
Grant, Michael Lee 111x81321
Grant, Rose Marie Lee 111x8132
Grantham, Jane Elsie Bryant 6311412
Grantham, M. W. Ley (Lee?) 6311412
Grattan, James B. Ferguson 54116
Grattan, Jane Elvira 5411a
Grattan, Jane Elvira Bolling Ferguson 5411
Grattan, Jane Gay 54118
Grattan, Lavinia Payne 5411x
Grattan, Lucy Gilmer 54113
Grattan, Mary Peachy 54117
Grattan, Peachy Ridgeway Gilmor 5411
Grattan, Robert R. 54119
Grattan, Sallie Gay 54112
Gray, Carol Diane Gordon 24222133111
Gray, Catherine Whittet 24222133113
Gray, Cristi Gail Williamson Lovegren
                      5111111142
Gray, Dennis W. 5111111142
Gray, Frederica Crane Prior 24222133112
Gray, Hannah Louise 242221331111
Gray, Horace Alfred III 2422213311
Gray, Horace Alfred IV 24222133111

Gray, Lawrence Lewis 24222133112
Gray, Lawrence Lewis, Jr. 242221331121
Gray, Louise Wise Lewis 2422213311
Gray, Tamera Gail Lovegren 51111111421
Green, Blain Patrick 222334112
Green, Carol Rattan 514243121
Green, Carolyn Louise Lawwill 22233411
Green, Christopher Scott 514241212
Green, Constance Victoria Bartram 6311432
Green, Gertrude 1331442
Green, Henry 6516
Green, Jean Davidson 6516
Green, Kathleen Lorraine Perkins 222334112
Green, Kendra Michelle 5142431211
Green, Kenneth Ray 514243121
Green, Linda Carolyn 511111351
Green, Mark Randolph 222334111
Green, Orrin Nobel 22233411
Greffard, Helen Carter Hopkins 17511211
Greffard, Marie-Helene 175112112
Greffard, Melanie Catherine 175112111
Greffard, Pierre 17511211
Gregory, Anna Elizabeth 4142831
Gregory, Anna Elizabeth McGarvey 414283
Gregory, Barbara Rousseau 41428322
Gregory, Brent Evans 414283211
Gregory, Dorothy Miller Shields 4142832
Gregory, Jan 17511312
Gregory, John Hannon 414283
Gregory, Lewis ("Lew") Winston 4142832
Gregory, Nancy Rae Hunter 41428321
Gregory, Peter Edward 41428321
Grendahl, Dennie T. 242453b112
Grendahl, Jane R. Evarts 242453b112
Grether, Bobbi Frances Nugent 51111122216
Grether, David Scott 51111222161
Grether, Kenneth John 51111122216
Grether, Layla Michelle 511111222162
Gribble, Robert Francis 3312333
Grider, Michael 5111113221
Grider, Teresa Lynn Williamson 5111113221
Griffeth, Saralee 13314444
Griffin, Amy Elizabeth 1113812133
Griffin, Bradley Kent (Anderson) 111381212
Griffin, Christopher Sean 111381213
Griffin, Cynthia Lynn (Anderson) 111381211
Griffin, Grace 1721a12
Griffin, Helen Patricia Robertson Anderson
11138121
Griffin, John Willard 11138121
Griffin, Kathleen Jean Ruth 111381212
Griffin, Kathleen Louise Philbrick 111381213
Griffin, Mary Louise 1113812132
Griffin, Sandra Lynn Hofman 111381212
Griffin, Virginia Ann Harrison 511111117
Griffiss, Margaret Mary 1117133
Griffith, Annie ("Nanny Puss") Bryant
6311414
Griffith, Fleicia Marion Victoria Bryant
6311415
Griffith, Llewellyn Downes 6311414
Griffith, Llewellyn Downes 6311415
Griffith, Marie Yorstoun Kennedy Stuart
63114151

Griffith, Maurice Edmund de Burgh 63114151
Griffith, W. S. 631141513
Griffith, Yrene Thorburn 63114151
Grisham, Rhonda Lynn 51111122113
Grooby, Christopher 64121281
Grooby, Mildred Chalkley Coleman 64121281

Groomes, Sallie W. 511112
Grove, Daniel Thor 5411311341
Grove, Eric Skelly 5411311342

Grove, Patricia Marie Ferguson Skelly
541131134
Grove, Stephen T. 541131134
Groves, Elizabeth Royal Robertson 623114
Groves, Joseph Asbury 623114
Grubb, Elisa Ann Bermudez 57456651
Grubb, John Gilbert III 57456651
Grubb, John Gilbert, Jr. 5745665
Grubb, Margaret Hall Mengel 5745665
Grubbs, Evelyn Gault 17834212
Grubbs, Harold Trennis 17834212
Grubbs, Harold Tennis, Jr. 178342121
Gruet, Eileen Lynn 111344411
Guest, Bernard Robertson 111762
Guest, Eliza Laurens Chisolm 111762
Guest, Mary Bernard 1117621
Gulledge, Lillian Estelle Jones 1331457
Gulledge, Mr. 1331457
Gurley, Samuel Eldridge 5142431121
Gurley, Sara Eldridge Lansden 514243112
Gurley, Timothy 514243112
Guzanki, Nancy Elizabeth 51111122323
Gwathmey, Harriet White 111x6451
Gwyn, Claiborne Watkins Beattie 1117621
Gwyn, Mary Bernard Guest 1117621

-H-
Hadden, Alexander Carter 111x212313
Hadden, Ann 111x21233
Hadden, Carol Wolgemuth 111x2121
Hadden, David 111x2123
Hadden, David, Jr. 111x21231
Hadden, Gavin III 111x21211
Hadden, Gavin, Jr. 111x2121
Hadden, John David 111x212311
Hadden, Katherine Carter 111x212312
Hadden, Linda 111x21212
Hadden, Loris Jeffries 111x2123
Hadden, Lyn Carter 111x21231
Hadden, Patricia 111x21211
Hadden, Peter 111x21214
Hadden, Reilly 111x212411
Hadden, Susan Gay 111x21213
Hagerdon, Leontine 13141
Hagerman, Gabriel 1113462122
Hagerman, Zachary Chancellor 111346121
Halcomb, Patricia Ware McGriff 511111472
Hale, Charlette ("Schatzie") 51424422
Hale, Jo Ann Burgin 5111111132
Hale, Terrance Alan 5111111132
Haley, Andrew Clarke 1113441312
Haley, Kellen Emily 1113441313

Haley, Megan 1113441321
Haley, Patrick 1113441311
Haley, Timothy Sean 1113441322
Hall, Glada Fay 511111117
Hall, Nellie Alene 511111116
Hamilton, Andy 178375
Hamilton, Bessie Earl Watson Creely 178375
Hamilton, Bilbo 1783751
Hamilton, Charles E. Patrick 641x
Hamilton, Cleta 1783755
Hamilton, Dallas 1783752
Hamilton, James 1783754
Hamilton, Jane Catherine Coleman 641x
Hamilton, Oscar 1783753
Hamilton, Pat 1783756
Hammer, Sandra Diane Samples 5111114121
Hammer, Wayne 5111114121
Hammerman, Constance Gay Morenus 4142211
Hammerman, Daniel Aaron 41422112
Hammerman, Herbert 4142211
Hammerman, Joseph Richard 41422111
Hamner, Mary Jane 1721
Hamner, Orin 1783734
Hankins, Richard 111x2623
Hankins, Susan Constant Blackford 111x2623
Hanson, Bertha 1331448
Hanson, Valerie Jean 111424513
Hardin, Barbara Rousseau Gretory 41428322
Hardin, Cary Elizabeth 414283221
Hardin, Catherine Baylor Fields 414283222
Hardin, Walter Reade III 41428322
Hardison, Harriett 64111342
Harfst, Alice Flournoy Fitzgerald 1535412
Harfst, Dabney 15354122
Harfst, David Littleton 15354124
Harfst, Elizabeth Baukages 15354121
Harfst, Helen Spoehr 15354121
Harfst, Martha Venable 15354123
Harfst, Meade Boswell 15354121
Harfst, Pat Shae 15254124
Harfst, Richard David 1535412
Harfst, Richard Frederick Fitzgerald
                                     153541211
Harfst, Richard Herndon 15354121
Hargrave, Pearl 51111113
Hargrave, Rosa 5111198
Hargrove, Arnold 511111221
Hargrove, Demetrius Deray 5111112211
Hargrove, Doyal Ray 5111112213
Hargrove, Gracie Clara Carroll Browning
                                     51111122
Hargrove, Joann Nelson 5111112213
Hargrove, Katie Ruth 5111112211
Hargrove, Lisa Renee 5111112121
Hargrove, Morris Wade 5111112212
Hargrove, Nancy Gail Tallent 5111112212
Hargrove, Patricia Upton 5111112213
Hargrove, Ruth Orlene 51111128
Hargrove, Thomas Wesley 51111122
Hargrove, Virgia Loretta Browning 511111221
Harkey, Donald Jeffery 5634422
Harkey, Leslie Faye Eldridge Gill Bullis
                                     5634422

Harman, Austin Stanley 5111113532
Harman, Charity Christa 5111113531
Harman, Patsy Lawan Teague 511111353
Harman, Samuel Elias 5111113533
Harman, Seth Elisha 5111113534
Harman, Stephen Erl 511111353
Harmon, Helen Louise 1721227
Harnate, Cheryl Lynn Combee 5111112343
Harnate, Tony 5111112343
Harrington, Ann Hunley 2135242111
Harrington, Ann Randolph Hurst 213524211
Harrington, Myron Charles III 2135242112
Harrington, Myron Charles, Jr. 213524211
Harris, Cynthia Lynn (Anderson) Griffin
                                     111381211
Harris, Janice Marie Jabaga 1113812111
Harris, Kelly Robert 11128121111
Harris, Millicent 514111
Harris, Miss M. 161181
Harris, Richard Roger 111381211
Harris, Routy Darin 1113812111
Harrison, Archibald Irwin 242221
Harrison, Arthur 178346
Harrison, Benjamin, Jr. 215
Harrison, Caroline Pearson 641212332
Harrison, Deborah Jopson 64121233
Harrison, Elizabeth 133146
Harrison, Elizabeth Lawrence Sheets 242221
Harrison, Elizabeth Lewis Carter 1114182
Harrison, Elizaeth Irwin 2422213
Harrison, Emily Barclay McFadden 242453b1
Harrison, Eva Merle Eldridge 5142421
Harrison, Howard Paul 5142421
Harrison, Howard William 51424211
Harrison, Jean Carter 2422214
Harrison, John Randolph 242453b1
Harrison, Josephine Clement 242453b11
Harrison, Lulu 133148
Harrison, Mary Randolph 2422211
Harrison, Maude Creilly 178346
Harrison, Rema Doris 24222131
Harrison, Richad Logan 64121233
Harrison, Sarah Powell 64121232
Harrison, Susannah Randolph 215
Harrison, Susie Ruffin Coleman 6412123
Harrison, Thomas Randolph 6412123
Harrison, Thomas Randolph, Jr. 64121231
Harrison, Virginia Logan 641212331
Harrison, William Sheets 2422212
Harriss, Diana Binford 133144433
Harriss, Jean Abbitt 133144431
Harriss, Jean Dixon Abbitt 13314443
Harriss, John Riddick 13314443
Harriss, Margaret Dixon 133144434
Harriss, Sarah Riddick 133144432
Hart, James L., Jr. 111x64212
Hartman, Ann David Dandridge Stiffler
                                     111x21111
Hartman, Christopher 111x21111
Hartsill, Lucia Fatina 5111113242
Harvey, Benjamin Curry 13314455
Harvey, Chatham 13314452
Harvey, Frances Plunkett 13314455

Harvey, Frankie Nell Melton 5111117x1
Harvey, Iva Childs Jones 1331458
Harvey, Jane Abbitt 133144551
Harvey, Jesse Jennings 1331445
Harvey, Jesse Jennings, Jr. 13314453
Harvey, Kenneth Wayne 5111117x1
Harvey, Lola Virginia 13314451
Harvey, Lola Virginia Abbitt 1331445
Harvey, Lucy Downs 13314453
Harvey, Martha A. 133144553
Harvey, Mary Frances 133144552
Harvey, Mr. 1331458
Harvey, Shari Dawn 5111117x11
Harvey, William Clifton 13314454
Harville, Marion Gail Warren 511111461
Harville, Steven Robert 5111114611
Harville, Tracey Lynn 511114612
Harville, William Robert 511111461
Harville, William Scott 5111114613
Harwell, Roberta A. 57352
Haskins, Helen ("Dee") Wallace 4142613
Hassell, Andrew Morrison II 111326513
Hassell, Dorothea 111326512
Hassell, Hugh Senn 111326512
Hassell, James 1113265122
Hassell, Joanna 1113265121
Hassell, Virginia 1113265123
Hatch, Lemuel Durant 6231112
Hatch, Willie Georgine Adams 6231112
Hatcher, Charles 62311115
Hatcher, Olive Hill Dobbins 62311115
Hatchett (child, died infancy) 51111983
Hatchett (Dau., died infancy) 51111933
Hatchett, Alvin 51111932
Hatchett, Amanda Lenora 5111194
Hatchett, Amanda Susan 511118
Hatchett, Ann Buckner 5111162
Hatchett, Arvie Alsy 511119c
Hatchett, Austin 51111931
Hatchett, Ava 51111631
Hatchett, Avis Hovis 51111663
Hatchett, Bamma Chaney 5111195
Hatchett, Billie 51111672
Hatchett, Bulah 51111622
Hatchett, Chamoa 51111623
Hatchett, Charles 51111633
Hatchett, Charles A. 51111
Hatchett, Charley Sanford 5111197
Hatchett, Claire 5111165232
Hatchett, Clarence Earl 511119x
Hatchett, Clifton 5111167
Hatchett, Daryl 5111165212
Hatchett, Debby 511116631
Hatchett, Dennis 511116521
Hatchett, Dillard 51111663
Hatchett, Dorothy Grace Marion 511119a
Hatchett, Edna 41111621
Hatchett, Edsel E. 51111652
Hatchett, Edward Lee 511119
Hatchett, Effie Lee Renegar 5111165
Hatchett, Elbert Lee 5111198
Hatchett, Elizabeth Pettigue 511116614
Hatchett, Elmiry A. 511117

Hatchett, Emmett Earl 5111165
Hatchett, Erna Agusta Augh 511119c
Hatchett, Ethel Sophrona 5111192
Hatchett, Fortune 5111163
Hatchett, Frances 51111635
Hatchett, Gay Sharp 5111193
Hatchett, Geneva Luraleen 51111651
Hatchett, Gerald Wayne 511119x2
Hatchett, Geraldine Henry 511119a
Hatchett, Gertrue 51111634
Hatchett, Ginger 511116632
Hatchett, Harlin Oswald 51111982
Hatchett, Helen Frances 51111954
Hatchett, Holden 5111162
Hatchett, Illene 5111164
Hatchett, J. D. 511116633
Hatchett, James T. 511113
Hatchett, Jan 511116524
Hatchett, Jeff Davison 511116
Hatchett, Jerrell 51111636
Hatchett, John C. 51111x
Hatchett, John Edwin 5111195
Hatchett, John Edwin, Jr. 51111951
Hatchett, John Oscar 5111168
Hatchett, Kathleen 51111671
Hatchett, Kathy 511116621
Hatchett, Katy 5111165231
Hatchett, Keth 511116634
Hatchett, Ladelle Mary 511119a1
Hatchett, Lara 51111612
Hatchett, Lera Faye Jackson 511119a
Hatchett, Lester Dillard 5111199
Hatchett, Libby Melvin 511116521
Hatchett, Lila 5111161
Hatchett, Lillian Lee 5111196
Hatchett, Lillie Bell 51111624
Hatchett, Lisa 511116622
Hatchett, Louie 5111169
Hatchett, Loyal 51111632
Hatchett, Lura Mary Williamson 511116
Hatchett, Maggie ("Mag") Williamson 5111163
Hatchett, Margaret ("Maggie") Catherine 511111
Hatchett, Margie Barnett 51111652
Hatchett, Margie McKee 5111166
Hatchett, Martha E. 511115
Hatchett, Mary Alice 5111191
Hatchett, Mary Arnold 511119
Hatchett, Mary Coggins 5111163
Hatchett, Mary Jane 511114
Hatchett, Mary Susan Bridges 511119
Hatchett, Mildred Louise 511119x1
Hatchett, Minnie Johnson 5111167
Hatchett, Modena Estelle 51111953
Hatchett, Mollie Gatlin 5111161
Hatchett, Morris Clinton 511119a
Hatchett, Morris Clinton, Jr. 511119a2
Hatchett, Neva Beth 51111955
Hatchett, O. J. 51111662
Hatchett, Olita Farice 51111952
Hatchett, Owen Jefferson 5111166
Hatchett, Pauline Felton 511119x
Hatchett, Randy 511116522

Hatchett, Reed 51111613
Hatchett, Robbie 5111165221
Hatchett, Ronnie 511116523
Hatchett, Rosa Hargrave 5111198
Hatchett, Roston 5111161
Hatchett, Sallie W. Groomes 511112
Hatchett, Sametha 511116623
Hatchett, Sherry Bryson 511116522
Hatchett, Sophrona B. Eldridge 51111
Hatchett, Sophrona Nadine 51111981
Hatchett, Stephen 5111165222
Hatchett, Stephenie Cantrell 511116523
Hatchett, Thelma Scarborough 511119x
Hatchett, Thomas Russell 5111193
Hatchett, Velma Nelcine 511119b
Hatchett, Virginia 51111661
Hatchett, Wesley 5111165211
Hatchett, William H. 511112

Hathaway, Brantley Davis 24222133113
Hathaway, Brantley Davis, Jr. 242221331131
Hathaway, Catherine Whittet Gray 24222133113
Hawk, Bessie Vestal 21181242
Hawkins, Eric Todd 51111126412
Hawkins, JoAnn 1721b22
Hawkins, Tracy Shannon Smith 51111126412
Haxell, Billie Neal Eldridge Riggs 51424421
Haxell, Bobby Joe 51424421
Hay, Jean 63114271
Hayes, Carolyn Ann Williamson 5111111121
Hayes, Charles Dennis 5111111121
Hayes, Charles Dennis, Jr. 5111111211
Hayes, Earl 511111222
Hayes, Linda Evans 17837811
Hayes, Lula May Catherine Browning McGuire
511111222
Hayne, Jack 1722352
Hayne, Mary Frances Culpepper 1722352
Hazelwood, Kathy Hickman 1113324123
Heard, Elma 511116611
Heart, Carrie 178333
Heathman, Wendy Carol 2221314132
Hedrick, Betty Lou 5745662
Heffner, Amy Clinton 6411131131
Hefner, Margaret Ruth 51111132
Helfrich, Rosemary 5111112713
Hem, John 414231
Hem, Rebecca Gay 414231
Henckels, Mr. 35111181
Henckels, Ann Elizabeth Evans 35111181
Henderson, Ashley Carroll 51111241221
Henderson, Barbara Allen Garner 5111112412
Henderson, Beth Calloway 51111124122
Henderson, David Earl 5111112411
Henderson, Donna Lynn 51111124111
Henderson, Earl Amery 511111241
Henderson, Emma Margaret Williamson Hill
51111177
Henderson, Jan Leota Hudson 5111112411
Henderson, Jeanne Ann 5111112415
Henderson, Katherine Grace Jones 51111124121
Henderson, Kyle David 51111124212
Henderson, Martha Jane 5111112414
Henderson, Mary Adeline 5111112413

Henderson, Maurice Strange 511111241
Henderson, Micah Dewayne 51111124211
Henderson, Patricia Joan Segrest 51111124122
Henderson, Sandra Jo Gilbert 5111112421
Henderson, Thomas S. 51111177
Henderson, Toni Wynell Curles 5111112412
Henderson, Violet Lowris Strange 511111242
Henderson, Walker Aaron 511111241212
Henderson, Wilburn Maureice ("Maury")
51111124122
Henderson, William Carroll, Jr. 51111124121
Henderson, William Carroll, Sr. 5111112412
Henderson, William Jesse 51111241211
Henderson, Willie Marvin, Jr. 5111112421
Henderson, Willie Marvin, Sr. 511111242
Hendrix, Mr. 1783553
Hendrix, Ernestine Shofner 1783553
Henley, Mattie 563443
Hennessy, Patricia Lynn Duncan 111344125
Henry, Geraldine 511119a
Henshaw, Eliza 6311534
Henshaw, Ellen Hannah 6311531
Henshaw, Eva Stella 6311535
Henshaw, Frederick Thomas 6311532
Henshaw, Joseph Frederick 631153
Henshaw, Joseph William 6311536
Henshaw, Margaret Yuille 6311537
Henshaw, May Victoria 6311533
Henshaw, Victoria Leonard Yuille 631153
Hepburn, Tara Jean 414261122
Herbert, Brandon 5111126111
Herbert, Marisa Dawn Howard Enslinger
51111126111
Herbert, Sara Elizabeth 511111261112
Herford, Elizabeth Ann Dandridge 1733
Herford, William 1733
Herlong, Kathryn 41426331
Herring, Elizabeth Cushing 11142421
Hester, Tonya 51111181522
Hewitt, Hector Norman Simson 6311413
Hewitt, Mary ("May") Elizabeth Bryant
6311413
Hibbs, Jerrie Elaine 51111122214
Hicks, Tammie Lynn 5111112744
Hightower, Inez 178336
Hilderbrandt, Grace Brooks 1116132313
Hilderbrandt, Margaret Ann 11161332312
Hilderbrandt, Margaret Stewart Gordon
111613231
Hilderbrandt, Philip Merrill 111613231
Hilgers, Gretchen Butter 111344374
Hilgers, Heidi Louise 1113443742
Hilgers, John 111344374
Hilgers, Margaret Jean 1113443743
Hilgers, Spencer Robinson 1113443741
Hill, Alan Craig 511111775
Hill, Brenda Smith 511111772
Hill, Connie Compton 511111772
Hill, Doris Whetstone 511111774
Hill, Elbert S. ("Speck") 51111177
Hill, Emma Margaret Williamson 51111177
Hill, Jane Sharon 511111771

Hill, Karissa Michelle 5111117733
Hill, Kelley Margaret 5111117731
Hill, Kyla Marie 5111117732
Hill, Leora Ann Agnew 511111773
Hill, Lisa Godwin 511111775
Hill, Paul Kelly 511111773
Hill, Rodger Garren 511111772
Hill, Rodger Garren II 5111117721
Hill, Steven Gregg 511111774
Hill, Tracy Ann 5111117742
Hill, Wendy Nicole 5111117741
Hilliard, Elizabeth Murdock 111344334
Hilliard, Mr. 111344334
Hillman, Mr. 17835122
Hillman, Betty Low Bates 17835122
Hilton, Victoria 1331446221
Hilyer, Mary Lucille 51111146
Hines, Donna Lea 5111117131
Hines, Mary A. 2118
Hinkle, Jeanette 51111126
Hinson, Rhonda Elaine 5111112341
Hintennach, Beate 15354823
Hodel, Jennifer Lynn 5111126431
Hodel, Kenneth 5111112643
Hodel, Teresa ("Terri") Gayle Smith
    5111112643
Hodges, Henryetta 1783733
Hodgson, Dorothy 1331464
Hodnett, Carolyn Rangeley 17212422
Hodnett, Elizabeth 172124211
Hodnett, James Fontaine 1721242
Hodnett, James Fontaine, Jr. 17212421
Hodnett, Tiffany Ann Hearfort 17212421
Hodnett, Virginia Rangeley Puckett 1721242
Hodnett, William Fontaine 172124212
Hofman, Sandra Lynn 11381212
Hoge, Virginia Randolph Bolling 24244521
Holland, Elizabeth Cushing Watts 17511512
Holland, George Randolph 17511511
Holland, Thomas Wilson 175115121
Hollenbeck, Jane Masters 351121111
Hollenbeck, John F. 351121111
Holmes, Alexander Rutherford 241c11423
Holmes, Alexander Rutherford II 241c1142311
Holmes, Anne Rutherford 241c114232
Holmes, Gaylord Clark 241c114231
Holmes, Gordon McHenry 241c1142312
Holmes, Laura Miller 241c114231
Holmes, Mathilde Keyser Clark 241c11423
Holmes, Sarah Carrington 241c1142313
Holmes, Virginia Carrington 241c114233
Holzer, Frank 1722343
Holzer, Margaret Dandridge 1722343
Hooker, Debra Lynn Cheatham 1113324132
Hooker, Pamela Elizabeth 11133241321
Hooker, Raymond Cottrell III 1113324132
Hooper, Daniel Paul 5111114531
Hooper, Harry, Jr. 511111453
Hooper, Helen Marie 511111441
Hooper, Holly Ann Smith 5111114631
Hooper, Judith Lynn 5111114532
Hooper, Margaret Eloise Toney 511111453
Hooper, Paul Jeffrey 51111145311
Hooper, Scott William 51111145312

Hoover, Elizabeth Cushing 241c114221
Hopkins, Alice Jean Stewart 17511243
Hopkins, Byrd Willis 1751121
Hopkins, Chelsea Marie 175112131
Hopkins, Elizabeth Young Cannon 17511212
Hopkins, Evangeline Marie Fisher 17511213
Hopkins, Fortescue Whittle 1751122
Hopkins, Garland James 175112
Hopkins, Garland James III 17511242
Hopkins, Garland James, Jr. 1751124
Hopkins, Harriot Duval 17511214
Hopkins, Harriot Hamilton Rutherfoord 17511₂
Hopkins, Helen Carter 17511211
Hopkins, James Talbot 17511221
Hopkins, Jane Ellison 17511222
Hopkins, Jean Dixon Talbot 1751122
Hopkins, Jean Talbot 17511224
Hopkins, Judith Hale Wilhoit 1751124
Hopkins, Katharyn Douglass 17511241
Hopkins, Katherine Roseborough 1751121
Hopkins, Lewis Willis 17511212
Hopkins, Lora Crutchfield McWorter 1751122
Hopkins, Maud Matthews Logan 175112
Hopkins, Nancy Washington 1751123
Hopkins, Regina Leigh Ferris 17511242
Hopkins, Robert Whittle 17511243
Hopkins, Shelly Moore 17511221
Hopkins, Susan DuVal 17511223
Hopkins, William Jacob 175112132
Hopkins, William Roseborough 17511213
Horn, Garrie Dawn Williamson 5111113241
Horn, Geoffrey Garth 51111132411
Horn, Kevin 5111113241
Horn, Valarie Mitchell 51111132412
Horner, Alexander Brown 161136212
Horner, Jackson Coghill 161136212
Horner, James ("Jimmy") Byrd 161136212
Horner, Maria Randolph Brown 161136212
Horsley, A. Davidson 1611a2
Horsley, Annie 1611a3
Horsley, John Rolfe 1611a2
Horsley, Michael 172234133
Horsley, Patricia J. Cossett 172234133
Horsley, William Hunt 1611a1
Hounschell, Christina Marie 6412122243
Hounschell, Tommy 641212224
Hounschell, Virginia Carter Allen Van Orden
    641212224
Houston, Gary Allen 51111132111
Houston, Gina Michelle McElvain 51111132111
Hovis, Avis 51111663
Howard, Anne Katherine 211812522
Howard, Bessie Vestal Hawk 21181252
Howard, Dale 5111112611
Howard, Freida 1783341
Howard, Holly Carroll Combee 5111112342
Howard, Kathleen Cordia 57456642
Howard, Kathrine 21181251
Howard, Marisa Dawn 51111126111
Howard, Martha June Carroll 5111112611
Howard, Miriam Ethel Sowers 2118125
Howard, Randy 5111112342
Howard, Stephanie Carroll 51111123421

Howard, William Thomas 2118125
Howard, William Thomas III 211812521
Howard, William Thomas, Jr. 21181252
Hower, Frankie Rebecca 51111123
Hubbard, Bolling 13428
Hubbard, Eugene 13412a
Hubbard, Felitia Chapman 13428
Hubbard, Felitia Pickett 134281
Hubbard, James Lenaeus 13423
Hubbard, William 13424
Hucks, Allen Keith 17511522
Hucks, Katharine Logan Shiell 17511522
Hudson, Andrew Weldon 153548213
Hudson, Angell Nora 153548211
Hudson, Charles 15354821
Hudson, Elizabeth Blair Baldwin 15354821
Hudson, Ethel Elsie Vincent Yuille 63114x3
Hudson, Jan Leota 5111112411
Hudson, Martha Caitlyn 153548212
Hudson, Mary Burgoyne 63114x32
Hudson, Pamela Burgoyne 63114x33
Hudson, Philip Burgoyne 63114x3
Hudson, Philip Burgoyne, Jr. 63114x31
Huffman, Eunice 1611x21
Hughes, Constance Eldridge Totty 56344111
Hughes, Kathleen Dynel 511111762
Hughes, Richard 56344111
Hughes, Shawna 111622254
Hulcher, Carter robertson 1113621212
Hulcher, Charles Clay 1112621211
Hunt, Bobby Carl 17217231
Hunt, Leslie Susan 172172311
Hunt, Melissa Lynn 172172312
Hunt, Sandra Anne Wilborn 17217231
Hunt, Teri Lynn 17223562
Hunter, Alice Lee Smith 13314x1
Hunter, Aubrey 13314x6
Hunter, Charles Jones 13314x1
Hunter, Charles Jones, Jr. 13314x11
Hunter, Constance Rattan 514243123
Hunter, Emma Lillian Jones 13314x
Hunter, Eoline 13314a2
Hunter, Evelyn 133141
Hunter, Frederick Campbell Stuart III 24142x231
Hunter, Howlett 13314x
Hunter, Hubert 13314a1
Hunter, Ida West Jones 13314a
Hunter, John Morris 24142x232
Hunter, Juliet King Lehman 24142x232
Hunter, Lacey Lee 133145
Hunter, Nancy Rae 41428321
Hunter, Oscar 13314a
Hunter, Peter James 13314x5
Hunter, Rachel Wood 13314x1
Hunter, Raymond E. 13314x3
Hunter, Ruby 13314x4
Hunter, Terry Ashton 514243123
Hunter, Virginia 13314a3
Hunter, William B. 13314x2
Hurd, Hetty Wray 1721232
Hurst, Ann Randolph 213524211
Hurst, Edward Hunter 21352421

Hurst, Elizabeth Hunter 213524213
Hurst, Emma Randolph Elebash 21352421
Hurst, Jean Perrin 213524212
Hurt, Ellen Carter 64121222
Hurt, Jane Caroline 641212
Hurt, Rebecca Leigh 64121221
Hurt, Rebecca Leigh Coleman 6412122
Hurt, William Walker 6412122
Hutcherson, Gloria Ann 111344111
Hyams, Eliza Bolling Skipwith 1116222
Hyams, Henry Michael 11162223
Hyams, John Skipwith 11162222
Hyams, Mathilde Skipwith 11162221
Hyams, Myrtis Juanita Temple 11162222
Hyams, Ouite Gayle 111622222
Hyams, Valery Gaienne 1116222
Hyams, Valery Gaienne Hyams III 1116222461
Hyams, Valery Gaienne, Jr. 11162224
Hyatt, Ben A., Jr. 178351913
Hyatt, Dayna Marie Smith 178351913
Hyde, Dorothy 1721a13
Hyde, Ruth 17221722

-I-

Iglehart, Alison Lewis 11179422
Iglehart, Robert Anderson 111794222
Iglehart, Robert Iden 11179422
Ince, Anna Fielding 17511111
Ince, Charles Kitchell 17511112
Ince, Jean Dandridge Logan 1751111
Ince, William Kitchell 1751111
Ince, William Logan 17511113
Indian Queen iv
Ingram, Jimmie Ophelia Dandridge 1721a2
Ingram, Marvin 1721a2
Inman, Iska Lynn ("Aunt Mickey") Alexander 1783513
Inman, W. P. 1783513
Irish, Thelma Fay 2223341
Isinger, Robert Davis II 1113442212

-J-

Jabaga, Janice Marie 11133812111
Jackson, Bennett Riddell 5142442111
Jackson, Brandon Ray 5142442112
Jackson, Brett Russell 5142442113
Jackson, Cassandra Desdemona 4133
Jackson, Charlie Richard 1331211922322
Jackson, Jackie Ray 514244211
Jackson, Julie Annette Riggs 514244211
Jackson, Lera Faye 511119a
Jackson, Pauline Elizabeth 1331211922321
Jacobsen, Charles H. 1611x22
Jacobsen, Pocahontas Virginia Farrar Saunders 1611x22
James, Dorothy Ann Dandridge 174
James, Frederick William 174
James, Mary Lee Cunningham 6231161
James, Peter Conrey 6231161
James, Robin Lynn 5111118132
Jameson, Glyn 511111771
Jameson, Jane Sharon Hill 511111771
Jameson, Jarod Matthew 5111117712

ordan, James Donald 511111272
ordan, James Donald, Jr. 5111112722
ordan, Jeannie 5111114722
lordan, Jim 178338
ordan, Jimmie 1783382
lordan, Lelia 1783383
ordan, Lelia Barton 178338
lordan, Levi Benjamin 51111127221
ordan, Rebekah Brianne 51111127222
lordan, Robert 1783381
ordan, Sarah Rose 51111127223
lordan, Susan Lorraine Loomis 5111112722
ordan, Vera Lee Carroll 511111272
lordan, Victoria ("Vikki") Leigh 5111112723
losephs, Patricia 111324131
Joyner, Francis Leonidas, Jr. 15341322
loyner, Margaret Anne Dulin 15341322

-K-

Kalergis, Natasha Marie 111x44314
Kallenbach, Amy Elizabeth Butler 574566351
Kallenbach, Mark Joseph 574566351
Kammler, Diane Renee 21924611
Kanich, Louise Scott Steele 133112551
Kanich, Robert E. 133112551
Karpus, Peggy 111324123
Kauffman, Betty Gay Symington 111x2143
Kauffman, Sanford Byrd 111x2143
Keams, Kathleen 242453b115
Kean, Elvira Grattan 541121
Kean, Otho G. 54112
Kean, Sallie Gay Grattan 54112
Kean, William Gilmer 541122
Kearfort, Tiffany Ann 17212421
Keen, Dianna 5111113145
Keen, Jimmie Glynn 511111314
Keen, Kaylinn 5111113143
Keen, Linda Lou 5111113141
Keen, Sharon 5111113145
Keen, Shirley Ann Pusley 511111314
Keen, Tricia 5111113142
Keeney, Caroline Gay Poggie 1113321142
Keeney, Gerald 1113321142
Kelly, Gloria Dandridge 1721b11
Kelly, John 1721b11
Kelly, Susan 5111114223
Kendig, Anne Randolph 21182611
Kendig, Emily Virginia Parker 2118261
Kendig, Mary Emily Corgin 21182612
Kennedy, Amy Marie Seibel 172122311
Kennedy, Andrew Randolph 172122312
Kennedy, Dale Keith 17212231
Kennedy, Iris Jean Yates 17212231
Kennedy, Mathew Keith 172122311
Kenney, Barbara Jean Rowland 51424231
Kenney, Edward 5142423
Kenney, Edward F., Jr. 51424231
Kenney, Irene Agatha Eldridge 5142423
Kenney, Michael Edward 514242311
Kenney, Stephen O'Neal 514242312
Kenney, Susan Lee 514242313
Kenwright, Margaret June 631152222

Kettler, Caroline Canfield 1113443253
Kettler, Forest Walker 1113443252
Kettler, Robert Peyton 1113443254
Key, Caroline Maclin 111x41412
Key, Daniel Robertson 111x414121
Key, Timothy 111x41412
Keyes, Renate Marina 24151343111
Keyser, Julia Brent 241c1142
Keyworth, Constance 1113812
Kilburn, Adela 631143
Kilgore, Amanda Leigh 5111117323
Kilgore, Betty Helen 511111311
Kilgore, Lana Jo Williamson 511111732
Kilgore, Michael W. 511111732
Kilgore, Misty Jane 5111117322
Kilgore, Nathan Oran 5111117321
Kimbrell, Aaron William 22213141222
Kimbrell, Andrea Brown 2221314122
Kimbrell, Dena Bennett 2221314124
Kimbrell, Eleanor Miller Smith 222131412
Kimbrell, Elizabeth Marie 22213141221
Kimbrell, Marc Alfred 2221314122
Kimbrell, Margaret Miller 2221314123
Kimbrell, Marian Caitlin 22213141241
Kimbrell, Robert Aaron Hayden 22213141242
Kimbrell, Robert Dodd 2221314124
Kimbrell, Steve Morris 222131412
Kimbrell, Steve Morris, Jr. 2221314121
Kime, Florence Susanne 1751152
Kindig, Edwin Lawrence, Jr. 2118261
King, ANnie Randolph 219243
King, Byran 511116524
King, Charla 5111165241
King, Diane Renee Kammler 21924611
King, Eliza Custis Leatherbury 219246
King, Emily Jill 51111132431
King, Ethel Carman 219246
King, George Henry III 219245
King, George Henry, Jr. 21924
King, Jan Hatchett 511116524
King, Jason 5111165244
King, Kevin 5111165242
King, Marilyn June Smith 2192461
King, Mary Margaret ("Margie") Williamson
                                   5111113243
King, Mary Meredith ("Mamie") 219241
King, Michael Glen 5111113243
King, Nancy Elizabeth 21924612
King, Rachel 5111165243
King, Richard Bolling 219242
King, Robert Skipwith 219246
King, Robert Skipwith II 2192461
King, Robert Skipwith III 21924611
King, Susan Christian 219244
King, Susan Christian Bolling 21924
King, Suzanne ("Suzy") Marie 21924613
Kingham, Frank 511111816
Kinikin, Sharon 15354622
Kinzy, Georgia Afton Hurt 5142443
Kirchoff, Elizabeth Thornton Maull
                                   24222132121
Kirchoff, Gary 24222132121
Kirchoff, Lindsey Marie 242221321211

Limbock, Sara Elyce 51111111712
Lindbloom, Maude Elvira 514244
Lindenblad, Ann Bolling Terry 13314468
Lindenblad, Beth Ann 1331446821
Lindenblad, Irving Werner 13314468
Lindenblad, Irving Werner, Jr. 133144681
Lindenblad, Nils Bolling 133144682
Lindenblad, Susan Lieber 133144682
Linville, Joyce Marie 1331121512
Lipsey, Jewel 1721721
Litcher, Cameron Jaye 5735223111
Litcher, Cathryn Anne Wilkinson 573522311
Litcher, Jade John 573522311
Litcher, Shane Wilkinson 5735223112
Little, Anne Drake 111x2632
Little, Betty 51111179
Littlejohns, Ellen 63115
Liung, Karen 17834224
Livingston, Anne 251
Lloyd, Arthur Selden, Jr. 111x215
Locke, Carlene Worley 5111112432
Locke, Charlene Price 5111112432
Locke, David Brent 51111124321
Locke, Donnie Alton 511111243
Locke, Gregory 51111124323
Locke, Joe Alton 5111112432
Locke, John Wayne 51111124312
Locke, Lisa Shuster 51111124321
Locke, Mary Frances Strange 511111243
Locke, Melanie 51111124311
Locke, Melissa Sanders 51111124312
Locke, Michael Edward 51111124322
Locke, Thomas Wayne 5111112431
Locke, Waltraud 5111112431
Lockhart, Howard 211812514
Lockhart, Miriam Katherine Biggs Campbell
211812514
Logan, Anna Aylett Anderson 1751162
Logan, Anna Clayton 17511611
Logan, Beverley Haskins 17511612
Logan, Charles Markley 175113
Logan, Charles Markley Logan, Jr. 17511131
Logan, Diana Gail Graham 175112
Logan, Fielding Lewis 175111
Logan, Fielding Lewis III 17511121
Logan, Fielding Lewis, Jr. 1751112
Logan, Florence Susanne Kime 1751152
Logan, Frances Wilson McNulty 175116
Logan, George Willis 1751163
Logan, George Willis, Jr. 17511631
Logan, Georgine Washington Willis 17511
Logan, Georgine Willis 175117
Logan, Helen Harmon Best
Logan, Jacqulyn Cundiff 1751113
Logan, Jean Dandridge 1751111
Logan, Jean Markley 175111
Logan, John Lee 175115
Logan, John Markley 17511122
Logan, Jon Davies 17511231
Logan, Joseph Dandridge 1751152
Logan, Joseph Dandridge 175116
Logan, Joseph Dandridge III 1751161
Logan, Joseph Dandridge IV 17511613

Logan, Joseph Davies 17511
Logan, Julia 64121
Logan, Katharine 17511522
Logan, Laura Oglesby Burks 1751161
Logan, Marjorie Jean 1751151
Logan, Marjorie Wood 175115
Logan, Martha Ann Wade Byrd 17834272
Logan, Mary Graham 17511123
Logan, Mary Margaret Coleman 6412
Logan, Maud Matthews 175112
Logan, Michelle 17511523
Logan, Nancy Clayton 175114
Logan, Richard, 6412
Logan, Sallie Strother 175113
Logan, Stephen Davies 17511523
Logan, Susanne Lee 17511521
Logan, Tom 17834272
Logan, William Cundiff 17511132
Lomasito, Lori Margaret 41426131
Long, Carol Calkin 1535481
Long, Flynn Vincent 153548
Long, Flynn Vincent III 15354812
Long, Flynn Vincent, Jr. 1535481
Long, Gloria 1535481
Long, Gloria Long 1535481
Long, Gracie Lillian 1722414
Long, Martha 15354811
Long, Martha Venable ("Teeka") 1535482
Long, Martha Venable Fitzgerald 153548
Long, Sarah ("Sally") 15354813
Loomis, Susan Lorraine 5111112722
Loper, Mr. 17223672
Loper, Teresa Anne Byrd 17223672
Lopez, Karen Jean Mckeon 153541123
Lopez, Miguel Angel 153541123
Love, Miss 6413
Love, Robert 1722361
Love, Sue Ella 5111113
Love, Virginia Elizabeth Dandridge 1722361
Lovegren, Cristi Gail Williamson 51111114
Lovegren, Ralph A. 5111111142
Lovegren, Tamera Gail 51111111421
Lovell, Annie Delmar 172122
Lowe, Golia V. Williamson 51111183
Lowe, Liston Wayne 51111183
Lowery, Elizabeth 111x8131
Lowery, Mildred Hamner Dandridge 1721b1
Lowery, Perrin 1721b1
Lowrie, Margaret Gaye 631156131
Ludlow, Dorothy Martin 63115221
Ludlow, Roy 63115221
Luebcke, Holly Carroll Combee Howard
5111112342
Luebcke, Jamie 5111112342
Lukens, Charles Edward 1751131
Lukens, Charles Edward II 175113131
Lukens, Courtland Gregory 175112121
Lukens, Dawn Patsell 17511313
Lukens, Elizabeth 175113123
Lukens, Fara Virginia 175113132
Lukens, Jan Gregory 17511312
Lukens, John Dunlap 17511213
Lukens, Mary Wilson 17511314
Lukens, Patricia Allen 17511312

Montgomery, J. W. 1722355
Montgomery, Virginia Pearl Culpepper 1722355
Moore, Alice May Callaway 35116712
Moore, Alison 41426214
Moore, Amanda Catherine 51111143221
Moore, Arthur 35116712
Moore, Brandi Kay 351167123
Moore, Bulah 178332
Moore, Catherine Elaine Bost 5111114322
Moore, Charles Michael 172235611
Moore, Charles Milton 17223561
Moore, Clay 5111113151
Moore, Cynthia Kohler 351167121
Moore, Danny M. 5111114322
Moore, Helen Merle 514242
Moore, Jennifer Leah 172235612
Moore, Lois Amelia 111x813
Moore, Lottie Bell 3511671
Moore, Mary Elizabeth Lewing 17223561
Moore, Matthew Hollis 3511671211
Moore, Melony 5111113151l
Moore, Michael Hollis 351167124
Moore, Patrick Arthur 351167121
Moore, Richard Reynolds 111348121
Moore, Samuel Alexander, Jr. 11134811
Moore, Sara Beth Story 5111113151
Moore, Sara Beth Story Pusley 5111113151
Moore, Shelly 17511221
Moore, Sherri Diane 351167122
Moore, Traci Wolf 111348121
Moore, Vicky 514243221
Moore, Vicky Lynn 5111112742
Moorman, Virginia Judith 13314
Moran, Katherine 6412124
Morash, Victoria 242453b114
Morenus, Carlyn Gay 41422122
Morenus, Constance Gay 4142211
Morenus, Constance Mary Gay 414221
Morenus, Daniel Hastings 41422123
Morenus, David Rutherford 41422121
Morenus, Marjorie Rose Rutherford 4142212
Morenus, Richard Cousins 4142212
Morenus, Richard Thomas 414221
Moretz, Charles Hugh 21924612
Moretz, Nancy Elizabeth King 21924612
Morgan, Mr. 1783554
Morgan, Mary Shafner 1783554
Morris, Beverly Carroll 5111112631
Morris, Camille 11162256
Morris, Cloe Marie Lawrence 511111713
Morris, CLurtis Ray 511111713
Morris, Curtis Clyde 51111171
Morris, Deborah Ann 51111122313
Morris, Donna Kay Brown 5111112632
Morris, Donna Lea Hines 5111117131
Morris, Jeanettie Elnora Carroll 511111263
Morris, Joy Ann 511111712
Morris, Joy Delores Browning Myrick 5111112231
Morris, Lawrence Craig 5111117131
Morris, Leslie Erin 51111126323
Morris, Lori Ann 51111126321
Morris, Louis Lambkin 11162256
Morris, Mary Malva Williamson 51111171

Morris, Matthew William 51111126322
Morris, Odis 51111263
Morris, Ronald 5111112231
Morris, Rosemary 511111711
Morris, William ("Billy") Odis 511111263
Morris,Tracey Larue 5111112633
Moss, Mary Frances 1331443
Motley, Bonner 1783811
Motley, Ed 178381
Motley, Frank Robertson, Jr. 111x4434
Motley, Hugh Douglas Camp 111x4432
Motley, Julie Clark 111x4434
Motley, Kathleen Buchanon 111x4432
Motley, Katy Robertson 111x441
Motley, Minnie Raines 178381
Mounts, Freddie 511111281
Mounts, Jeffery Alan 5111112811
Mounts, Sarah Ann Carroll 511111281
Mullen, Anne Rives Mengel 5745664
Mullen, Cheryl Ann Garrison 57456643
Mullen, Cindy Lakey 5745663
Mullen, David Lloyd 574566412
Mullen, Elizabeth Rives 574566432
Mullen, Jennifer Anne 574566421
Mullen, Joseph Gerald III 57456641
Mullen, Joseph Gerald IV 574566411
Mullen, Joseph Gerald, Jr. 5745664
Mullen, Kathleen Cordia Howard 57456642
Mullen, Linda 57456641
Mullen, Mary Elizabeth Rice 57456641
Mullen, Michael Randolph 57456643
Mullen, Michael Scott 574566433
Mullen, Robert Rives 57456642
Mullen, Sandra Elizabeth Farris 5745664
Mullen, Sarah 574566431
Munn, Catherine Virginia Warren 5111114
Munn, Edward Earl 511111421
Munn, Edward Earl 511111431
Munn, Edward Earl, Jr. 5111114311
Munn, Mary Elizabeth Warren Williams 511111421
Munn, Patricia Arnold 5111114311
Munn, Scott 5111114311
Munn, Tracy 5111143112
Munoff, Ann Hadden 111x21233
Munoff, Sam 111x21233
Munson, Elizabeth 1722359
Munster, Cameron Carr 1113443132
Munster, Charlotte Robertson 11134431
Munster, Colleen Gavin 111344313
Munster, Drayton 1113443131
Munster, Walter Nelson 11134431
Munster, Walter Nelson, Jr. 111344313
Murallon, Maria Ana 111381223
Murdock, Elizabeth 111344334
Murff, Betty Jane 17834253
Murff, Daniel Thomas 178342521
Murff, Elmo 1783425
Murff, Etoil 17834251
Murff, Ettie Jean Neal 17834252
Murff, Guy Thomas 17834252
Murff, Janet 178342524
Murff, Michael 178342523
Murff, Mildred Creilly 1783425
Murff, Richard 178342522
Murff, Stanley N. 178342525

Norris, Timothy 111x214322
Norris, Velma Odell 51111921
North, Mary 1722369
Norwood, Elizabeth 1782
Nugent, Becky Lou Vertrees 51111122214
Nugent, Bobbi Frances 51111122216
Nugent, Darryl Fredric (Sattich) 51111122214
Nugent, Jerrie Elaine Hibbs 51111122214
Nugent, Kimberley Louise 51111122213
Nugent, Marjorie Frances McGuire Sattich
　　　　　　　　　　　　　　　　　　5111112221
Nugent, Robert Darryl 51111222141
Nugent, Robert Hevern 5111112221
Nugent, Samantha Nicole 51111222142
Nugent, Sheri Diane (Sattich) 51111122215

-O-

O'Brien, Patricia Ann 54113121
O'Callagahan, Elizabeth S. 178342741
O'Callagahan, Eugene 17834274
O'Callagahan, Michael Wade 178342742
O'Callagahan, Virginia ("Jennie") Wade
　　　　　　　　　　　　　　　　17834274
O'Hea, Anne Agnes Yuille 631145
O'Hea, Charles Phillip Randolph 6311458
O'Hea, Charlotte Augusta 6311455
O'Hea, Eileen Martha Sicily 6311457
O'Hea, Foliola Lucy Linda 6311451
O'Hea, Francis Andrew Llewellyn 6311459
O'Hea, George Fitz Henry 6311456
O'Hea, George Henry 631145
O'Hea, Reginald Archibald Jerome 631145x
O'Hea, Sebastian John Adolphus 6311454
O'Hea, Stella Cecilia Marguerita 6311453
O'Neal, Harry L. 1783782
O'Neal, Linda Joyce Burgin 5111111131
O'Neal, Mary Low Armstrong Parker 1783782
O'Neal, Michael Eugene 5111111131
O'Neal, Michael Eugene II 51111111312
O'Neal, Terri Lynn 51111111311
O'Rea, Elizabeth Agnes Catherine 6311452
O'Rielly, Catherine 6311425
Ogilbee, Dessie Creilly 178345
Ogilbee, Mitchell 178345
Ohl, James Dean 511111344
Ohl, Joshua Dathon 5111113441
Ohl, Justin Tyler 5111113442
Ohl, Sharon Kay Williamson 511111344
Oldacker, Mildred 511111411
Oliver, Dena Chesley Branch 57456636
Oliver, Elizabeth 57456633
Oliver, Elizabeth Ann 57456634
Oliver, Elizabeth Sterling 574566382
Oliver, Harry Diggs III 57456633
Oliver, Harry Diggs, Jr. 5745663
Oliver, Jacqueline Alexander 574566361
Oliver, John Patton 57456636
Oliver, Jonathan Edwards 574566381
Oliver, Kay Edwards 57456638
Oliver, Loretta 57456635
Oliver, Martin Vianey 57456638
Oliver, Mary Elizabeth Mengel 5745663
Oliver, Mary Frances 57456631
Oliver, Mary Frances 57456632

Oliver, Perry 57456636
Oliver, Theresa Martin 57456637
Olleo, Gay Frances Reif 111344431
Olleo, Kimgberley 1113444311
Olleo, Lisa 1113444312
Olleo, Mr. 111344431
Olson, Janet Alise 1113321112
Ooghe, June Adelaide Walker 11142431
Ooghe, Lydia Adelaide 111424314
Ooghe, Robert Barksdale 11142431
Ooghe, Robert Barksdale, Jr. 111424313
Osterman, Miss C. 1611614
Otwell, Gloria Jean 11138122
Ousley, Stephen Lee 5111114412
Overton, Charles Jay III 17212212
Overton, Grace 172121
Overton, Kelly Jensen Sofield 172122122
Overton, Martha Ann Dandridge Sofield
　　　　　　　　　　　　　　　17212212
Overton, Martha Shannon Sofield 172122121
Owen, Jennie 3511211
Owens, Carla Dell Riggs 514244214
Owens, Dan Hewlett 17212242
Owens, Donald Keith 514244214
Owens, Francis Elizabeth Cehan 17212242
Owens, Janae Dawn 5142442141
Owens, Jill Dean 5142442143
Owens, Joey Dell 5142442142
Owens, Kent 11133243
Oxley, Anne Page 222335
Oxley, Benjamin Franklin 22232
Oxley, Evelyn Byrd Randolph 22232
Oxley, Franklin 222333
Oxley, Jennie Willing 222334
Oxley, John Jefferson 222331
Oxley, Mary Louise ("Lulu") 222332

-P-

Page, Anna Bolling Archer 12152
Page, James A. 12152
Palmer, Glen 17223582
Palmer, Holly Stuart 11133212312
Palmer, Jane Elizabeth 41426115
Palmer, Joshua 172235821
Palmer, Judith Young 17223482
Palmer, Mabel 63114a1
Palmer, Peter 1113321231
Palmer, Sarah Turner Blackwell 1113321231
Palmer, Trent Richard 11133212311
Para, Lisa Marie 1113441212
Paris, Cathy June 5111111123
Paris, Anne Corbin 2118262
Parker, Bobby Russell 1783782
Parker, Cythia Marilyn 17837822
Parker, Emily Virginia 2118261
Parker, Gawin Lane 211821
Parker, John Robert 21182
Parker, John Russell 211822
Parker, Joseph Henry 211824
Parker, Margaret Carrier 211826
Parker, Mary Lou Armstrong 1783782
Parker, Nancy Angela 17837821
Parker, Robert Randolph 211826

Ramey, Jean Perrin Hurst 213524212
Ramey, Thomas Crawford 213524212
Ramsey, Jamie Katherine 1331445531
Ramsey, Martha A. Harvey 133144553
Ramsey, Paula 51111122622
Ramsey, R. Kent 133144553
Randolph, Miss 31
Randolph, Addie 222136
Randolph, Alexander Dressler 1114212211
Randolph, Ann E. 22216
Randolph, Anna Elizabeth ("Bettie") 222131
Randolph, Anne ("Nancy") Meade 21
Randolph, Anne Meade 222
Randolph, Anne Meade Randolpy 222
Randolph, Brett III 2224
Randolph, Brett, Jr. 222
Randolph, Cornelia K. Wright 22213
Randolph, Elizabeth Jane 26
Randolph, Elizabeth Page Craven 11142122
Randolph, Emily Ann 1114212221
Randolph, Emily Vaughan 22217
Randolph, Evelyn Byrd 22233
Randolph, George Washington 222137
Randolph, Jane 216
Randolph, Jane 216
Randolph, Jane Bolling 21
Randolph, Jane Silounce 22234
Randolph, John 233
Randolph, John Mickelborough 222133
Randolph, Lucy A. 22218
Randolph, Maria L. 22219
Randolph, Mary Skipwith 24222
Randolph, Mary Susan 22231
Randolph, Mary Susan Rositzke 111421222
Randolph, Mary Willing Byrd 2223
Randolph, Montague Mickelborough 22213
Randolph, Nancy ("Nannie") W. 222132
Randolph, Patric Henry 2223
Randolph, Richard 21
Randolph, Richard Bolling 11142121
Randolph, Richard Kidder 2221
Randolph, Richard Montague 222135
Randolph, Richard Nichols 111421222
Randolph, Sarah Anne 22232
Randolph, Susannah 215
Randolph, Thomas E. 22215
Randolph, Virginia 222134
Randolph, William Barksdale 11142122
Randolph, William Byrd 2114
Rangeley, Susan Webster 17212
Rankin, John Beverley 211826121
Rankin, Mary Emily Corbin Kendig 21182612
Rankin, Thomas Kendig Parker 211826122
Rankin, Thomas Taplin 21182612
Rapinchuk, Linda 5111112642
Rasier, Anne Dorsey Toth 1113441213
Rasier, Mr. 1113441213
Rattan, Carol 514243121
Rattan, Catherine Lansden 51424312
Rattan, Clarence Travis 51424312
Rattan, Constance 514243123
Rattan, Cynthia 514243122
Raynor, Carolyn Fay Yates 17212232
Raynor, Jack L. 17212232

Reade, Frank 111x411
Reade, Heather 1113321232
Reagan, Dorothy Mae 511111231
Reed, Ann Hayden Skelly 541131131
Reed, Benjamin Skelly 5411311311
Reed, Elizabeth Gay Brown 41426333
Reed, Katherine Elizabeth 414263331
Reed, Mike 541131131
Reed, Norma Masie June 63115613
Reed, Shawn Edward 41426333
Reeves, Chester 178351911
Reeves, Ed 1113263212
Reeves, Elizabeth Dawn Smith 178351911
Reeves, Susan Lunsford Lynn 1113263212
Reid, Kelly Deann 511111845
Reif, Gay Frances 111344431
Reif, Karen Neeley 111344432
Renegar, Effie Lee 5111165
Renfro, Nellie Jane 51111173
Revel, David 563441112
Revel, Kelly Noel Totty 563441112
Revel, Sarah 5634411121
Rexrode, Barry 111344411
Rexrode, Eileen Lynn Gruet 111344411
Reynolds, J. Sargeant, Jr. 211826111
Reynolds, Margaret Randolph Young 211826111
Reynolds, Virginia Randolph 2118261111
Rhodes, Ann Hayden Skelly Reed 541131131
Rhodes, Christopher Nelson 1113324142
Rhodes, Don 541131131
Rhodes, Isaac Nelson 11133241422
Rhodes, Jacob Nelson 11133241421
Rhodes, Mary Katherine Doyle 1113324142
Rice, Mary Elizabeth 57456641
Richard, Kasandra Lynn 51111134221
Richard, Keri Lane Williamson 5111113422
Richard, Mark 5111113422
Richards, Walter Scott 1113324112
Richardson, Alicia Francine 3511671221
Richardson, Hibernia McIlwaine Friend
1113263616
Richardson, James Arthur 11132635
Richardson, Jean 15354112
Richardson, Jenny Rona 1113263641
Richardson, John Friend 111326362
Richardson, Kenneth Ray 351167122
Richardson, Margie Roadman 111326362
Richardson, Marguerite ("Cricket")
1113263621
Richardson, Sherri Diane Moore 351167122
Richardson, Sonya Kay 3511671222
Ridgeway, Bobbie 1722353
Riggs, Billie Neal Eldridge 51424421
Riggs, Bradley Michel 511111226211
Riggs, Breanna Meaghan 511111226212
Riggs, Carla Dell 514244214
Riggs, Cory Elizabeth 5142442121
Riggs, Denise Annette Sillivan 514244212
Riggs, Julie Annette 514244211
Riggs, Kelly Bullard 514244212
Riggs, Kris Alan 514244213
Riggs, Rachel Alison 5142442122
Riggs, Richard Dale 514244212
Riggs, Richard Riddell 51424421

Robson, Charles Baskervill 64111342
Robson, Charles Baskervill II 641113421
Robson, Charles Baskervill III 6411134211
Robson, George 6411134
Robson, George, Jr. 64111341
Robson, George M., III 641113412
Robson, Harriett Hardison 64111342
Robson, Lucie Lea Wurtz 641113421
Robson, Marianna 641113411
Robson, Naomi Fithian 64111341
Robson, Patrick Lea 6411134212
Rock, Hillard 1611362222
Rock, Howard 161136222
Rock, Lydia deJarnette Poland Selby 161136222
Rodgers, Margaret Abbitt 1331446232
Rodgers, Sally Ann Terry 133144623
Rodgers, Warren Lee 133144623
Rodgers, Warren Lee, Jr. 1331446231
Rodgers, William Nathaniel 1331446233
Rodland, Gail Brashears Gibson 111344423
Rodland, Paul 111344423
Roe, Connie 1721725
Rogers, Anna Mae Miller 172123621
Rogers, Frank Stagg 17212362
Rogers, Katherine Galt Miller 17212362
Roller, Dessie 1783381
Romaine, Anne Corbin Parker 2118262
Romaine, Anne Mason 211826232
Romaine, Douglas Patteson 21182623
Romaine, Douglas Randolph 211826233
Romaine, Jane Hundley 211826231
Romaine, Jane Williams Collins 21182623
Romaine, Jean Kollen 211826211
Romaine, Jean Kollen Gillander 21182621
Romaine, Mason III 2118262
Romaine, Mason IV 21182621
Romaine, Mason V 212826212
Romaine, Randolph Parker 21182622
Romieux, Marilyn ("Mickey") 54113112
Roseborough, Katherine 1751121
Rosenberg, Catherine Leigh 641212212
Rosenberg, Elizabeth Powell 641212211
Rosenberg, Michael Albert Hans 64121221
Rosenberg, Rebecca Leigh Hurt 64121221
Rosi, Celia 5735222
Rositzke, Mary Susan 111421222
Ross, Sallie Ruth 1721226
Rouse, Robert Wayne 51111122641
Rouse, Tina Michele Thornton 51111122641
Rowe, Charles Daniel 111344342
Rowe, Elizabeth Averett Robertson 111344232
Rowe, Henry Alan 111x41411
Rowe, Jonathan Reade 111x414111
Rowe, Mary Louise 111x414112
Rowe, Reade Maclin 111x41411
Rowland, Barbara Jean 51424231
Rubio, Amanda Josephine Cortes 17223621
Rubio, Cortes 1722362
Rubio, Margaret Rebecca Dandridge 1722362
Rubio, Nancy Lucille Cortes 17223622
Rucker, Elizabeth B. 14232242
Rus, Mary Cornell 6411131111

Russell, Cleta Hamilton 1783755
Russell, Mary Katherine 111x6462
Russell, Woody 1783755
Ruth, Kathleen Jean 111381212
Rutherfoord, Harriot Hamilton 1751121
Rutherford, Marjorie Rose 4142212
Ryder, Diedra Diane 24151343212
Rye, Susan 133144411

-S-

Sahling, Claire Stone White 111x6422
Sahling, Mr. 111x6422
Salah, George Anthony 641212x1
Salah, Susan Caroline Coleman 641212x1
Samples, Amanda Nicole 5111114131
Samples, Donna Susan 511114122
Samples, Forrest Marion 511111413
Samples, Janet Anne Preston 511111413
Samples, Katelyn Elaine 5111114132
Samples, Marion Colleen Ponder 511111412
Samples, Mark Patrick 5111114141
Samples, Milton Forrest 511111412
Samples, Patricia Mary Langford 511111414
Samples, Sandra Diane 511114121
Samples, Steven Mark 511111414
Sampson, Bruce Carroll 1116132312
Sampson, Margaret Ann Hilderbrandt 1116132312
Sampson, Sherry Lynn 514241112
Sanderlin, Terri Elaine 5111112313
Sanders, _____ Gay 41634
Sanders, Alexandra Marie 5142432221
Sanders, Beverly Marie Dinkel 514243222
Sanders, Collins Frank 514243222
Sanders, Dillon Christopher 5142432222
Sanders, Evangella Louise 5142432223
Sanders, Inman 41634
Sanders, Krista Lynne Ingerson 5111118131
Sanders, Lori 514242212
Sanders, Melissa 5111124312
Sanders, Pamela Ann 5111117114
Sartin, Earline 511111322
Sattich, Amanda Brooke 51111122213
Sattich, Anthony Wayne 51111122213
Sattich, Daniel DeBoe 51111122112
Sattich, Deborah Sue Allen 51111122211
Sattich, Gayla Kaye 51111122132
Sattich, James Jason 51111122111
Sattich, Jesse Edward 51111122133
Sattich, Kimberley Louise Nugent 51111122213
Sattich, Marjorie Frances McGuire 5111112221
Sattich, Michelle DeBoe 51111122112
Sattich, Patricia Darlene Sea 51111122212
Sattich, Richard Terry 51111122211
Sattich, Ronald Eugene 51111122212
Sattich, Stanley Eugene 5111112221
Sattich, Steven Nicholas 511111222121
Sattich, Teresa Riley 51111122213
Sattich-Nugent, Becky Lou Vertrees 51111122214
Sattich-Nugent, Darryl Fredric 51111122214

Watts, Marjorie Jean Logan 1751151
Watts, Patricia Matthews Stebbins 17511511
Watts, Richard Jennings 241c11421
Watts, Richard Thomas III 1751151
Watts, Richard Thomas VI 17511511
Weilgus, Andrew Howard 5411311331
Weisiger, Miss M. 1611x2
Weiss, Nancy 111613225
Weisser, Jacob Charles 1113443712
Weisser, Jessica Katherine 1113443711
Welborn, Bessie V. Wilborn 172174
Welborn, Clary 1721742
Welborn, LeFon 1721741
Welborn, Locke LaFon 172174
Welborn, Mary Nell 1721743
Wellborn, Nan Overton Mahone 17511231
Wellborn, William Revere 17511231
Wells, Henry 12141
Wells, Martha Covington 12141
Wells, Marvin Clay 5111118154
Wells, Susan J. 5735
Wells, Theresa Jane Christian 5111118154
Werth, Elie Maury 153541
West, Elizabeth Bolling 1332
Whateley, Deborah Kay 5111112234
Whetstone, Doris 511111774
White, Benjamin Briscoe III 2422213313
White, Benjamin Briscoe IV 24222133131
White, Brandy Rene Christian 51111181511
White, Claire Stone 111x6422
White, Elizabeth Harrison 24222133132
White, Elizabeth Lane 111x64622
White, Elizabeth Lewis Carter Harrison 1113182
White, Frances Mary 1113324131
White, James Lowery II 111x6463
White, Jane Poythress 111x64631
White, Jesse Kenan 24222133133
White, Jessie Kenan Lewis 2422213313
White, Kathleen Brown 111x646
White, Kathleen Robertson 111x641
White, Kathleen Sanders 111x6461
White, Linda Lee Marbury 111x6463
White, Martha Norton 111x6421
White, Mary Alice 5111112433
White, Mary Faukerson 111x643
White, Mary Katherine Russell 111x6462
White, Shad Eugene 51111181511
White, William Beckler 1114182
White, William Young Conn, Jr. 111x646
White, William Young Conn III 111x6462
White, William Young Conn IV 111x64621
Whittington, Robin 1113441112
Whittle, Emily Cary 6528
Whittle, Fortesque 652
Whittle, Francis McNeece 6528
Whittle, James Murray 6523
Whittle, Mary Ann Davies 652
Whittle, Powhatan Bolling 6529
Whitworth, Alison Lynn 5142411121
Whitworth, Chad Clayton 5142411124
Whitworth, Charles Darwin 514241112
Whitworth, Chase Allen 5142411122
Whitworth, Kimberly Leigh Allen 514241112

Whitworth, Mark Thomas 5142411123
Whitworth, Sara Landman 51424111
Whitworth, Sherry Lynn Sampson 514241112
Whitworth, Taylor Elizabeth 5142411125
Whitworth, Thomas Jerome 51424111
Whitworth, Thomas Jerome, Jr. 514241111
Wickersham, Janice Carolyn 5142443
Widner, Laura Joanne 111381224
Wiese, Martha Norton White 111x6421
Wiese, Mr. 111x6421
Wigginton, Anne Eliza 1241
Wilborn, Anita Stratten 1721725
Wilborn, Anna Davis 172171
Wilborn, Beatrice Dandridge 172173
Wilborn, Beatrice Dandridge 1721c3
Wilborn, Bessie V. 172174
Wilborn, Connie Roe 1721725
Wilborn, Diana Sue 17217232
Wilborn, Eva Smart Powell 172173
Wilborn, James Durward 172172
Wilborn, James Harris 1721721
Wilborn, James Thomas 17217
Wilborn, Jewel Lipsey 1721721
Wilborn, Mabel 172176
Wilborn, Mabel Elizabeth 1721724
Wilborn, Mamie Allen 172172
Wilborn, Marcus Eugene 1721723
Wilborn, Marcus Samuel 172173
Wilborn, Marcus Samuel 1721c3
Wilborn, Marjorie 1721711
Wilborn, Mary Louise Triplett 1721723
Wilborn, Mary Pocahontas Dandridge 17217
Wilborn, Ora 172175
Wilborn, Ruth Hyde 1721722
Wilborn, Sandra Anne 17217231
Wilborn, Thomas Henry 1721725
Wilborn, William ("Willie") Clark 172171
Wilborn, William Allen 1721722
Wilborn, Willodean 1721712
Wilbourn, Adeline Kenon 1737
Wilburn, Sallie L. 51424
Wilcox, Frances Delores Alexander 1783519
Wilcox, Jared Mann 1783519
Wilcox, Virginia Lynn 17835191
Wildasin, Charles Edward 1331412
Wildasin, Charles Edward 13314123
Wildasin, Evelyn Hunter 13314121
Wildasin, Jamie Jones 1331412
Wildasin, Jamie Jones 13314124
Wildasin, Margaret Handy 13314122
Wilhoit, Judith Hale 1751124
Wilkes, Margaret Marie 51111122322
Wilkinson, Ann Elizabeth 5735225
Wilkinson, Ann Elizabeth 57358
Wilkinson, Ann Elizabeth Wilkinson 5735225
Wilkinson, Beth Allison Davis 573522312
Wilkinson, Caroline Paige 5735223121
Wilkinson, Cathryn Anne 573522311
Wilkinson, Celia Rosi 5735222
Wilkinson, Edgar Claiborne 5735225
Wilkinson, Gene Cox 57352232
Wilkinson, George Carroll 5735223
Wilkinson, George Carroll, Jr. 57352231
Wilkinson, George E. 57352

Williamson, Jason Keith 5111113242
Williamson, Jeff Davis 5111117
Williamson, Joan Bowden 511111114
Williamson, Joshua Keith 51111132421
Williamson, Julie Rae 5111117611
Williamson, Katherine Alexandra 51111111541
Williamson, Katherine Vaughn 51111175
Williamson, Kathleen Dynel Hughes 511111762
Williamson, Katie Mae 5111114
Williamson, Keli Vonne 5111113431
Williamson, Kenneth Dean 51111179
Williamson, Kenneth Lloyd 511111322
Williamson, Keri Lane 5111113422
Williamson, Kevin Glenn 5111117521
Williamson, Lana Jo 511111732
Williamson, Larry Don 5111111154
Williamson, Laura Elizabeth Fox 511111791
Williamson, Laura Katherine Bradford
                                 5111111154
Williamson, Laurel Elaine 51111765
Williamson, Leah 51111111731
Williamson, Leta Jo Robison 511111321
Williamson, Lucia Fatina Hartsill 5111113242
Williamson, Lucretia Magdalene 51111131
Williamson, Lula Losson ("Lossie") 5111112
Williamson, Lulu Winona 511111113
Williamson, Lura Mary 511116
Williamson, Mable Connor 5111119
Williamson, Macon Oscar 5111192
Williamson, Maggie ("Mag") 5111163
Williamson, Marcie 51111174
Williamson, Margaret ("Maggie") Catherine
                        Hatchett 511111
Williamson, Margaret Ruth Hefner 51111132
Williamson, Mary Alice Baxter 511111324
Williamson, Mary Helen 51111753
Williamson, Mary Lou Nicholson 511111733
Williamson, Mary Malva 51111171
Williamson, Mary Margaret ("Margie")
                                 5111113242
Williamson, Mary Sue Gibson 511111121
Williamson, Melissa 5111113222
Williamson, Michael Gene 5111111211
Williamson, Mickey Sue 5111111221
Williamson, Mildred McLary 51111113
Williamson, Nancy Louise 511111764
Williamson, Nellie Alene Hall 511111116
Williamson, Nellie Jane Renfro 51111173
Williamson, Odis Keith 511111324
Williamson, Oran Odis 51111173
Williamson, Patsy Ruth Trapp 511111115
Williamson, Pauletta Jean Collins 511111343
Williamson, Pearl Hargrave 51111113
Williamson, Percy Jeff 51111175
Williamson, Rachel Dynel 5111117622
Williamson, Radford Turner 51111111
Williamson, Radford Turner, Jr. 511111114
Williamson, Ray 51111191
Williamson, Reubin Murrell 51111134
Williamson, Rhonda 5111111173
Williamson, Richard Kyle 511111752

Williamson, Roxie Vernell 51111178
Williamson, Royal Glynn 511111117
Williamson, Ruby Ann Baxter 511111323
Williamson, Ruth E. Taylor 51111132
Williamson, Sandra Jean 5111111222
Williamson, Sandra Sue 511111792
Williamson, Sarah Elizabeth 51111111532
Williamson, Sarah Shawn 5111117911
Williamson, Scott Allen 5111117522
Williamson, Sharon Kay 511111344
Williamson, Shelby Penn 51111111542
Williamson, Sue Ella Love 5111113
Williamson, Tammy Nell 511111731
Williamson, Teresa Lynn 5111113221
Williamson, Terry Dean 5111111161
Williamson, Terry Neal 511111762
Williamson, Thomas Leroy 5111116
Williamson, Tressie Jane Warren 5111118
Williamson, Trevor Alan 5111117612
Williamson, Velma Derotha Kirkland 51111133
Williamson, Vicki Ann 5111111212
Williamson, Vicki Lynn 5111111151
Williamson, Virginia Ann Harrison Griffin
                                 511111117
Williamson, Walter Clyde ("W.C.") 51111176
Williamson, Walter Eugene 511111
Williamson, Wanda Gail Davis 5111111153
Williamson, Wanda Lou 51111135
Williamson, William Eugene ("Gene")
                                 511111121
Williamson, Willie Beatrice 51111181
Willis, Annie Irene 511111225
Willis, Annie Lelia Toler 1722416
Willis, Frances Virginia 11161322
Willis, Frank Elery 1722416
Willis, Georgine Washington 17511
Wilson, Annie Frankie 5111117
Wilson, Bryan Branson 1722424
Wilson, Claire 178342232
Wilson, Creely Neal Myatt 17834223
Wilson, Ellen MacCorkle 13314472
Wilson, Franklin Wayne, Jr. 111x8881
Wilson, Franklin Wayne III 111x88812
Wilson, Hazel Bernice Dandridge 1722424
Wilson, Helen Yuille 6311429
Wilson, James Blair 1331447
Wilson, James Blair, Jr. 13314471
Wilson, Lynn Worden 111x8881
Wilson, Melanie 178342233
Wilson, Norman Leslie Galloway 6311429
Wilson, Sarah Lewis 111x88811
Wilson, Stella Watkins ("Billie") Abbitt
                                 1331447
Wilson, Susan Hay 641212x
Wilson, William 17834223
Wilson, William, Jr. 178342231
Wineroth, Joel 111344222
Wineroth, Joel, Jr. 1113442221
Wineroth, Linda Leslie Lewis 111344222
Wineroth, Whitney Caroline 1113442222
Wingfield, Elizabeth Virginia Terry 13314467
Wingfield, Herman Cleveland 13314467

Winston, Betty Benfer 17212321
Winston, Lena Virginia Jones 1331451
Winston, Mr. 1331451
Wisdom, Amanda Michelle 511111243111
Wisdom, George 51111124311
Wisdom, Melanie Locke 51111124311
Wise, Louise Clisby 24222133
Wold, Traci 111348121
Wolff, Edith Gaylord Clark 241c114253
Wolff, Robert Brent Keyser 241c114252
Wolff, Sally Cary Clark 241c11425
Wolff, Stewart MacKay 241c11425
Wolff, Stewart MacKay, Jr. 241c114251
Wolgemuth, Carol 111x2121
Woltz, Rita Holmes Robertson 11134413
Woltz, Robert Kyle 11134413
Woltz, Sarah Kyle 111344135
Womack, Edmund Wilson 133112151
Womack, Frank 1331433
Womack, Joseph Wilson 1331121512
Womack, Joyce Marie Linville 1331121512
Womack, Katherine Anne Booker 133112151
Womack, Mary ("May") Price 1331433
Womack, Susan Glenn 1331121511
Womble, Brandi Elizabeth 5745664321
Womble, Charles Randall 574566432
Womble, Elizabeth Rives Mullen 574566432
Wood, Alden Randolph 1113451121
Wood, Anna Chalmers 6315
Wood, Brackston Ewing 1113451221
Wood, Caroline Fairfax 1113451122
Wood, Carroll Goodman 111345122
Wood, Catherine Carlisle Canada 332425213
Wood, George Twyman III 1113451
Wood, George Twyman IV 11134511
Wood, George Twyman V 111345112
Wood, Hunter Whitney 1113441122
Wood, Jennifer Lynn Gagnon 1113441122
Wood, Katherine Suttles 111345112
Wood, Laura Kathleen 1113451222
Wood, Linda Ellen Leonard 11134512
Wood, Louise Fairfax Robertson 1113451
Wood, MacArthur 332425213
Wood, Marjorie 175115
Wood, Mary Ann 133112121
Wood, Mason 11134411221
Wood, Melanie Ann 1113321111
Wood, Melissa Carolyn 3324252132
Wood, Michael Anderson 3324252131
Wood, Nora E. 57355
Wood, Rachel 13314x1
Wood, Walter Wyvill 11134512
Wood, Walter Wyvill, Jr. 111345122
Wood, Whitney 11134411222
Woodcock, Susan Gay Hadden 111x21213
Woodcock, Theodore 111x21213
Woodruff, Frances 13314631
Woodson, Nannie 222311
Wooldridge, Caroline 33242
Worden, Florence 111x8842
Worden, Lynn 111x8881
Worden, Mary Stuart 111x8882
Worden, Wyndham Robertson 111x881

Worley, Carlene 5111112432
Worn, Beverley Anne 631156115
Worthen, Della Rene 5111118151
Worthington, Jane Atkinson Clark 241c114243
Worthington, Peter Laurenson 241c114243
Worthington, Peter Laurenson, Jr. 241c114243
Worthington, Sarah Jane 241c1142432
Wright, Betty Jane Murff 17834253
Wright, Cornelia K. 22213
Wright, Joe M. 17834253
Wright, Joseph ("Jody") Marshall Murff
178342532
Wright, Sherribeth 178342531
Wurtz, Lucie Lea 641113421
Wyant, Dominique ("Dom") Homan 4142632
Wyant, Julie Gaston Gay 4142632
Wyant, Margaret Homan 41426321
Wyatt, Carolyn Rangeley Hodnett 17212422
Wyatt, Charles Kelly 17212422
Wyatt, Constance Ann 24151343213
Wyatt, David Fontaine 172124221
Wyatt, Virginia Nelson 172124222
Wyatte, Johnson 51111671
Wyatte, Kathleen Hatchett 51111671
Wyer, Elizabeth Fenwick 111713342
Wyer, Rolfe 111713342
Wysocki, Catherine Marie 5111112822

-X-

-Y-

Yates, Carolyn Fay 17212232
Yates, Chealsea Elizabeth 172122331
Yates, Chesley Randolph 1721223
Yates, Chesley Randolph, Jr. 17212233
Yates, Ellen Baskerville 6411137
Yates, Iris Elizabeth Dandridge 1721223
Yates, Iris Jean 17212231
Yates, Jacob Randolph 172122332
Yates, Janet Lynn McDaniel 17212233
Yates, Orville 6411137
Yensho, Edward Andrew 241c114222
Yensho, Julia Brent 241c1142221
Yensho, Letitia Lee Sexton 241c114222
Yensho, Victoria Lee 241c1142222
Young, Almeda 36653
Young, Anne Corbin 21826112
Young, Anne Randolph Kendig 21182611
Young, Barbara 511116512
Young, Bobbie Louise Culpepper 1722358
Young, Eugenia Lou Adams 13311253
Young, Franklin L. 1722358
Young, Hendrix Alan 17223584
Young, Judith 17223582
Young, Kelly 172235812
Young, Margaret Randolph 211826111
Young, Mr. 133112531
Young, Patricia 17223583
Young, Robert 17223581
Young, Ronald Faris 21182611
Young, Sandy 41426222

Young, Sherry 172235811
Young, Sue Mason 17223581
Yuille, Adela Kilburn 631143
Yuille, Adrienna Lynn 631156116
Yuille, Alan Binnie 63114653
Yuille, Albert Alexander 6311561
Yuille, Albert Lodden 6311467
Yuille, Albert Loddon 63114x
Yuille, Alexander 63119
Yuille, Alexander Bremner 63115623
Yuille, Alexander George 631156
Yuille, Alexander Lodden 63114671
Yuille, Allen Neil 6311465
Yuille, Amelia Gladys Muriel Curran 6311561
Yuille, Ann Bollingbroke Buchanan 63111
Yuille, Ann McMillan 631142
Yuille, Anna Cross 6311
Yuille, Anne Agnes 631145
Yuille, Annie Denny 631146
Yuille, Annie Ellen 631152
Yuille, Annie Elsie 6311427
Yuille, Annie Veronica 63114241
Yuille, Anthony Ashley Angus 631142a
Yuille, Archibald 631146
Yuille, Archibald Binnie 63114651
Yuille, Archibald Denny 6311462
Yuille, Arthur D. Buchanan 63114x51
Yuille, Arthur Leonard 6311562
Yuille, Barbara 63114622
Yuille, Betsy ("Bessie") 631141
Yuille, Beverley Anne Worn 631156115
Yuille, Bruce 63114673
Yuille, Catheine O'Rielly 6311425
Yuille, Charles Henry 631148
Yuille, Clara Bindi Margetts 6311467
Yuille, Constance Victoria Bartram Green 6311432
Yuille, Dannielle 631156114
Yuille, Darys Alexander John 631156115
Yuille, Dianne Amelia 631156113
Yuille, Donald Reginald 631142b
Yuille, Doris Audley 6311563
Yuille, Dorothy Vernon 63114253
Yuille, Eileen Ann 6311552
Yuille, Elana Beatrice Mary 6311431
Yuille, Elizabeth Ann 63114x52
Yuille, Ellen Littlejohns 63115
Yuille, Ethel Elsie Vincent 63114x3
Yuille, Ethel Maria Clarissa Pike 63114x
Yuille, Fanny De St Helier Cox 631143
Yuille, Florence Isabel 6311423
Yuille, Florence Nita Scott 6311466
Yuille, Frank Archibald 6311425
Yuille, Gaylord Anthony 631156117
Yuille, Geoffrey Buchanan 63114x4
Yuille, George 63113
Yuille, George 631142
Yuille, George 63114251
Yuille, George Arthur 6311424
Yuille, George Binnie 63114652
Yuille, Guy Ulick 6311464
Yuille, Harry Leonard 6311554
Yuille, Heather 63114623
Yuille, Helen 6311429
Yuille, Helen 63118
Yuille, Helen Buchanan 63114x1

Yuille, Helen Catherine 63114252
Yuille, Helen Mary 63114a
Yuille, Jack Buchanan 63114x5
Yuille, James 63114
Yuille, Jeffrey Leighton 631156131
Yuille, John Cross Buchanan 63117
Yuille, John Oliphant 6311426
Yuille, John Richard Randolph 631149
Yuille, Joyce Ellen 63115622
Yuille, Kate Malone 631155
Yuille, Kelvin Alexander John 63115611
Yuille, Leighton Eldred Truscott 63115613
Yuille, Mabel Lois Berthon 63114x5
Yuille, Margaret 63114621
Yuille, Margaret 631157
Yuille, Margaret Gaye Lowrie 631156131
Yuille, Margaret Murdock 63112
Yuille, Margory Agnes 63115621
Yuille, Marion Hilda Strugnell 63115611
Yuille, Marjorie Cross 63114x2
Yuille, Mary 631147
Yuille, Mary Casey 6311424
Yuille, Mary Denny 63114
Yuille, Mary Denny 6311421
Yuille, Mary Ellen 6311551
Yuille, Mary Ellen Truscott 631156
Yuille, Max 6311466
Yuille, Milicent Beatrice 631142x
Yuille, Muriel Ethel Bremner 6311562
Yuille, Muriel Margaret 6311428
Yuille, Murray 631156232
Yuille, Nancy May 6311463
Yuille, Nellie Sherrard 6311462
Yuille, Nelson Albert Slade 63115612
Yuille, Neville 631156233
Yuille, Norma Masie June Reed 63115613
Yuille, Peter 631156231
Yuille, Ravenna Anne 6311461
Yuille, Rhona Eleanor Miller 63115623
Yuille, Richard Cross 6311x
Yuille, Robert 6311
Yuille, Robert 63115
Yuille, Robert 631155
Yuille, Robert Joseph 6311553
Yuille, Robert William 631151
Yuille, Slade Bruce Nelson 631156121
Yuille, Tannis Margaret Rose 631156112
Yuille, Thomas 63116
Yuille, Vaughan Albert Archibald 631156111
Yuille, Victoria Leonard 631153
Yuille, Violet Binnie 63114654
Yuille, Violet Marion Wilson Binnie 6311465
Yuille, William 631143
Yuille, William Cross 63115
Yuille, William Cross 6311422
Yuille, William Douglas 6311432
Yuille, William Lodden 63114672
Yuille, William Robert 631154

-Z-

Zeller, Jeremy Scott 511111113111
Zeller, Jordan Michael 511111113113
Zeller, Nicholas O'Neal 511111113114
Zeller, Paul 51111111311
Zeller, Ryan Paul 511111113112
Zeller, Terri Lynn O'Neal 51111111311

CPSIA information can be obtained
at www.ICGtesting.com
Printed in the USA
BVHW040240170419
545729BV00021B/261/P